Understanding Business
Series Editor: Richard Barker

The Economy and Business Decisions

D. R. Myddelton

 Longman

LONGMAN GROUP LIMITED
Longman House
Burnt Mill, Harlow, Essex CM20, 2JE, England
and Associated Companies throughout the World

© Cambridge Business Studies Project Trust, 1977, 1984

First published under the title The Economy and Decision Making 1977
New edition 1984

ISBN 0 582 35454 5

Filmset in 10/12 Monophoto Plantin
by Northumberland Press Ltd, Gateshead

Printed in Great Britain
by Richard Clay (The Chaucer Press) Bungay

Contents

Introduction to the Series

This series produces a new approach to the teaching of business. It is suitable for young managers, students and academic sixth-formers. It has been developed over the last decade to give understanding of the nature and purpose of business activity, whilst also stimulating the minds of the more academically gifted members of society.

The material provides for an analytical understanding of people's problems and behaviour within organisations. The texts discuss the nature of problems, and explore concepts and principles which may be employed to aid their solution. Test materials have been selected from industrial and commercial organisations; from the private and public sector; from non-profit-making institutions. The material is as much to provide general understanding about industrial society and the workings of organisations, as it is to help those who are already engaged in their business or professional career.

The approach of decision-making has been used to draw together ideas, and produce significant elements of reality; the approach gives purpose and challenge to the reader. Any organisation is striving towards more or less closely defined objectives by deciding how to carry out, and control, its activities within constantly changing conditions. The programme looks carefully at these processes of decision-making; it provides the student with an understanding of their overall nature. Ideas from the four functional areas of human behaviour, quantitative data, accounting and the economic environment are drawn together within a decision-making framework; the approach is then applied to different areas of business activity, particularly to those of finance, marketing and production.

This series of eight books has been designed to meet the needs of students (and their lecturers/teachers) studying the business world. The up-to-date materials within each book provide many ideas and activities from which the teacher can choose. Lecturers on management courses may use the book to introduce analytical concepts to practitioners; tertiary management courses may use them as a first text and as a source of well-tried and up-to-date cases; BEC and 'A' Level students may use the books as complete courses.

To meet these different needs, each book in the series has been designed to stand either as a part of the whole, or complete in its own right.

All books have the same chapter format:

a chapter objective and synopsis so that the purpose and pattern are clear;
a factual/explanatory text with case examples where applicable;
a participative work section to provide materials for learning, application and discussion.

The participative sections are an integral part of the whole text and allow students to gain understanding by doing. They are usually divided into three parts. Firstly, some simple revision questions to enable the students to check their own basic understanding. Secondly, a series of exercises and case problems to test their application and to increase their knowledge of the area. Thirdly, a set of essay questions.

There is a teachers' booklet accompanying each student text which introduces the topic area, clarifies possible objectives, suggests approaches to the selected materials and adds additional ideas. The teachers' booklets also provide solutions, where appropriate, to the participative work sections.

The philosophy, approach and materials have been forged in discussion with businessmen, lecturers and teachers. Trial and error has refined much of the text and most of the participative work. The whole venture has been co-ordinated by the Cambridge Business Studies Project Trust. Initial work developed from a link between the Wolfson Foundation, Marlborough College and Shell International Ltd. Trustees for the Project include Professor John Dancy, Sir Michael Clapham and Sir Nicholas Goodison; much early guidance was also given by Professor Sir Austin Robinson.

The series can be used as the basis for an 'A' Level examination run by the Cambridge Local Examinations Syndicate and established in 1967. The examination syllabus and objectives are in line with the materials in these texts.

Richard Barker
Series Editor

Preface to this Edition

Viewpoint

This book is for people who are studying business decisions. It is intended to be useful for people in business as well as for students in business schools, polytechnics and colleges of further education, and for sixth-formers on business studies courses. The text has been completely rewritten compared with the earlier version, *The Economy and Decision Making*, by Peter Donaldson and Jim Clifford.

Economics is normally divided between macro- (Greek 'big') covering national aggregates and governments and micro- (Greek 'small') looking at individuals and firms. The subject of this book is macro-economics (or the business economic environment). Unlike most other business subjects, such as accounting or marketing, in macro-economics we cannot always adopt the viewpoint of the firm. We also need to discuss 'the economy' as a whole, though using aggregates has its dangers (as Ch. 3 explains).

The main focus of this book is not 'the government'. In Part III we discuss governments and their objectives; but our main concern is how governments affect business firms and the economy as a whole. Even without government (if that were possible) there would still be economic growth, international business, money, and a labour market.

Contents

The book contains plenty of factual information. About half of the 100 tables and charts contain *facts*, mostly about the British economy and covering the past 10 or 20 years. I have tried to include essential theory without being too superficial, but the book is meant to be an *introduction*. Most readers will want to grasp the main issues, and those who want more details will find that there are many books available.

Detailed contents are shown on the first page of each chapter. The book is split into four parts: Economic Background, Economic Topics, Government, and an Industry Study.

I. Economic Background

Chapter 1 describes the market economy and how it works; lists the main groups comprising the business community; and outlines reasons why governments intervene in the market. Chapter 2 deals with the circular flow of incomes in the economy: wage income and personal consumption, savings and investment, exports and imports, taxes and government spending. Chapter 3 discusses economic aggregates such as 'national income'; and looks at savings, consumption, and investment from the point of view of individuals and firms, as well as in total.

II. Economic Topics

Chapter 4 covers economic growth: the historical record, some causes of growth, and future prospects. Chapter 5 deals with international trade and money, and national 'balance of payments'. Chapter 6 describes the functions of money, and the causes and effects of the world-wide post-war inflation. Chapter 7 discusses first employment, then unemployment and its causes.

III. Government

Chapter 8 looks into government spending and tax revenue; it also discusses local authorities and nationalised industries, and certain government controls. Chapter 9 describes the trade cycle and fiscal policy, monetary policy, and overall government economic objectives and constraints.

IV. Industry Study

Chapter 10 contains a fairly detailed study of the housing market. It shows how complex an industry appears when one looks below the surface of aggregate statistics.

How to use the Book

Each of the 10 chapters contains three kinds of question at the end.

The A Revision Questions, about 35 per chapter, are related to the text material, and are set out in the same order. They are meant to be helpful as 'instant' revision after reading a chapter, or part of one. Between them they cover nearly all the main points made in the text. Many readers should find them useful; and it may sometimes be a good idea to *write down* your (brief) answers.

Most chapters have about 10 B Exercises and Case Studies, usually requiring some sort of number work. Some of the B Questions refer to tables and charts in the text, asking you to explore their meaning or to update them; others are short exercises related to parts of the text; and finally a few represent case studies which may be suitable for work in groups.

Most chapters contain about 15 C Essay Questions, covering topics for discussion. They may be worth looking through even if one is not actually planning to spend time writing an essay. There are many more B and C questions than any one person is likely to want, so there is a need to be selective in their use.

A feature of the book, as of others in this series, is the glossary (on pages 210 to 223). This aims to define about 240 of the key words and phrases used. They are shown in **bold type** the first time they appear. A working definition is usually also given at a suitable point in the text. I have tried to avoid jargon; but economics has plenty of its own terminology, which one cannot completely escape. When you come across a word or phrase you don't understand, it is good practice to *look it up at once* in the glossary. By the time you finish the book you should be able to define most of the glossary items. There is also (on page 209) a list of common abbreviations (acronyms).

Finally there is a fairly extensive index (on page 224). The letter G as the first item after the index entry means that the word or phrase is shown in the glossary.

For teachers an extensive Teacher's Guide is available from the publishers. It contains answers to the B Questions, detailed summaries of key points in each chapter, and suggestions about ways to use the text.

Acknowledgements

I would like to acknowledge several debts. Professor Peter Forrester at Cranfield kindly made available the time (and, to some extent, the money) which enabled me to write the book. My colleagues Marek Kwiatkowski and Ron Stevens at Marlborough and Charles Grant and Frank Fishwick at Cranfield and my brother Alexander all made extremely helpful detailed comments on drafts of most chapters. My editor, Richard Barker, was generous with encouragement. Finally, several students at Cranfield made useful comments, and in particular I am grateful to Charles Awdry, Geoff Foster and Alasdair Johnston at Marlborough who spent a good deal of time and effort making detailed and constructive suggestions on how to improve a draft version of the book.

D. R. Myddelton

Part I   Economic Background

Chapter 1

The Market Economy

Objective: *To explain how scarce resources imply (opportunity) cost and choice; to stress the importance in the market process of prices, competition, and entrepreneurs; to describe the groups comprising the business community, and how they interact; and to explain the main reasons why governments intervene in the market.*

Synopsis: *Economic goods are scarce, so choices must be made. The key political question is who chooses? In the market system it is consumers, in a centrally planned economy it is the government. In the market, prices balance what producers supply and what consumers demand. Profit is a major incentive for entrepreneurs managing competing businesses: they combine various factors of production in trying to provide goods and services which will satisfy consumers.*

The main groups in the business community are consumers, producers, employees, and investors. Consumers decide how much of their income to consume currently, what to spend it on, and from whom to buy. The main sectors of production are primary (extractive), secondary (manufacturing), and tertiary (services), with many firms' output being the input *to other firms. Sole traders and partners are fully liable for all their firms' debts; while companies are incorporated as separate legal entities, and the shareholders have only* limited *liability.*

Government intervention in the market has greatly increased this century. Among the economic reasons for this are: public goods, market 'imperfections', and demand management. Political reasons include paternalism and egalitarianism.

1.1   The Market Process

1.1.1   Scarcity and Choice

Resources count as 'economic' only if they are scarce as well as valuable. Air, for example, is literally vital to all of us; but when it is plentiful it is a **free good**.[1] When it is scarce, however (as for deep-sea divers or astronauts), air becomes an **economic good.**

Scarcity implies the need for *choice*. People can't have everything they want, so in the **market** system consumers choose which goods and services they prefer. An increase in the demand for, say, video-recorders may increase their **price**. This helps to restrain the demand for them, as well as encouraging producers to increase the supply. Thus the changing market price balances the strength of consumers' desires for certain goods against the scarcity of the resources needed to produce them.

In **centrally planned economies** it is governments who decide what should be produced. But without market prices the central planners may find it hard to co-ordinate all the complex inter-related production decisions. Moreover government orders may not coincide with consumers' preferences. So there may be shortages of goods people desire and surpluses of unwanted articles. The basic *economic* point is that even 'all-powerful' dictators have to choose between scarce resources. The key *political* question is: *who* chooses?

In all countries there is a mixture of market economy and government decision. In this sense all are **mixed economies**. The balance depends on the political climate as well as on the sway of different economic theories. But in practice we regard the Western democracies as market economies and the Communist countries of Eastern Europe and Asia as centrally planned.

Which is 'better' depends on one's political views. Most people tend to prefer their own system; but we may observe one solid piece of evidence.

[1] Words in bold type are defined in the Glossary (pages 210 to 223).

The Berlin Wall was built by the communists to stop East Germans escaping from a centrally planned economy into the Western market economies. It is a grim, if unintended, tribute to the value of freedom.

Figure 1.1 shows for a hypothetical country a **production possibility curve** (AB) for two representative goods, clothes and food. The total supply of economic goods is limited, by definition. In this case it is assumed that making more clothes leaves fewer resources for producing food. One can be provided only at the expense of the other, so the 'cost' of more clothes is the foregone output of some food. This is the basic idea of **opportunity cost**. The combination of clothes and food which consumers prefer is point C on the curve AB, representing OM clothes and ON food.

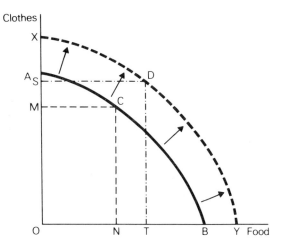

Fig. 1.1: Production possibility curves for clothes and food.

Shifting the AB curve upwards and to the right (to XY) makes it possible to produce *both* more clothes and more food. Thus point D means OS clothes (> OM) and OT food (> ON). As we shall see in Chapter 4, **economic growth** means either increasing the *amount* of resources available or *combining* existing resources better.

1.1.2 Markets and Prices

In a competitive market people choose to make bargains with each other. Since *both* buyer and seller expect to gain from such a voluntary market deal, a producer's profit is not made 'at the expense of' consumers. Producers compete to *satisfy* consumers, not to reduce their well-being! (Indeed the Greek word for 'exchange' also means 'change from enmity into friendship'.)

Rivalry between several potential buyers tends to drive prices up, while competition between potential sellers tends to drive prices down. In theory the price will settle at a level which precisely 'clears' the market. Thus Fig.

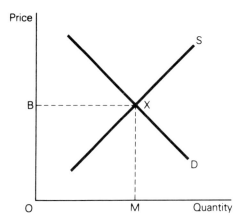

Fig. 1.2: Supply and demand for eggs in a competitive market.

1.2 shows a competitive market, say for eggs, with many sellers and many buyers. Price is shown on the vertical axis and quantity on the horizontal axis.

The demand curve D shows how many eggs buyers will demand at any price; and the supply curve S shows how many eggs sellers will supply at any price. As the price falls, people want more eggs; so the demand curve is 'downward-sloping' from left to right. But as the price falls fewer eggs are supplied. The demand curve crosses the supply curve at the point X, at the 'market-clearing' price OB. This means that consumers will demand the same number of eggs (OM) as producers will supply.

Competitive markets will tend towards **equilibrium**, but may never actually reach it in practice. This is due to imperfect knowledge of ever-changing conditions, together with time-lags in adjustment. Change, uncertainty and time are three important aspects of the real world which are sometimes overlooked by economic theories.

Economic rent is any surplus received above what suppliers require to prevent them transferring a **factor of production** to some other use. (This latter amount is called **transfer earnings**: it is another name for opportunity cost.) In many markets the amount a factor of production receives thus consists of two elements: transfer earnings plus economic rent.

The item which corresponds to economic rent on the demand side is called **consumer surplus**. This is the excess of the maximum price someone would be prepared to pay for a good (its 'value' to him) over the price actually asked. For example, someone prepared to buy a hardback book priced at £15 might find a paperback version in the same shop priced at £6. If he is indifferent between the two, then buying the paperback will provide him with consumer surplus of at least £9 (= £15 minus £6). ('At least' £9 because he might have been willing to pay *more* than £15 for the hardback.)

Fig. 1.3: Consumer surplus and economic rent.

Figure 1.3 shows the relationship between economic rent, consumer surplus, and actual market price. Economic efficiency consists of maximising the difference between the most the consumer is willing to pay ('value') and the opportunity cost of production ('cost'). Clearly the market price should normally fall between value and cost, the actual price depending on market conditions. If the price were above 'value', the consumer would not buy; but if it were below 'cost', the producer would not sell. This shows how important it is for producers to *know* both what their own costs are and how highly consumers value particular goods and services.

In the short run many factors of production may have few alternative uses, and it may also be difficult to expand supply. OPEC can charge $30 per barrel of oil, much above the Middle East cost of production; but in the long run developing other energy sources may help reduce the price of oil. The large increases in the price of oil in the 1970s converted much of the previous consumer surpluses into economic rents for producers. Hence the ambiguous effect on the UK, which is both a consumer and a producer of oil.

1.1.3 Competition

The market economy is not static, it is a dynamic *process*, always adapting itself to changing conditions. The market may tend towards equilibrium, but never reaches it. New disturbing features continually appear, such as the quadrupling of oil prices in the 1970s or the microchip revolution in the 1980s.

Competition is central to the market system. It involves not only short-term price competition, but what has been called 'the gale of creative destruction'. This is longer-term competition from new commodities, new technologies, new sources of supply, or new types of organisation. Such challenges to existing products and ways of business may command a *decisive* cost or quality advantage. If so, they can strike at the very foundations of the profits and outputs of existing firms. Some apparent restrictions, such as patent protection or long-term contracts, have the effect of reducing risk. By so doing they may actually encourage the long-run process of expansion and change, just as motor cars travel faster *because* they have brakes.

Market competition benefits consumers because it minimises production costs. It also ensures that market prices reflect those costs, and that producers are responsive to consumers' demands for product variety and product quality. A competitive market provides signals and incentives for businesses to allocate scarce resources efficiently to maximise consumer welfare.

Perfect competition is a technical term referring to idealised conditions. It implies identical goods, perfect knowledge, no transaction costs, and buyers and sellers small enough to have no influence on prices. 'Perfect competition' actually means the *absence* of 'competition' as normally understood: it excludes advertising, price-cutting, and improving the quality of goods.

Real ('**imperfect**') competition mainly involves long-term rivalry for *reputation*. It is a 'discovery procedure' to show *who* can be relied on to serve customers well. In comparing the competitive market system with a centrally planned economy, a common mistake is to suppose the decision-makers to be omniscient. Of course then one can criticise competition as being 'wasteful'. But this assumes away the main economic problem, the 'division of knowledge'. Making a better or a cheaper mousetrap is a good start, but consumers have to *find out* about it. Hence advertising is an essential part of the market system, spreading *knowledge* about new products (and reminding people about old ones).

Freedom of entry into different industries is vital, since it allows innovators a chance to outdo existing firms. Encouraging such rivalry tends to reduce costs to the lowest possible level. It thus contrasts with a monopoly, where there is only a single seller. For example, allowing foreign producers to compete in the domestic market is likely to benefit domestic consumers (see 5.1.3). And the presence of several competing domestic producers allows workers a choice of employers and may provide alternative sources of supply for other producers.

Figure 1.4 shows an outline of some major factors affecting competition within an industry. In analysing any market a key question to ask is what, if anything, is obstructing potential competition. Examples might be: legal restrictions on entry, by licensing or other means; restrictions on conditions of business, such as Sunday opening times for shops; statutory monopolies, as for the Post Office; limitations on advertising, as in many professions; etc.

The central dotted box in Fig. 1.4 contains an 'industry' (which may not be easy to define). Within it, we assume that different enterprises compete with each other. The basis for competition may be price, probably based on differences in cost; quality, possibly based on differences in technology or design; or service, possibly based on different market segments. All these ultimately depend on correctly identifying consumers' wants.

Outside the central box are external forces affecting the industry: potential

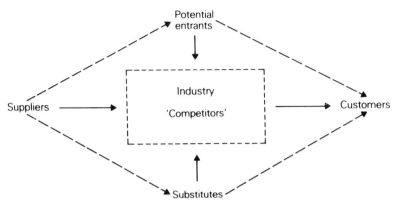

Fig. 1.4: Industry competition.

entrants, preventing the possibility of monopoly profits; suppliers, who also compete with each other; and substitute products, which either now or potentially compete with the industry's products. Changes in any of these three external forces can significantly affect an industry.

1.1.4 Entrepreneurs

If competition is central in the market, the **entrepreneur** is the key figure in driving the competitive process. He acts as the 'go-between' (= 'entrepreneur') linking resource-owners ('capitalists') with customers. His function is to bring together the various factors of production in order to produce goods and services which will satisfy customers.

The prospect of **profit** for entrepreneurs is a major incentive in the market system to foresee and satisfy consumers' wants. This implies private ownership and control of the factors of production, freedom to use them, and hence inequality of wealth. Even if everyone were to start equal, those who succeed in making profits, while others fail, will have more wealth, at least for a time. That is not to say, of course, that 'making money' is the only worthwhile objective in life. But if nobody is allowed to make and keep profits, there can be no market system.

Suppressing the profit incentive, by too much taxation or by other means, can stifle the market. There is no point in 'playing shop', as in a children's game, if the counters you win during the game are all taken away at bed-time. Moreover private ownership of the factors of production makes people take care to avoid **losses**. Thus scarce resources will tend not to be wasted. In contrast, it is notorious that few people feel much responsibility for 'public' property.

The entrepreneur is a 'general manager', concerned with Marketing, Production, Personnel, Finance, and Control. He must make, or appoint others to make, key decisions in all these areas:

a. *Marketing*: what market(s) to enter or develop; product quality; product range; pricing, distribution methods, promotion.
b. *Production*: size, location, and type of facilities; technical equipment and production processes; sources of supplies.
c. *Personnel*: selection of managers; key promotions and dismissals; type of organisation.
d. *Finance*: sources of finance; balance between short-term and long-term finance, and between equity share capital and borrowing.
e. *Control*: co-ordinating the various parts of the business; planning ahead; monitoring performance.

Entrepreneurs need to have energy, self-confidence, and imagination. They should be good at forecasting the direction and timing of future events, and quick to respond to changing circumstances. In modern conditions they need to be politically sensitive. Their two essential characteristics are *alertness* to identify new profit opportunities and the *courage* to act. It also helps if they are *lucky*!

1.2 The Business Community

The simplest view of the 'business community' would show only Producers (sellers) and Consumers (buyers). Figure 1.5 is rather more complex. The dotted box indicates that both employees and investors may in a sense be

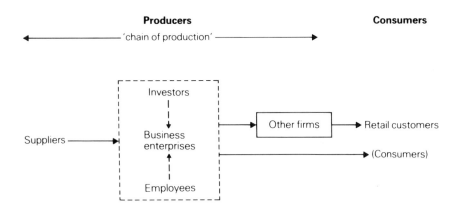

Fig. 1.5: An outline of the business community.

considered to be 'members' of a producer firm. Outside suppliers and customers, however, are quite separate.

A producer firm may sell to retail customers, but the **chain of production** (including distributors) is often more complex. Many firms sell to *other* firms who themselves (perhaps after more such 'intermediate' transactions) finally sell to the ultimate retail customers. Thus a street artist may sell his product direct to the final customer. But a manufacturer of printing inks sells his product to printers, who provide services for publishers, who sell to newsagents or booksellers or libraries, who sell to the final customer.

We now consider each part of the business community in turn: first consumers, then producer firms, employees and investors. We treat each separately, though one individual may perform more than a single role. For example, many employees are also consumers of their firm's products.

We are not concerned only with the United Kingdom. Many firms sell their products abroad, and many buy factors of production from abroad. And of course many consumer products are imported. A few of the largest firms also own production facilities abroad: these are sometimes called **multinationals**. Such firms may be owned by shareholders of many different nationalities. Their managements have to deal not with one, but with several different national governments.

1.2.1 Consumers

The purpose of business is to provide goods or services which will satisfy consumers at a profit. Hence businessmen must always have their customers in mind.

Consumers make a number of important economic decisions: how much of their income to spend on current consumption, and how much to save (see **3.2.4**); which goods and services to consume; and from which competing suppliers to buy these goods and services. The customer (purchaser) may not always be the same as the ultimate 'consumer'. For example, children (like pet animals) consume goods which they do not themselves buy.

Consumers need not be residents of the United Kingdom: nearly one third of all UK production is now exported to foreigners. Business nowadays is more international than ever (see Ch. 5). The UK population, however, can be a useful starting basis for analysing the total 'consumer market' into distinct groups.

Selling firms nearly always need to 'segment' the total market in some way in order to focus their marketing effort. For most products only certain parts of the population comprise the potential market. It would be optimistic, for example, to regard everyone as a potential buyer of this book.

Market segments should be distinct from others, large enough to be profitable, and practically reachable. Grouping people by age and sex could be suitable for such goods as clothes or books. Other divisions might be by occupation, by income level, or by geographical region.

In considering a product there are several levels to examine. For instance,

in Fig. 1.1 we looked at 'food' and 'clothing'. One kind of food might be
fruit, rather than meat; one kind of fruit might be apples, rather than pears
one kind of apple might be Golden Delicious, rather than Cox's Orange
Pippins. We also need to identify place and time: apples in Worcester rather
than in Newcastle; apples today rather than in a week's time.

In a developed economy consumers make very fine distinctions. Peas, for
example, are proverbially alike; yet in the market intermediate buyer
distinguish different grades. Indeed, one well-known television advertisement
shows a large pea being excluded from a packet of smaller peas. As suggested
earlier, part of the function of advertising is to *educate* consumers, not only
about what is available, but about why it may be desirable.

1.2.2 Producers

Three different kinds of productive business are usually distinguished
primary, **secondary**, and **tertiary**. They account respectively for about
10 per cent, 30 per cent, and 60 per cent of national output.

a. *Primary*. These are mainly *extractive* industries: they include agriculture
fishing, forestry, mining, quarrying, and extraction of oil and natural gas.

b. *Secondary*. These include *manufacturing* industries producing: (i) capital
investment goods (for use in further production), such as industrial robots
(ii) consumer durables, such as cars and washing machines; (iii) single-use

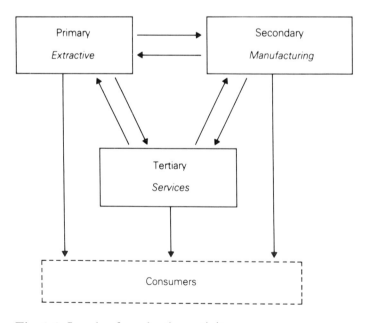

Fig. 1.6: Levels of productive activity.

consumer goods, such as food and newspapers; (iv) other consumer goods, such as books or clothes, which last for some time but are not normally classed as 'durable'. The secondary sector also includes construction businesses (see Ch. 10).

2. *Tertiary.* These include *service* industries, such as wholesale and retail distribution; transport and communication; gas, electricity and water utilities; and financial services, such as banking, insurance, and accountancy. The UK government provides some of the main services, such as defence and police, and welfare services such as schooling and health.

As noted earlier, the output of many producing firms represents *inputs* to other producing firms. This is called **intermediate** output. Not every firm sells its output directly to the consumer market; and many firms, especially large ones, also transfer goods between stages of production *within* their own organisations. Figure 1.6 outlines the position.

1.2.3 Employees

Employees earn income by selling their labour services to producer firms (or to government producers). They then spend most of it in their capacity as consumers, and save the rest (see **3.2**). There are some 22 million employed workers in the UK, many of them part-time, in addition to about 2 million 'self-employed' persons. The variety of their skills is enormous.

Maintaining the aggregate level of employment is an important economic objective (see Ch. 7). This is both because of the *waste* if resources are unused, and because most people of working age *want* to be employed in order to earn their living. But in a changing world, not everyone can be guaranteed the same job for life; hence even employees may need entrepreneurial 'alertness'.

1.2.4 Legal Structure of Enterprises

The most important distinction is between business enterprises which are 'incorporated', normally with limited liability for the owners, and those which are not. The process of incorporation creates a separate legal entity, apart

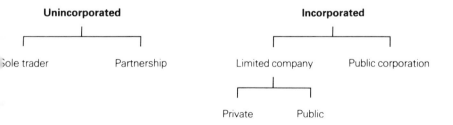

Fig. 1.7: The main kinds of business enterprise.

from the persons who own the business. Figure 1.7 sets out the main kind
of business enterprise.

a. *Unincorporated businesses.* The two main types of *unincorporated* busines
are **sole traders** and **partnerships**. A sole trader, or a partner in a firm
has *unlimited* personal liability to make good any amounts owed by the firm
Thus his entire personal wealth can be at risk, in addition to the capital h
has actually invested in the firm.

A 'sole trader' (an individual person) is the simplest form of busines
enterprise. He might be a dentist, taxi driver, or management consultant
Partnerships are common forms of enterprise, especially for small units (suc
as building or retailing) or in professions (such as medicine or law).

In a partnership firm:

1 There is usually a verbal or written partnership *agreement*, stating the basi
   for sharing profits or losses. Where there is no other agreement, all partner
   share equally in profits or losses, and contribute capital equally to the firm
2 Each partner, by his actions on behalf of the firm, legally binds all hi
   fellow-partners, whether he consulted them or not. Hence absolute *trus*
   is essential.
3 The death of any partner automatically dissolves a partnership, since
   firm has no separate legal existence of its own. But the remaining partner
   can easily establish a new firm, under the old name, if they wish.

b. *Incorporated businesses.* There are two main kinds of *incorporated* busines
enterprise: (1) limited companies, and (2) public corporations.

1 Limited companies

A **limited company** is created by two documents: the Memorandum an
Articles of Association. The Memorandum is the company's constitution
setting out its name, registered office, authorised share capital, and objects
The Articles are the detailed rules of the company, dealing with election o
directors, rights of shareholders, procedures for meetings, etc.

A company can perform legally binding acts in its own right, such as ownin
property, suing people, etc. As a separate legal entity, a company can continu
to exist beyond the life of its present owners. On a shareholder's death, hi
shares will be transferred to some other person, either by legacy or whe
his estate is 'realised' (turned into cash).

There are two kinds of limited company: (1) private, and (2) public.

1 Private limited companies are usually fairly small, with a maximum of 5
   members (shareholders). This arrangement may well suit the small o
   medium-sized family business, which may want to expand beyond the siz
   or financial resources of a partnership. At the same time, control of th
   enterprise can remain in the hands of a single family.
2 Public limited companies (known as 'plc') have no maximum number o
   shareholders. Their shares are quoted on the stock exchange and can b
   transferred between members of the public. If such companies wish t
   expand, they can raise more capital by issuing new shares to members o

the public. The managers running the company often own very few shares themselves.

2 Public corporations

Public corporations are better known as **nationalised industries** (see **8**.4). In effect they are corporations, rather like public limited companies, in which the government owns all, or most, of the shares. The legal constitution of each nationalised industry is set up in a separate statute.

1.2.5 Investors

There are two main kinds of financial *investment* in business enterprises: loans, consisting of fixed sums of money and bearing interest; and ordinary share capital (**equity** capital), which represents residual *ownership*.

The main lenders to sole traders, partnerships, and private limited companies are the commercial banks. In addition to banks, other large financial institutions (such as pension funds and insurance companies) also lend to public limited companies. Individuals may also lend to all kinds of business enterprise.

Figure 1.8 outlines the overall pattern of *ownership* of business enterprises.

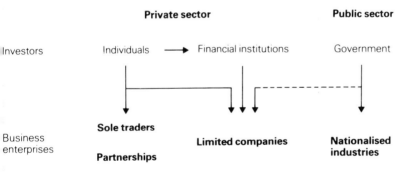

Fig. 1.8: Owners of business enterprises.

Individual persons own unincorporated firms (sole traders and partnerships), which they often manage as well. Individuals also own most of the shares in private limited companies. In public limited companies, however, individuals now own less than half of the ordinary shares. More than half is owned by various **financial institutions**, such as unit trusts, investment trusts, pension funds and insurance companies. The government owns at least a majority of the capital of the nationalised industries (usually all of it), and may also own some shares in certain public limited companies.

The capital invested by enterprises is often represented by fixed physical assets, such as equipment, buildings, or roads. Thus workers in a business may tend to be 'anchored' to a particular location or type of business. But shares in the ownership of these assets, in the case of public limited companies can be bought and sold on the stock exchange. So the ultimate investor possesses wealth which is 'mobile'. He can sell his shares to someone else if he needs the cash, or if he wants to invest in another kind of business or in another country.

1.2.6 The Market System

We have now described all the main actors in the market system (consumers, producers, employees, and investors), and the legal structures of business enterprises. Producers aim to make a profit by selling their output for revenue (income) which exceeds their total costs. Consumers also aim to gain from voluntary market transactions: when they buy goods and services, they expect the benefits (satisfactions) yielded to exceed the costs. We saw earlier (see 1.1.2) how in a competitive market the *price* mechanism tends to bring 'supply' and 'demand' into balance. Figure 1.9 summarises the overall position. It also includes government, which sometimes acts as a producer and sometimes as a consumer.

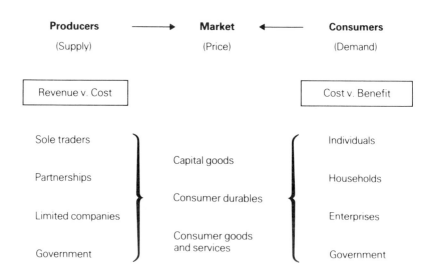

Fig. 1.9: The market system.

1.3 Government Intervention

From 1485 to 1815 it was unusual for England not to be at or near war against Scotland, France, Holland, or Spain. Tudor and Stuart governments both intervened extensively in the national economy. By means of **mercantilist** policies they tried to harness the nation's trade, industry, and commerce for the purpose of war potential. Tocqueville wrote of France, where the same policy was carried to extremes: 'It never occurred to anyone that any large-scale enterprise could be put through successfully without the intervention of the State.'

Adam Smith and the **classical economists** in Britain argued against these policies after 1776 and during the first half of the nineteenth century. Advocates of **laissez-faire** thought that governments needed to *justify* intervening; they argued that an 'invisible hand' led businessmen to benefit society even though that was not their intention. The voluntary competitive market system, they believed, could make everyone better off; and detailed government regulation, even if well-meant, was likely to make things worse not better.

Such views slowly came to prevail in Britain, and throughout the Victorian era government spending amounted to only about 10 per cent of the national income. *Laissez-faire* was less influential in other countries: France maintained a centralist tradition; the German states were being united into a single nation; and the United States, while thought of as the home of 'free enterprise', still needed a strong central government to forge a new nation.

The twentieth century has seen a striking increase in the extent of government. This is partly as a result of two world wars, and partly because of changed social conditions and political views. Developments in economic theory also contributed to the change of emphasis. It must be understood that *laissez-faire* and other philosophies of government depend on political opinion at least as much as on economic theory.

Since 1945 total UK government spending has increased from about one third to more than one half of national income. Government itself, including nationalised industries and local authorities, directly carries out much production and investment. Government is also a major customer of many firms, for example for military equipment, buildings, medical supplies, etc.

We shall be looking at details of government spending and taxation in Chapter 8. They are not the only kind of intervention (price controls, for instance, may be far more important), but they are the easiest to measure and compare over time and between countries.

In this section we briefly examine five main kinds of reason why governments intervene in the modern economy: (1) public goods; (2) market 'imperfections'; (3) demand management; (4) paternalism; (5) egalitarianism. As set out in Fig. 1.10, the first three may be considered as being mainly 'economic', and the last two as being mainly 'political'. But a clear distinction may not always be possible in a subject which used to be called 'political economy'.

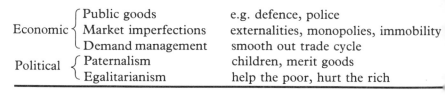

	Public goods	e.g. defence, police
Economic	Market imperfections	externalities, monopolies, immobility
	Demand management	smooth out trade cycle
Political	Paternalism	children, merit goods
	Egalitarianism	help the poor, hurt the rich

Fig. 1.10: Five kinds of reason for government intervention.

1.3.1 Public Goods

Public goods cannot be withheld from non-payers: they are available to everyone regardless of payment. An increasing number of people can consume them without reducing the amount left for others. Examples of public good are: military defence; police and the courts; street lighting. If the marke provided such goods, 'free riders' could share the benefit without bearing any of the cost. But government provision is financed out of compulsory taxation which falls on everyone.

The market system requires a certain framework of laws, to enforce contract and to maintain peace. Thus police, justice, and defence are widely agreed to be tasks that only government can fulfil. But few goods or services are wholly 'public', so it is often a matter of opinion which ones the government should provide.

1.3.2 Market 'Imperfections'

Most actual markets do not meet the stringent conditions needed for 'perfect competition (see **1.1.3**). Among the most important **market imperfections** are: (a) externalities, (b) monopolies, and (c) immobility. Each of these is discussed below.

Merely because the market is less than 'perfect', however, may not be enough to justify government intervention. For government too has its faults: red tape inflexibility, waste, lack of incentive, secrecy, use of compulsion, unresponsiveness to consumers' wishes. Thus the benefits from government action need to outweigh its costs. We should not compare an 'ideal' government with the actual market (any more, of course, than we should compare ar 'ideal' market against the actual government).

We should also remember a recently-retired senior civil servant's comment 'In a free society the economy consists of fifty million people beavering away doing pretty well what they want to, whether the government likes it or not.

a Externalities. **Externalities** refer to **social costs** (or benefits) resulting from market transactions but not borne (or not solely) by those directly involved Such costs or benefits can be difficult to measure. An example would be pollution of a river by a nearby factory. In theory, suitable laws of property rights might require a polluter to pay damages to compensate neighbours who were harmed. In practice, however, this may not be possible, so governments may either forbid pollution or limit its extent. Other examples might concern safety and health rules to protect employees or customers.

b Monopolies. **Monopolies** may find it pays them to restrict output and increase prices, compared with what would happen if there were competing suppliers. Two kinds of government action may try to prevent monopolies from harming the interests of consumers: (i) public ownership (nationalisation), or (ii) public regulation of privately-owned monopolies. Governments may also prevent proposed **mergers** that might lead to monopolies. But unless they have government protection, most monopolies are subject to long-run competition either from substitute products or from rival businesses.

c Immobility. Some factors of production may be slow to adapt to changing conditions. Government attempts to improve mobility of resources may help the market to work better. Thus workers may be unwilling to move from areas where traditional industries have declined. Suitable government housing policy could help labour mobility (though in the UK subsidised council housing has probably hindered it). The government may also provide 'regional incentives' to attract new industries to declining areas; or retraining to help workers acquire new skills.

1.3.3 Demand Management

The market system is not completely stable. Periods of above-average growth tend to be followed by periods of relative decline. These fluctuations, known as the **trade cycle**, cause problems to businesses as well as to governments. As a result, post-war governments have often tried to 'smooth out' the trade cycle. We discuss later (in Ch. 2) which economic aggregates governments may try to influence, and (in Ch. 9) the methods they may use.

In practice it has proved difficult to know (a) where the economy is now, (b) where it 'ought' to be, (c) which policy instruments would have the desired effect, and (d) with what time-lags. Indeed, it seems that some government actions intended to stabilise the economy may actually have been de-stabilising instead! So 'fine-tuning' policies are now rather out of fashion. Recent emphasis has been more on trying to improve the 'supply side' of the economy rather than on boosting aggregate demand.

1.3.4 Paternalism

Some people may be unable to look after themselves; for example, children and the mentally ill. Failing suitable family arrangements, the government is generally agreed to have a residual responsibility to take care of them. But does everyone need such government **paternalism**? Does education, for instance, need to be controlled and largely provided by the state? Or should the government simply provide (out of tax revenue) *finance* for children whose own families are unable or unwilling to pay for their schooling?

Perhaps even more contentious are so-called **merit goods** for adults. It is widely argued that certain services, such as health, are best provided collectively in kind. Otherwise some people might not choose to spend 'enough' of their own money to buy them. (If this were just a question of consumer *ignorance*, the government could simply *publish* its 'superior' knowledge.) Others object to the notion that 'the gentleman in Whitehall knows best'. They would prefer the government to limit itself to providing *finance* for the minority of people unable to afford a decent minimum level of welfare services.

1.3.5 Egalitarianism

The market system disperses incomes and wealth unequally. In principle, people whose incomes are thought to be 'too small' can simply be given more cash out of tax revenue. Thus redistribution in cash can mitigate absolute poverty. Paternalists, however, would still want the welfare state to provide benefits *in kind*, not in cash.

If some people are thought to have 'too much' wealth, or incomes that are 'too high', any 'excess' can be taken away by taxation. But thus over-riding consumers' market preferences may dampen incentives and as a result reduce consumer welfare. Incomes are not 'distributed' by a process separate from how they are earned; and forcibly changing the dispersion may reduce the *amount* of income generated.

Even in a completely 'egalitarian' society one would expect significant differences in incomes and wealth, due to age. And *relative* poverty is impossible to eliminate, in the sense that presumably there will *always* be some people whose incomes are 'below average'. There is also a question whether an egalitarian approach should be applied universally, or only within a nation.

Evidently the issues discussed in the last two sub-sections are highly political. They cannot be avoided in considering government intervention in the economy; but it should be emphasised that economists do not know the 'right' answers. Ultimately these depend on one's political views.

Work Section

A. Revision Questions

A1 How are consumer preferences reflected in the market?

A2 What are the key differences between a centrally planned and a market economy?

A3 How would you expect a fall in the price of a commodity to affect (a) demand? (b) supply?

A4 What is a 'mixed' economy?

A5 How does scarcity give rise to the phenomenon of 'opportunity cost'?

A6 How does growth affect an economy's 'production possibility curve'?

A7 Why is a seller's profit *not* normally made 'at the expense of' the buyer?

A8 Why is a demand-curve normally downward-sloping?

A9 Why does the market economy never reach 'equilibrium'?

A10 Why may competition be called a 'discovery procedure'?

A11 What is 'economic rent'?

A12 What are 'transfer earnings'?

A13 Why does the market price normally fall between cost (to producers) and value (to consumers)?

A14 Explain how the quadrupling of the price of oil converted much of previous consumer surpluses into economic rents.

A15 Name three important elements in long-term competition.

A16 Why is freedom of entry into industries important for competition?

A17 What is the major incentive in the market system causing producers to try to satisfy the demands of consumers?

A18 Why does private ownership of the factors of production imply inequality of wealth between individuals?

A19 Identify four different kinds of entrepreneurial decision.

A20 Why is 'alertness' a characteristic of successful entrepreneurs?

A21 Identify the main groups which are members of the 'business community'.

A22 Why don't all producers sell directly to consumers?

A23 What is the fundamental purpose of business activity?

A24 Why is 'consumer' not necessarily the same as 'purchaser'?

A25 Name three important kinds of economic decision made by consumers.

A26 Name the three main sectors of production. How do they differ?

A27 Give an example of a business in each of the three sectors of production.

A28 How does a partnership differ from a limited company?
A29 Name the three main groups of financial investors in productive enterprises.
A30 What is the main difference between 'equity' and 'loan' capital?

A31 What does *laissez-faire* mean?
A32 Why may government spending (as a percentage, say, of gross domestic product) not accurately measure government intervention?
A33 Give two examples each of government as (a) producer, (b) investor, (c) customer.
A34 What are public goods?
A35 What are externalities?
A36 Why may governments wish to regulate monopolies?
A37 Why does the existence of 'market imperfections' not necessarily justify government intervention in the market economy?
A38 Name three difficulties for governments aiming to smooth out the trade cycle by means of stabilisation policies.
A39 What are 'merit goods'?
A40 What problems may be caused by redistribution away from people with higher incomes?

B. Exercises and Case Studies

B1 Figure 1.11 represents the production possibility curve for an economy which produces only television sets and hospitals.

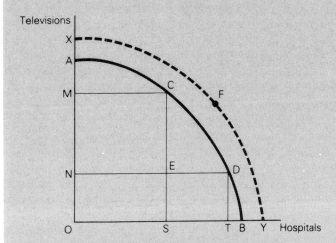

Fig. 1.11: Production possibility curves

   a. If the country were at point C on the curve AB, what quantity of televisions and hospitals would the economy be producing?
   b. If the country were at point D on the curve AB, in what way would its production differ from that at point C?
   c. Is it more beneficial for the community concerned to be at point C or at point E? Why?
   d. How might the economy concerned move from AB to XY?
   e. If it did so, would point F represent a possible point of optimum allocation of resources? Why or why not?

B2 Refer to Fig. 1.6 (page 10). There are nine arrows shown in the figure. Give two specific examples of a business transaction for *each* of the arrows.

B3 Refer to Fig. 1.8 (page 13). There are six arrows shown in the figure. Give one example of an 'investment' for *each* of the arrows. Be as specific as you can.

B4 Figure 1.12 shows the number of births and deaths per thousand population in the UK between 1945 and 1981. Deaths per thousand varied between 11 and 13 throughout the period, but the pattern for births was more varied. After a post-war spurt over 20, the birth rate fell to 15 per thousand by the mid-1950s; it then rose to $18\frac{1}{2}$ at the peak of the 'bulge' in the mid-1960s; and fell as low as $11\frac{1}{2}$ in the late 1970s.

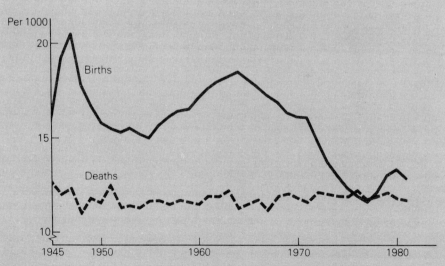

Fig.1.12: UK births and deaths per thousand, 1945 to 1981.

a. Ignoring migration, approximately what would be the annual change in the UK population (assume a base of 50 million throughout, for simplicity):
   i. in 1947? ii. in 1955? iii. in 1964? iv. in 1977?

    b. Identify one government-run and two privately-owned industries which you would expect to be affected by fluctuations in the birth rate. How might managers in each industry try to cope with the resulting problems?

B5 The price of oil is $30 per barrel. Suppose that Saudi Arabia, the main OPEC producer, has a marginal cost of production of $3 per barrel, while North Sea oil is produced at a marginal cost of $18.

    a. What is the economic rent per barrel for:
      i. Saudi Arabia
      ii. North Sea producers?
    b. What would happen if the market price of oil fell to $15 per barrel:
      i. to Saudi Arabian production?
      ii. to North Sea production?

B6 Figure 1.13 shows simple supply and demand curves in a market for leather brief-cases.

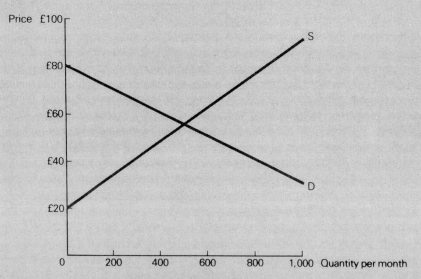

Fig. 1.13: Supply and demand for leather brief-cases.

    a. What is the 'market-clearing' price? How many brief-cases will be bought and sold at that price?
    b. Starting from the point identified in (a) above, by what percentage does demand for brief-cases change if:
      i. the price rises by 10 per cent?
      ii. the price falls by 20 per cent?
    (This is measuring the 'price-elasticity' of demand.)

C. Essay Questions

C1 Oil is scarce. Should national governments therefore control it to prevent the world supply running out?

C2 Does private ownership of the factors of production, as compared with government ownership, provide a powerful incentive for people to avoid wasting resources?

C3 Why are prices important in the working of the market economy?

C4 What are the advantages of a command economy over a market economy?

C5 Rolls-Royce and Ford are both in the 'car industry', but do they compete with each other?

C6 Why do sole traders and partnerships continue as useful forms of business enterprise in spite of their disadvantages?

C7 'The principle of limited liability is necessary for business enterprises to flourish in the modern economy.' Discuss.

C8 Discuss the proposition that consumers are the key members of the business community.

C9 How can government intervention in the 'mixed economy' be justified?

C10 How can successful entrepreneurship be encouraged?

C11 Is the 'century of *laissez-faire*' (from 1815 to 1914) best regarded as an atypical interlude in five centuries of mercantilism and extensive government intervention in national economies?

C12 'Government assistance to mitigate the social costs of declining industries or areas may tend to perpetuate the problem.' Discuss.

C13 What might be the advantages and disadvantages to a conglomerate firm of splitting up into several smaller units?

C14 Isn't competition wasteful? What are its advantages?

C15 Why is bankruptcy an essential feature of the market system?

Chapter 2

The Circular Flow

Objective: *To describe a simple 'circular flow' model of the national economy; to show how changes affect 'equilibrium'; to explain the 'multiplier'; and to review the model's basic assumptions.*

Synopsis: *The 'circular flow' model of the national economy analyses short-term fluctuations away from 'potential national income', which is taken to be constant.* Withdrawals – *Savings* (S), *Imports* (M), *Taxes* (T) – *are assumed to be a constant* proportion *of national income, while* Injections – *Investment* (I), *Exports* (X), *Government Spending* (G) – *are assumed to be a constant* amount. *'Equilibrium' occurs when total withdrawals equal total injections, i.e. when S + M + T equals I + X + G.*
  An increase in an injection, or a reduction in a withdrawal, exerts expansionary

pressure on the economy; while a reduction in an injection, or an increase in a withdrawal, exerts contractionary pressure. Thus withdrawals tend to reduce national income, injections to increase it; though we need to distinguish between temporary and permanent changes.

The 'multiplier' concept implies that a change in one of the component parts may lead to a larger change in national income. The 'multiplier' in practice probably amounts to less than $1\frac{1}{2}$, but the time-lags involved may vary.

In two basic respects the model is clearly unrealistic: in the real world relative prices can change, and economic resources are scarce. But the model's assumptions to the contrary need to be interpreted in the context of the short run rather than the long run.

2.1 The Basic Model

Throughout the book it will be convenient to have a **model** of a national economy. The 'macro-theory' of national income deals with aggregates, such as consumer spending or capital investment, which it treats as being **homogeneous**. This chapter outlines a **circular flow model** which should help to show in general terms how the various aspects of the national economy relate to each other.

We must remember, however, that in the real world nobody actually deals with such 'aggregates' (see also 3.1.1). They merely represent an artificial device to allow us to grasp some overall aspects of the market system. Failure to recognise this led to the famous 'paradox of value' which the classical economists could never resolve. The question was: since diamonds are luxuries while water is vital, why are diamonds more valuable than water? The answer is that no doubt in the aggregate 'water' is more valuable than 'diamonds'; but it is *marginal* demand and supply which determine market prices, rather than *total* demand and supply.

The circular flow model makes two critical basic assumptions: that prices do not change, and that unemployed supplies of all factors of production are freely available. For the purpose of analysis we also assume that **potential national income** is constant. While in the long run these assumptions are clearly unrealistic, they can be useful in letting us employ a fairly simple 'static' model to look at short-term fluctuations in national income.

Later chapters will discuss in more detail some of the matters which this chapter touches on only briefly: savings and investment in Chapter 3, imports and exports in Chapter 5, and taxes and government spending in Chapter 8.

2.1.1 A Simple Circular Flow Model

Imagine a self-sufficient country which requires no imports from other countries, and exports nothing itself. Its inhabitants manage without any economic interference from government. Finally, assume that people earn their incomes entirely from wages, and devote all their incomes to buying consumer goods and services, like cars and holidays. Thus there is no saving.

As a first step towards understanding more complex systems, we can divide this simple economy into two sectors: households and firms. Figure 2.1 shows that the connections ('flows') between households and firms are both physical ('real') and monetary. Later diagrams of the circular flow will show only the *money* flows.

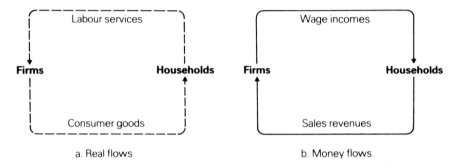

Fig. 2.1: The circular flow between households and firms.

Figure 2.1(a) shows households providing the labour services which firms employ to produce the goods which households buy in their role as consumers. Figure 2.1(b) shows the monetary counterparts to these 'real' (physical) flows. Firms pay wages in money to households, who then spend the money in buying goods and services from firms. (The use of money means that households do not literally exchange their labour services for consumer goods. They need not spend all their money wages in buying goods only from the same firm which employs them.)

In this very simple model the firms, by producing output, create household incomes just sufficient to buy that output. ('Supply creates its own demand.') Thus total income (Y) exactly equals consumption (C). Even this simple outline is enough to show that *all expenditure must be someone else's income.*

2.1.2 Saving and Investment

We now start to build up a more complex picture, stage by stage. Households now spend only *part* of their wage incomes on buying consumer goods from firms; they *save* the rest. **Saving** is 'income not spent on current consumption goods and services'. As well as making consumer goods, firms now also invest in **capital goods**. These are not themselves for immediate consumption, but are used to produce goods for later consumption.

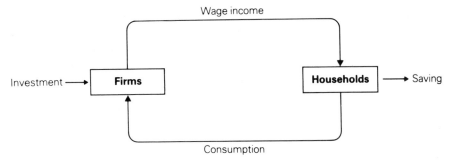

Fig. 2.2: The circular flow including saving and investment.

To begin with we assume that all saving is done by households and all real capital investment by firms. Household savings become **financial investments**, which do not directly increase the stock of capital goods. The capital market channels them through financial institutions, such as unit trusts, pension funds, or industrial companies, to finance real investment (fixed capital formation) by firms.

Savings represent household income which is *not* directly spent on consumer goods and services. This is an example of a **withdrawal**, which is defined as 'any income which is not passed on in the circular flow'. Fixed capital investment is an example of an **injection**: this is defined as 'An addition to the income of domestic households or firms which does not arise from the spending of domestic firms or households respectively.'

In our model, withdrawals tend to *reduce* national income, and injections to *increase* it. We shall see later precisely how this works. The point where withdrawals *equal* injections is defined as the equilibrium level of national income. Thus at this stage our simple economy is said to be 'in equilibrium' if household savings are equal to firms' capital investment.

2.1.3 Foreign Trade and Government Intervention

So far, Savings (S) have been the only 'withdrawal', and Investment (I) the only 'injection'. Now we introduce foreign trade (which amounts to nearly one third of UK national income).

Another kind of *withdrawal* from the (domestic) circular flow is Imports (M). **Imports** represent goods or services produced abroad and purchased by domestic households or firms. And another kind of injection into the circular flow is Exports (X). **Exports** represent domestically-produced goods or services sold to foreigners.

We must also allow for government intervention, which is very significant in the modern economy. **Taxes** (T), which are paid to government by households or firms, represent a third kind of 'withdrawal' from the circular flow. And a third kind of 'injection' is represented by real **government spending** (G), either on consumption goods and services or on investment (capital) goods.

To keep the picture simple, Fig. 2.3 assumes that only households import and pay taxes, and that real government spending goes only to firms. (A more complex picture is shown in Fig. 2.4 at the end of this section.)

In the circular flow model, government spending does *not* include **transfer payments**. These are any payments made by the government to households or firms *other than* in return for the services of factors of production. Examples would be unemployment benefits or state pensions to households, or subsidies to firms. Such payments do not lead directly to any increase in output, though they may change the *composition* of aggregate output by switching purchasing power from taxpayers to 'tax-receivers'.

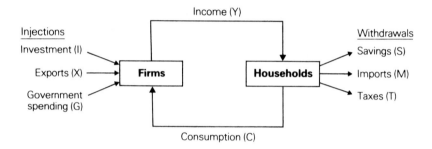

Fig. 2.3: The circular flow including foreign trade and government intervention.

2.1.4 The Overall Logic of the Model

According to the logic of the circular flow model, national income will be in equilibrium when:

WITHDRAWALS	=	INJECTIONS
Savings + Taxes + Imports		Investment + Government spending + Exports
S + T + M	=	I + G + X

And National Income (Y) can be expressed in terms either of Income

(= Consumption (C) plus Withdrawals) or of Expenditure (= Consumption (C) plus Injections). Thus, in symbols:

$$Y = C + S + T + M = C + I + G + X$$

National income = Income = Expenditure

2.1.5 A More Complex Version

To round off this section, Fig. 2.4 sets out a somewhat more complex version of the circular flow model.

The two inter-connected blocks labelled 'Firms' represent the very substantial amount of **intermediate goods** and services traded between firms. Firms' *profits* have been included, with their three-way split between business tax on profits, dividends to shareholders, and undistributed profits (= business savings). Part of consumption is seen to go in expenditure taxes, and part in imports. For convenience, imports and exports, tax and government spending, and savings and investment are connected with each other; but this should not be taken to imply that, in the short-term, they are necessarily equal (see **2.2.5**).

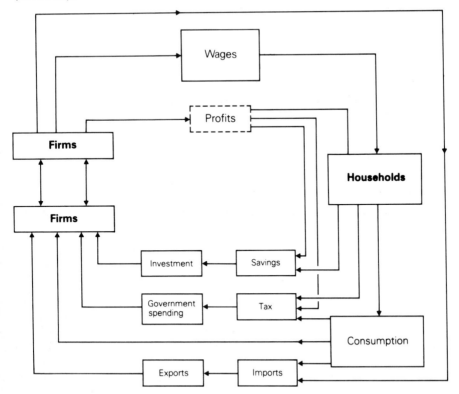

Fig. 2.4: A more complex version of circular flow.

2.2 The Effect of Changes

2.2.1 Equilibrium

In developing the circular flow model, we now make two further crucial assumptions: (1) That withdrawals are a constant *proportion* of national income; thus households save a constant proportion of their income, and taxes and imports are each a constant proportion of national income. (2) That injections – investment, government spending, and exports – are each constant *amounts*, not varying as national income changes.

Let us suppose, for example, that households save 20 per cent of their income, and consume the other 80 per cent. To begin with, investment spending is constant at 20 per week. (We don't need to specify units, but this can be thought of as £20 m. per week.) Figure 2.5 plots Savings (S) and Investment (I) on the vertical axis, against national income (Y) on the horizontal axis. (Notice that the two axes have different scales.) For simplicity, Fig. 2.5 refers only to savings and investment: strictly it could be 'withdrawals' and 'injections' respectively.

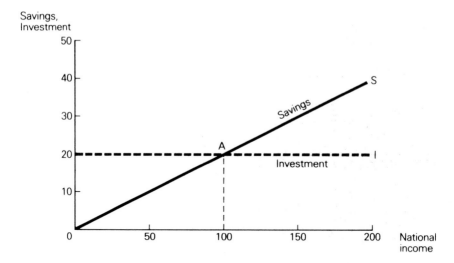

Fig. 2.5: Equilibrium.

In Fig. 2.5 equilibrium comes at the point (A) where the Savings line intersects the horizontal Investment line. This represents Savings (and Investment) of 20, and national income of 100.

If the amount which households wish to save is not the same as the amount which firms wish to invest, then the economy will not be in equilibrium (some economists argue that in practice this is very important). But there are supposed to be forces at work tending to push the economy towards equilibrium.

We can now go on to examine what happens to national income if there is a *change* in the behaviour of households, firms, or governments. We shall see how the model predicts that economic aggregates will change, if necessary, in order to move towards equilibrium. We consider first the *direction* of changes in national income (in the rest of this section); and then their *magnitude* (in the next section).

2.2.2 A Temporary Change in Injections

Starting from a position of equilibrium, what happens to national income if there is a *change* in one or more of the items? If there were no time-lags in the circular flow, adjustment to any changes would be instantaneous, and the economy would always be 'in equilibrium'. But we assume that income is paid to households *one week in arrear*, and that production adjusts to demand with *no* time-lag, so that there is no need for any change in stocks (inventories).

Figure 2.6 shows what happens when the amount of injections changes, for example through an increase in the amount of investment spending. The first two weeks show national income in equilibrium at 100. Savings (S) are equal to Investment (I), and both equal 20. According to our definitions:

National Income (Y) = Savings (S) + Consumption (C)

100 = 20 + 80

In week 3, firms decide to double their investment spending from 20 to 40. Household income in week 3 relates to week 2's production, and stays at 100. But production increases *immediately* to satisfy the increased demand for investment (capital) goods. Thus in week 3 national income = output = 120 (consumption 80 + investment 40). The excess of investment (an injection) over savings (a withdrawal) now exerts *expansionary pressure* on the economy.

Week	Disposable income (last week's Y)	S Savings (20%)	C Consumption (80%)	I Investment (constant)	Y National income
1.	100	20	80	20	100
2.	100	20	80	20	100
3.	100	20	80	40	120
4.	120	24	96	20	116
5.	116	23.20	92.80	20	112.80
6....					
n	100	20	80	20	100

Fig. 2.6: Temporary increase in investment.

In week 4, and later weeks, however, investment falls back to 20, so that national income gradually falls back to its starting level of 100.

As we can see, a once-off increase in investment spending causes an increase in national income. *But if the increase in investment is not sustained, national income gradually falls back to its original level.* The pattern of national income for this temporary increase in investment is shown in Fig. 2.8, as the dotted line.

2.2.3 A Permanent Change in Injections

What would happen if there were a *permanent* increase in investment spending, instead of a temporary increase as before? Figure 2.7 sets out the position week by week. The first three weeks' numbers are the same as in Fig. 2.6, but this time the increase in investment spending is maintained at the higher level of 40.

Week	Disposable income (last week's Y)	S Savings (20%)	C Consumption (80%)	I Investment (constant)	Y National income
1.	100	20	80	20	100
2.	100	20	80	20	100
3.	100	20	80	40	120
4.	120	24	96	40	136
5.	136	27.20	108.80	40	148.80
6....					
n	200	40	160	40	200

Fig. 2.7: Permanent increase in investment.

In week 4, household income rises to 120 (= last week's output), so savings rises to 24 (= 20 per cent of 120), and consumption to 96. Week 4 output therefore rises to 136 (= consumption 96 + investment 40). And so on ... The expansionary pressure is eliminated only when savings again become equal to investment. This *must* be at the point where 20 per cent of national income = 40; that is, when national income = 200 (= 40/20%).

Figure 2.8 shows the pattern of national income over time, both for a *permanent* increase in investment spending (solid line) and for a temporary increase (dotted line). A *fall* in investment spending would work in reverse: the resulting *contractionary* pressure ceases only when national income has *fallen* enough for savings (withdrawals) again to become equal to investment (injections).

Figure 2.9 shows the effect on equilibrium level of national income of a permanent increase in investment spending from 20 to 40 per week. As

National
income

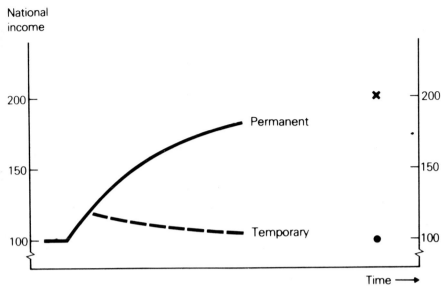

Fig. 2.8: Patterns of national income over time for increases in investment.

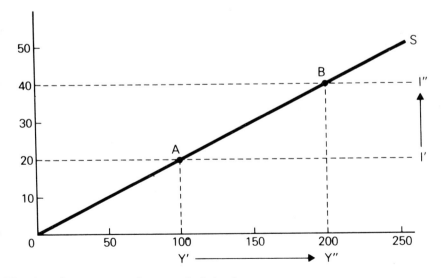

Fig. 2.9: A permanent increase in injections.

Investment (I) increases on the vertical axis from 20 (I') to 40 (I"), the equilibrium level of national income (Y) moves from 100 (Y') on the horizontal axis to 200 (Y"). The equilibrium point on the chart moves from A to B.

Instead of Savings and Investment, we should really have been using *total* withdrawals and *total* injections. The circular flow model defines national income as being in equilibrium when total withdrawals equal total injections; but this does not necessarily mean that Savings alone equals Investment alone (see **2.2.5**, below).

Thus the model predicts that a rise in Investment (I) or in Government Spending (G) or in Exports (X) will lead to an increase *in national income; and that a fall in I, G, or X will lead to a* reduction *in national income.*

2.2.4 A Change in Withdrawals

We have assumed that all kinds of injections (investment, government spending, and exports) are 'autonomous' constant *amounts* unrelated to national income. On the other hand, we have assumed that all three kinds of withdrawals (savings, taxes, and imports) are 'induced' constant *proportions* of national income.

Figure 2.9 showed the effect of a permanent increase in *injections*. Now Fig. 2.10 shows how a fall in *withdrawals* affects the equilibrium level of national income.

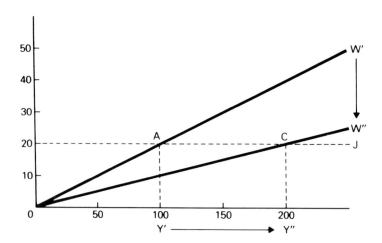

Fig. 2.10: A fall in withdrawals.

The original equilibrium level of national income (Y') was 100. At that point, withdrawals of 20 per cent of national income are equal to injections (J) of 20 at point A, where the W' line crosses the horizontal J line. Now the slope of the withdrawals line has changed from W' to W", representing a reduction from 20 to 10 per cent of national income. So at the original level of national income (Y') withdrawals are now *less* than injections. Hence national income will *rise* until at Y" (200) withdrawals – now at 10 per cent of national income – are again equal to injections. This is at point C, where the W" line crosses the J line.

Thus our model predicts that a fall in withdrawals (in Savings (S), Taxes (T) or Imports (M)) will lead to an increase in national income; and that an increase in S, T, or M will lead to a reduction in national income.

It may seem strange that a *reduction* in savings should lead to an *increase* in national income. What is generally supposed to be prudent behaviour in a single household, namely increasing savings, seems to lead to an undesirable result in the whole economy, namely a fall in national income. This is sometimes called the **paradox of thrift**. But this is a logical deduction from the model's assumptions (see **2.4**).

2.2.5 Compensating Changes

As we saw in **2.1.4** (page 28), according to the circular flow model, national income will be in equilibrium when total withdrawals equal total injections. That means when:

$$\text{Savings} + \text{Taxes} + \text{Imports} = \text{Investment} + \frac{\text{Government}}{\text{spending}} + \text{Exports}$$

$$S \quad + \quad T \quad + \quad M \quad = \quad I \quad + \quad G \quad + \quad X$$

But this is does *not* mean that each of the pairs is 'matched'. It does not imply that S = I, or that T = G, or that M = X in any given period. For example, the economy would be in equilibrium if the various items were as follows:

$$\text{Savings} + \text{Taxes} + \text{Imports} = \text{Investment} + \frac{\text{Government}}{\text{spending}} + \text{Exports}$$

$$S \quad + \quad T \quad + \quad M \quad = \quad I \quad + \quad G \quad + \quad X$$
$$40 \quad + \quad 70 \quad + \quad 50 \quad = \quad 30 \quad + \quad 90 \quad + \quad 40$$

Although S is not equal to I, nor T equal to G, nor M equal to X, *total* withdrawals are equal to *total* injections (= 160). That is what matters.

Now assume a *decrease* in investment by private firms. We have seen (Fig. 2.9, page 33, moving from I" to I') that the model predicts (other things remaining the same) that this will lead to a *fall* in national income. But other

36 *The Circular Flow*

things may not remain the same. Starting from a position of equilibrium, if one of the items changes, equilibrium may be restored *at its original level* by one of several possible 'compensating changes'.

Such restoration of equilibrium may well be an objective of government policy (rather than letting national income fall to the new, lower, equilibrium position). Hence it is common to consider possible *government* action to restore equilibrium, either by cutting taxes or by increasing government spending. This kind of government action, known as **demand management**, is illustrated in Fig. 2.11, and further discussed in **9.3.2**.

Event	Government response	leading to:
Contractionary pressure Investment falls Exports fall Savings rise Imports rise	Increase government spending or cut taxes	Budget deficit (or reduced surplus)
Expansionary pressure Investment rises Exports rise Savings fall Imports fall	Reduce government spending or raise taxes	Budget surplus (or reduced deficit)

Fig. 2.11: Government 'demand management'.

2.3 The 'Multiplier'

2.3.1 How the Multiplier Works

Section **2.2.4** dealt with the *direction* of changes in national income caused by changes in withdrawals or injections. We now consider their *magnitude*. Again we suppose government action – 'demand management' – to start the process.

We continue to assume that injections (I, G, X) are a constant *amount*, and withdrawals (S, T, M) are a constant *proportion* of national income. Suppose that total withdrawals amount to 40 per cent of national income. Starting from equilibrium, what then happens if government spending increases by, say, £500 m.? By how much will national income increase before equilibrium is restored?

Of course an increase in government spending of £500 m. will, in the 'first round', lead to an increase in national income of £500 m. But 40 per cent of that increase will be withdrawn from the circular flow (in savings, taxes, and imports). This leaves 60 per cent (£300 m.) in increased domestic spending. Output will rise to meet this demand (remember we are assuming no increase in prices). There will then be an increase of £300 m. in national income in the 'second round', of which 40 per cent (£120 m.) will be withdrawn. But 60 per cent (£180 m.) will lead to an increase in national income in the 'third round'. And so on ... Figure 2.12 sets out the position.

Round	Disposable income	$S + T + M$ Withdrawals	C Consumption	$I + G + X$ Injections	Y National income
1.	—	—	—	+500	+500
2.	+500	+200	+300	—	+300
3.	+300	+120	+180	—	+180
4.	+180				
5.					
...					
Σ 1 to n =	+1,250	+500	+750	+500	+1,250

Fig. 2.12: Effect of £500 m. increase in injections.

Equilibrium will be restored when increased withdrawals exactly equal increased injections. That will be when national income has risen by £1,250 m. (i.e. by £500 m./40%). At that point the increased withdrawals of £500 m. (= 40% × £1,250 m.) will exactly equal the increased injections (government spending up by £500 m.). So the **multiplier** in this case amounts to 100/40% = 2.5. Eventually the national income will have risen 2.5 times as much as the amount of the initial injection.

Although the *cumulative* increase in national income will be £1,250 m., since this was an isolated increase in government spending the *final level* of national income – in period *n* – will be the same as its starting point.

We can show the logic of the multiplier by repeating Fig. 2.9 from page 33. Here it is set out slightly differently, in Fig. 2.13.

Now the *slope* of the withdrawals line is $\triangle W / \triangle Y$. This shows the fraction of any new income that is withdrawn from the circular flow. The multiplier is simply $\triangle Y / \triangle J$, which is the increase in national income divided by the increase in injections. But $\triangle J = \triangle W$. So we can also define the multiplier as $\triangle Y / \triangle W$. In other words, the multiplier is the reciprocal of the slope of the withdrawals line.

$$\text{Multiplier} = \frac{\triangle Q}{\triangle Inj}$$

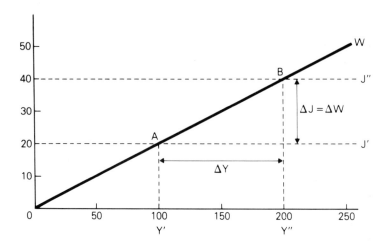

Fig. 2.13: The logic of the multiplier.

Thus the model makes a further prediction. The smaller the proportion of national income withdrawn (in S + T + M), the larger *the change in national income resulting from any change in injections. That is, the smaller the withdrawals percentage, the larger the multiplier.*

Of course the multiplier can work in *both* directions. A *reduction* in injections would cause a *larger fall* in national income.

2.3.2: The Size of the Multiplier

The multiplier is actually a lot *smaller* than one might expect, probably less than $1\frac{1}{2}$. The many 'leakages', by way of taxes and imports, cause the total fraction of income withdrawn from the circular flow to be much higher than merely the fraction of income *saved*. Since savings, taxes and imports have all risen as a proportion of income in many countries since the war, it follows that the value of the multiplier has *fallen*.

Figure 2.14 shows how the multiplier might work. Suppose the UK government increases spending by £100 m., by placing orders for frigates for delivery within one year. The leakages (withdrawals) from the circular flow might then increase as shown.

The secondary increase in consumption of domestic goods and services (C) can now be allowed for within the circular process. Figure 2.15 shows the *cumulative* increases, if the ratios remained constant.

		£ m.		Withdrawals		
				S	T	M
Initial gross expenditure	=	100	Y			
– Producers' imports		– 15	M			15
Domestic output		85				
– Company tax		– 4	T		4	
– Undistributed profits		– 4	S	4		
Personal incomes		77				
– Tax on incomes		– 26	T		26	
Personal disposable incomes		51				
– Personal saving		– 7	S	7		
Personal consumption		44				
– Indirect taxes (net)		– 4	T		4	
– Consumers' imports		– 10	M			10
Secondary increase in demand for UK goods and services	=	30		11	34	25

$$= 70\%$$

Fig. 2.14: Leakages from the circular flow.

The total increase in aggregate output (= income) is 1.43 times the initial injection. This ratio is the reciprocal of the proportion of each round of increased income which 'leaks' away in withdrawals (70%). Thus 100/70 = 1.43.

In this example the government recovers nearly half the extra £100 m.

	Y	G	C	S	M	T
1.	100	100*	–	–	–	–
2.	130	100	30	11	25	34
3.	139	100	39	14.3	32.5	44.2
4.						
...						
n	143	100	43	15.7	35.7	48.6	= 100.0*

Fig. 2.15: Cumulative increase in withdrawals.

spending in increased tax revenue (of £48.6 m.). If the extra work led to a fall in unemployment, with lower social security payments, the net cost to the Exchequer would be lower. This would reduce the total cumulative increase in national income.

Three aspects of the multiplier are of interest: the *direction* in which it operates, its approximate *size*, and the *time-lags* involved. In practice, the direction of the multiplier is not in doubt, and we may roughly estimate its order of magnitude. But the time-lags are often difficult to predict. Hence we may not be sure *how long* it will take for the effects of the multiplier to work through.

2.3.3 Criticism of the Multiplier

Keynes derived his famous 'multiplier' from an assumed *fixed* **marginal propensity to consume** (MPC). 'This quantity is of considerable importance, because it tells us how the next increment of output will have to be divided between consumption and investment.'

He went on to explain how to quantify the multiplier: '. . . if the consumption psychology of the community is such that they will choose to consume, e.g., nine-tenths of an increment of income, then the multiplier is 10; and the total employment caused by (e.g.) increased public works will be ten times the primary employment provided by the public works themselves, assuming no reduction of investment in other directions.'

People's income may be defined as equal to what they consume plus what they invest. If in a given period they spend nine-tenths of their income on consumption and one-tenth on investment, then their income *must* be ten times as great as their investment. *They are simply different ways of saying the same thing.* But this implies nothing about a *causal* relationship, nor need this proportion remain *fixed*.

Nor are we entitled to stand this supposed causal relationship on its head. We cannot conclude that the larger the proportion of income spent on consumption (the smaller the proportion spent on investment), the more the amount spent on investment will have to 'multiply itself' to create the total income!

There is no such constant mathematical relationship among the various elements – optimism, income, consumption, saving, and investment – which mutually interact. Indeed, the *aggregate* amounts do not interact at all. Investment decisions are made by many different people and firms, taking into account their own needs and views (see **3.3.4**).

The whole 'multiplier' concept rests on the assumptions that relative prices do not change and that suitable unemployed resources are always available. These assumptions are far removed from reality. A change in government spending may indeed have secondary effects; but their extent is not easy to predict, and the time-lags involved may vary. Thus we need to be suitably cautious in seeking to apply the notion of a multiplier.

2.4 The Assumptions Reviewed

At the start of this chapter we made two basic assumptions: that prices do not change, and that there are unemployed supplies of all factors of production. It may seem fair enough to ignore the complication of general inflation, for the purposes of a simple model. More important, however, is the assumption that even *relative* prices don't change. For that is one of the main adjustment mechanisms in the real world. By ruling it out completely, the model – which is really designed to apply only to the short run – takes a large step away from long run reality.

The second basic assumption was that there are unemployed supplies of all factors of production. This means we can always use 'spare' resources (including labour) to generate extra output at no (opportunity) cost. Assuming that economic resources are *not* scarce in the long run would again take us far away from the real world. Hayek has called this the assumption of 'full unemployment', which he says makes the whole price system 'redundant, undetermined and unintelligible'. But in the short run it may not be so unrealistic if mobility of factors of production takes *time*.

We made a third assumption at the start of the chapter: that potential national income is constant. Notice that we are not referring to *actual* national income, but to what is sometimes called 'full employment' national income. There will always be some **frictional unemployment** in a changing world (see Ch. 7). 'Potential' national income represents what actual national income *would be* if there were no labour unemployment above this unavoidable minimum level. It thus ignores the various phases of the trade cycle (see Ch. 9).

Most modern economies have been growing very rapidly by historical standards during the past 30 years (see Ch. 4), both in actual and in potential national income. But it makes it much simpler to ignore this growth, and again the assumption may be justified in a short-term context.

Two further crucial assumptions in 2.2.1 (needed for the model's 'multiplier' arithmetic to work) were that withdrawals represented a constant proportion of national income, while injections were a constant amount, whatever national income amounted to. Both these assumptions are completely false over a long period of time.

As far as withdrawals are concerned, savings in the UK since the war have risen significantly as a proportion of national income (see 3.2.4), so have imports (see 5.1.2), and so have taxes (see 8.2.1). With respect to injections, investment in the UK nearly doubled in real terms between 1960 and 1970, though admittedly it has been virtually constant since then (see 3.4.2). Both exports (see 5.1.2) and government spending (see 8.1.1) have grown substantially in real terms. But these facts do not necessarily invalidate the model in the short term.

Finally the 'paradox of thrift' (see 2.2.4) suggested that a *reduction* in saving would lead to an *increase* in national income. But of course this depends on the assumption that savings and investment are completely unrelated. Similarly the model predicted that an increase in spending – either on investment *or on consumption* – would lead to an increase in real national income. But such a prediction might not follow from different assumptions. For example, even with less than full employment, increased spending in reality would probably cause inflation, as Keynes himself recognised.

Any model inevitably has to over-simplify; and we have seen that the circular flow model essentially relates to the short run, not to the long run. At least it introduces some of the major economic aggregates, and tries to show their inter-relationships. But one of the problems is precisely that the *aggregates* themselves are *not* directly related to each other. What is required for 'full employment', for example, is a correspondence between supply and demand *in each sector* of the labour market (see Ch. 7). One can hardly expect an unemployed bus driver to carry out brain surgery! There are serious dangers in thinking in aggregates, as we now go on to discuss in the next chapter (see **3.1.1**).

Work Section

A. Revision Questions

A1 In the simplest version of the circular flow model, why do households pay money to firms?

A2 Why do firms pay money to households?

A3 Define (a) Saving, (b) Investment.

A4 What are 'capital' goods? How do they differ from 'consumer' goods?

A5 What is the difference between 'real' investment and 'financial' investment? Give two examples of each.

A6 In the circular flow model, define 'withdrawal'. Give an example.

A7 Define 'injection' in the model. Give an example.

A8 Define (a) imports, (b) exports.

A9 Define 'transfer payments'.

A10 In equilibrium, $S + T + M = I + G + X$. Express this in words, using the appropriate word(s) for each letter symbol.

A11 In the circular flow model, what is the assumed relationship between withdrawals and national income?

A12 What is the assumed relationship between injections and national income?

A13 Does an excess of injections over withdrawals exert (a) an expansionary or (b) a contractionary pressure on the economy? Why?

A14 Why does it make a difference, in the circular flow model, whether a change in injections is sustained, or for one period only?

A15 What is the 'paradox of thrift'?

What (and in each case why?) does the model predict will be the effect of:

A16 a fall in exports?

A17 an increase in government spending?

A18 an increase in the proportion of income saved?

A19 a fall in the proportion of income taken in taxation?

A20 Define 'demand management'.

A21 Define the 'multiplier'.

A22 What effect would a reduction in the proportion of income withdrawn from the circular flow have on the size of the multiplier? Why?

A23 What are the three kinds of 'withdrawal' from the circular flow? What are the three kinds of 'injection'?

A24 Which three aspects of the multiplier were suggested to be of interest?

A25 What is the 'marginal propensity to consume'?

A26 What assumption does the circular flow model make about prices?
A27 What assumption does the model make about unemployed factors of production?
A28 Define 'potential' national income. Why may it differ from actual national income?
A29 Why might the 'paradox of thrift' not be true in the real world?
A30 Why was it suggested that the circular flow model relates more to the short run than to the long run? Give as many reasons as you can.

B. Exercises and Case Studies

B1 Refer to Fig. 2.5 on page 30.
    a. Redraw the figure on the assumption that savings amount to 25 per cent of national income, and that investment equals 15.
    b. *From your chart* estimate the equilibrium level of national income.
    c. Confirm your graphical estimate of the equilibrium level of national income, by means of simple arithmetic.
B2 Refer to Fig. 2.6 on page 31. Complete lines 6 and 7.
B3 Refer to Fig. 2.7 on page 32. Complete lines 6 and 7.
B4 The text says (page 32): 'A *fall* in investment spending would work in reverse.'
    a. Construct a table along the lines of Fig. 2.7 setting out the numbers for the first 5 periods, assuming that savings amount to 20 per cent of national income, but that the amount of investment *falls* permanently from 20 to 12, as from period 3.
    b. Fill in line *n*, showing the details of the new equilibrium level.
    c. Explain the numbers in line *n*, by simple arithmetic.
B5 Refer to Fig. 2.9 on page 33.
    a. Construct a similar chart on the assumption that savings amount to 30 per cent of national income showing the original and final equilibrium positions of national income (Y' and Y") if the amount of investment increases from 18 to 24.
    b. How can you use the chart to explain what happens if the amount of investment falls from 24 to 18?
B6 Refer to exercise B4 above and to Fig. 2.6.
    a. Construct a table assuming that the fall in investment from 20 to 12 occurs in period 3 only, and that investment reverts to 20 for all subsequent periods. Show the numbers for the first 5 periods.
    b. Fill in line *n*.
B7 Refer to Fig. 2.10 on page 34.
    a. Construct a similar chart, on the assumption that withdrawals amount

to 25 per cent of national income to begin with, but fall to 20 per cent, with injections throughout amounting to 30.

b. What is the original and final equilibrium level of national income?

B8 What government action is needed to 'compensate' for these changes:
a. exports fall?
b. investment rises?
c. imports rise?
d. savings rise?

B9 In an imaginary economy, Y = £1,000; I is constant at £200; and households consume 80 per cent of any income received. What is:
a. the equilibrium level of national income (state: Y, S, C, I)?
b. the multiplier?

B10 Refer to exercise B9. The economy is in equilibrium, at a level of under-full employment. What new equilibrium figure would result in *each* of the following separate (and unrelated) situations:
a. a sustained rise in investment by 50 per cent?
b. a change in the marginal propensity to save from 20 to 25 per cent?
c. a permanent drop in investment by 30 per cent from its original level?

B11 Refer to Fig. 2.12 on page 37.
a. Assuming that one third of national income is 'withdrawn' in leakages from the circular flow, construct a table similar to Fig. 2.12 showing numbers for the first 4 periods in respect of a reduction in injections of 600.
b. Fill in line Σ1 to *n*.
c. What does the multiplier amount to?
d. How would your answers above differ if there had been an *increase* in injections of 600?

B12 Refer to Fig. 2.15 on page 39. Fill in lines 4 and 5.

B13 The following flow diagram represents the position of Country A when its resources are fully employed:

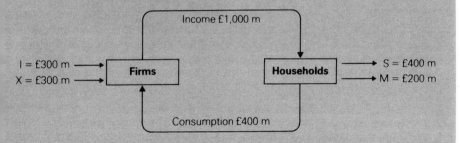

a. i. Is the country in equilibrium?
   ii. Does it have a surplus or deficit on its balance of trade?
   iii. What is the value of the multiplier?

b. What would be the effect on on Country A if (together):
   i. imports fell by 25 per cent;
   ii. savings fell by 10 per cent; and
   iii. I rose by 10 per cent?
   Explain how you reach your conclusions.

B14 Meticulousia was an economy where order and regularity were important, and where the state had always played a significant part in economic affairs. The following data applied to the economy: $Y = £10,000$, $C = £2,000$, $M = £2,000$, $S = £4,000$, $G = £2,000$, $T = £2,000$, $X = £4,000$, and $I = £2,000$.

Although the economy was in equilibrium, the government was worried about the high level of unemployment, and was determined to do something about it.

The government decided to start the ball rolling by spending an extra £2,000 of state money on new roads, schools, and port facilities. At the same time, the government would cut taxes on firms that exported and on personal incomes, so reducing taxation by 25 per cent. There was also to be a modest cut in the incentives on personal savings schemes, to bring about a $12\frac{1}{2}$ per cent fall in S.

a. Draw a flow model to indicate the nature and values of income flows at the original equilibrium position. What observations, if any, can you make about this position?
b. Consider the government measures, and then:
   i. illustrate the changes on a flow diagram;
   ii. explain the effects of these changes on the multiplier.

B15 Refer to Fig. 2.14 on page 39. Draw up a similar table, making the following assumptions:
1. Producers' imports equal 20 per cent of initial gross expenditure.
2. Company tax and undistributed profits *each* equal 5 per cent of domestic output.
3. Tax takes one third of personal incomes.
4. Personal saving is one sixth of personal disposable incomes.
5. Indirect tax accounts for 20 per cent of personal consumption.
6. Consumers' imports account for 25 per cent of personal consumption.
   a. What proportion of income is each of the three types of withdrawals?
   b. What is the value of the multiplier?
   c. What would the value of the multiplier become if taxes were changed to take one half, instead of one third, of personal incomes?

C. Essay Questions

C1 Why might the factors that influence the decisions to save and to invest not coincide in practice? What would be the consequences?

C2 In what ways might the introduction of foreign trade and government intervention influence the effect of business investment decisions on the general level of economic activity?

C3 What would you expect to be the overall effect on the multiplier of the post-war increase in the UK of the proportion of income going in savings, tax, and imports? Would it make government 'demand management' easier or more difficult? Why?

C4 What forces, if any, are at work in the economy which might tend, in time, to bring savings and investment towards equality?

C5 Why does it matter if the time-lags of the multiplier are difficult to predict? What might make them so?

C6 What factors might affect people's 'consumption psychology'?

C7 Discuss the strengths and weaknesses of the concept of the multiplier.

C8 The text (referring to Fig. 2.13) says on page 37: 'The multiplier is the reciprocal of the slope of the withdrawals line.' Try to express this in words which could be understood by someone who has not seen Fig. 2.13.

C9 What are the characteristics of a good model? Can a model be useful if it employs unrealistic assumptions?

C10 Why is it potentially misleading in economics to think in terms of aggregates?

Chapter 3

Consumption, Saving and Investment

Objective: *To describe three ways of estimating national income; to explain how 'income' is split between 'consumption' and 'saving'; to outline factors affecting capital investment; to discuss capital formation and consumption.*

Synopsis: *Aggregate estimates of national income are not complete or accurate measures of human welfare. Three ways to estimate 'national income' are by totalling (a) incomes, (b) expenditures, and (c) output.*
   'Consumption' normally means expenditure on consumer goods, not the amount of services consumed; while 'saving' – defined as income less consumption – may be related either to current or to 'permanent' income.
   The interest rate – the 'price of time' – affects the choice between consuming now or later. Neither classical nor Keynesian theories fully explain capital investment.

Many factors influence its level, including: demand for output, production capacity, supply of funds, etc.

Gross UK fixed capital formation (excluding dwellings) amounts to about 15 per cent of GDP, capital consumption to about 12 per cent. Real increases or decreases in stocks (inventories) are usually less than 2 per cent of GDP.

3.1 The National Economy

3.1.1 Measuring Economic Aggregates

Politicians may talk about a need for 'housing' or 'education' – in the **aggregate**. But this is not how real families think of them: they think of a specific kind of house or school. (And it is pointless in economics to talk about 'need' without mentioning *price*.) Moreover the 'British economy' is not guided by a single hierarchy of needs. Only in war-time, with one supreme 'national objective', was that state of affairs even remotely approached. When we talk about 'countries' doing this or that, we usually mean 'individuals' or 'groups of people' living in those countries.

In political economy we talk about 'governments', but their aims will not always be the same as those of each citizen. Indeed, the 'government' itself is not monolithic: in reaching decisions it has to combine many different opinions. There are countless examples of government departments having contradictory policies.

We lose *information* when we aggregate or **average**. For example, suppose there is heavy unemployment in one region but more or less 'full' employment in another. An increase in spending in the first region may well cause a real increase in national income, by increasing employment and output. But in the second region it may be more likely to cause an increase in prices, without much affecting real output. Thus the dispersion of the average level of unemployment may be crucial in interpreting the situation.

We also need to distinguish between **average cost** and **marginal cost**. The average cost of production is calculated by dividing the total cost of production by the number of units produced. The *marginal* cost is the cost of producing one more unit. Since many costs tend to be **fixed** – especially in the short run – the marginal cost may often be less than the average cost. (This concept is explained in more detail in *Production Decisions* by John Powell.) To the businessman, it is marginal cost that is relevant; but it may not be easy to decide what is the appropriate time-period to be looking at.

Similarly the *timing* of events in economics can be vital. Economics is not just a mathematical game played instantaneously via sets of simultaneous equations! Yet calculations of 'annual average' returns from investment projects can conceal such useful information. 'Static' models of the economy may be much simpler and easier to handle than 'dynamic' models, but they nearly always run the risk of being misleading.

Not everything of value can be traded on the market, nor is everything that is expressed in terms of money necessarily a *benefit*. Modern economies produce **bads** (such as pollution) as well as goods. Current concern with the 'quality of life' refers to this problem.

Assuming that 'cost implies value' may make sense for voluntary market transactions. Presumably 'cost' is normally *less* than 'value' as perceived subjectively by the buyer, otherwise why would he choose to buy? But where governments decide to spend other people's money, this may not be so. For instance, what if the government were to build and maintain a huge brick pyramid in the Shetland Islands? It would no doubt *cost* a good deal, but would it really be worth much?

Aggregates like **gross domestic product** or **national income** do *not* provide accurate measures of human welfare. They leave out many 'non-economic' factors that have value (such as a country's climate), while including some items whose value may be less than cost. And many 'economic' transactions may be recorded inadequately, or not at all, in official estimates of national income. Some of the main examples are listed in Fig. 3.1.

1. Depreciation of durable consumer goods
2. Illegal transactions
3. Barter transactions
4. Government-provided goods and services
5. Non-marketed agricultural goods
6. Notional rent of owner-occupied accommodation
7. 'Do-it-yourself' work done within families
8. Gifts
9. Leisure

Fig. 3.1: Items inadequately recorded in national income statistics.

Growth in items 2 and 3 has led to the expansion of what is called the **black economy**. (It is also sometimes referred to as the 'hidden', 'informal', or 'underground' economy.) But estimates of its size are mere guesses. Such unrecorded transactions can make it hard to compare national incomes of countries with very different social conditions. It can also be difficult to make comparisons over long periods of time for a single country.

Another serious problem is how to allow for changes in the general level of prices (that is, in the purchasing power of money). There are ways of 'deflating' money estimates of national income into **'real' terms**, in order to adjust for inflation (as discussed in Ch. 6). But the results can only be approximate.

It is worth having such problems in mind when we look at 'national income' statistics in the rest of this section. They can be useful, but they can also be misleading. The compilers of government statistics are well aware of the problems: indeed they publish estimated **reliability gradings** for various components of national income. These are shown in the left-hand column of

Figs 3.2, 3.3, and 3.4. Grade A means the margin of error is reckoned to be less than 3 per cent; Grade B between 3 and 10 per cent; and Grade C more than 10 per cent.

In principle 'national income' can be calculated in three different ways: by adding up (1) everyone's *income*, (2) everyone's *expenditure*, or (3) the value of total *output*. We now examine these in turn.

3.1.2 Income Estimates

Figure 3.2 shows the main items of national income (as percentages of the total) for 1960, 1970, and 1980. Between 1960 and 1980 total national income rose by 50 per cent in real terms, and national income per head of population by 40 per cent.

Reliability grading	*Percentages*	*1960* (%)	*1970* (%)	*1980* (%)
A	Employment	73	77	82
B	Self-employment	8	8	8
B/C	Company profits	14	9	6
B/C	Government trading	–	–	(2)
B	Rent, etc.	5	7	7
	Residual error	–	(1)	(1)
A	National income	100	100	100
In 1975 £b.: National income		59	78	88
In 1975 £: National income per head		1,120	1,400	1,565

Fig. 3.2: National income: income estimates.

Company profits and government trading results are shown after deducting **stock appreciation** (the increase in book value of stocks due not to physical volume increases but to price increases). They are also shown after deducting **capital consumption** (an estimate of depreciation of fixed assets, at current replacement cost). **Residual error** is simply a balancing item to reconcile the estimates of national income based on income with those based on expenditure (as shown in Fig. 3.3, below). In recent years this item has averaged about 1 per cent of national income. Numbers in brackets represent negative amounts.

It is clear that the share of employment income has been increasing, and that of company profits falling. It may also be noted that profits represent only a small proportion of total national income.

3.1.3 Expenditure Estimates

Figure 3.3 shows percentage estimates of national income based on expenditure for 1960, 1970, and 1980. They start by analysing total Domestic Spending at market prices between:

a. private and government;
b. **consumption** and **investment** (a distinction discussed later in this chapter).

Two adjustments are then made to the expenditure estimates:

c. exports are added, and imports deducted, to convert from domestic *spending* to domestic *production* (at market prices);
d. **expenditure taxes** are deducted, and **subsidies** added, to convert from domestic production at market prices to gross domestic product (GDP) at **factor cost**.

Reliability grading	Percentages	1960 (%)	1970 (%)	1980 (%)
A	Private consumption	81	80	81
C	Private fixed investment	12	14	17
C	Private stockbuilding	3	1	(2)
A/B	Government consumption	20	23	29
C	Government fixed investment	8	10	7
	Domestic spending	124	128	132
A/B	Add: Exports	25	29	38
A/B	Less: Imports	(26)	(28)	(35)
	Domestic production at market prices	123	129	135
A	Add: Subsidies	2	2	3
A	Less: Expenditure taxes	(16)	(21)	(22)
A	*Gross domestic product at factor cost*	109	110	116
C	Less: Capital consumption:			
	Private	(5)	(6)	(10)
	Government	(4)	(4)	(6)
A	National income	100	100	100

Fig. 3.3: National income: expenditure estimates.

Capital consumption estimates are then deducted separately, to arrive at national income.

As a percentage, gross private fixed investment has been increasing, but so has capital consumption. Private stockbuilding was negative in 1980, which means that the real value of stocks held *fell* in that year. Government consumption has been increasing, but government fixed investment fell quite sharply between 1970 and 1980. Exports and imports both rose noticeably between 1970 and 1980: they now represent about 27 per cent of GDP at market prices.

3.1.4 Output Estimates

It is sometimes easier to calculate output by adding up the output of all the various productive units, rather than by adding up the total amount of expenditure incurred in purchasing that output.

Merely aggregating each productive unit's *sales revenue* would produce a total far higher than the value of output actually available for consumption. This is because of all the **intermediaries** in a market economy. For example, adding together the sales value of (1) farmers' wheat plus (2) flour mills' sales plus (3) bakeries' bread plus (4) retail bread sales would count the value of the *same* wheat *four times*!

Reliability grading	Percentages	1960 (%)	1970 (%)	1980 (%)
A	Agriculture, forestry, fishing	4	3	2
A	Petroleum and natural gas	–	–	4
A	Other mining and quarrying	3	$1\frac{1}{2}$	2
A	Manufacturing	$36\frac{1}{2}$	$32\frac{1}{2}$	25
B	Construction	6	7	$6\frac{1}{2}$
A/B	Utilities	$11\frac{1}{2}$	12	11
B	Distributive trades	12	$10\frac{1}{2}$	10
B	Insurance, banking, finance	3	4	$4\frac{1}{2}$
B	Ownership of dwellings	4	$5\frac{1}{2}$	6
B	Professional and other services	10	13	$15\frac{1}{2}$
B	Government-provided services	10	12	$14\frac{1}{2}$
	Residual Error	–	(1)	(1)
	Gross domestic product	100	100	100
	Primary sector	7	$4\frac{1}{2}$	8
	Secondary sector	$42\frac{1}{2}$	$39\frac{1}{2}$	$31\frac{1}{2}$
	Tertiary sector	$50\frac{1}{2}$	57	$61\frac{1}{2}$

Fig. 3.4: National income: output estimates.

The concept of **value added** avoids this problem of 'double counting'. Each enterprise's 'value added' is the sales value of its output *minus* the value of the inputs it buys from other firms. Figure 3.4 shows the results analysed by industry for 1960, 1970, and 1980, as percentages, not of national income, but of gross domestic product at factor cost.

Agriculture represents only a small share of total output. The fall in manufacturing between 1960 and 1980 is very noticeable: it now represents under a quarter of total output. The main offsetting increases are in petroleum and natural gas (a new item in 1980), in professional and other services, and in government-provided services (which are public administration and defence, public health, and education).

3.2 Consumption and saving

3.2.1 Consumption

'Consumption' normally means *expenditure* on consumer goods or services in a period. Figure 3.5 sets out the main classes of consumer spending for 1960, 1970, and 1980, in terms of percentages.

Percentages	1960 (%)	1970 (%)	1980 (%)
Food	30	25	23
Drink and tobacco	12	13	11
Housing	10	13	15
Fuel and light	4	5	5
Clothing	10	9	7
Durable and household goods	11	11	12
Miscellaneous goods	7	6	8
Car expenses and travel	7	8	9
Other services	9	10	10
	100	100	100
Total consumer spending (1975 £ b.)	46	58	72

Fig. 3.5: Consumer expenditure, 1960 to 1980.

Many things other than income affect consumption, including family size and age spread, changes in tastes, in prices, and in interest rates. Even if people always consumed a constant proportion of their **disposable income**, the government could alter the rate of *tax* on gross incomes. That would change the ratio between disposable incomes after tax (and hence personal consumption) and the national income:

| Gross
Income | $-$ | Tax on
Income | $=$ | Disposable
Income | $\longrightarrow$ | Consumption
Saving |

3.2.2 Consumer Durables

There is a problem in classifying **durable consumption goods**, such as cars or washing machines. Money may be *spent* on them in one period, but the services are actually *consumed* (used up) in later periods. One could define 'consumption' as the amount of services *consumed* in a period. But it would be hard to tell how much of a durable consumer good had been 'used up' in any period (depreciation).

The only 'consumer good' where the national income statistics take a different approach is dwelling houses. These are treated as 'capital' expenditure, and estimates are made of the services used up in each period. This is possible because there is a well-established market for renting houses; and especially desirable because houses tend to last for a very long time, compared with most other durables (see Ch. 10).

In national income statistics, 'durable goods' mean those goods which are fairly costly and which can be bought on credit terms, such as: motor cars, furniture, radio, electrical, and other household appliances. Other goods are not included as **consumer durables** even though they may last just as long: jewellery and watches; curtains; clothing; crockery and glassware; and books.

For many of these goods there is an active **second-hand market**, which is more important in practice than in most text-books. Sales of second-hand goods between households (such as books or furniture) are not recorded; but purchases by consumers from other sectors are recorded (such as second-hand cars from business firms, or army surplus stores from the government).

3.2.3 'Permanent Income'

Consumption (however defined) may be related not to *current* income, but to some longer-term measure of **permanent income**. Then a change in a household's income might influence consumption only insofar as it affected the level of income expected to be sustainable in future. This notion of 'income' excludes occasional or windfall income, such as once-only income tax rebate or a non-recurring capital gain.

The 'permanent income' approach leaves open the question what happens to the relatively large proportion 'saved' out of a *temporary* increase in income. It may be spent either on durable consumption goods or on financial investments. The former involves real new spending, but the latter merely transfers the ownership of existing financial securities.

Figure 3.6 summarises the two possible definitions of 'consumption' and of 'income' discussed above. Changing the meaning of 'consumption' or of 'income' must clearly change the meaning of 'saving' as well – since it is merely 'income minus consumption'.

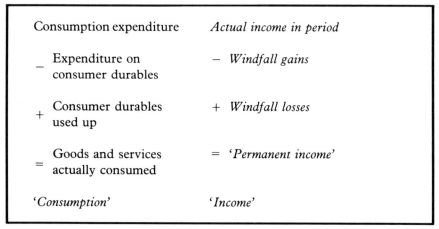

Fig. 3.6: 'Consumption' and 'Income'.

3.2.4 Saving

Saving is defined as income minus consumption. Many economists have believed that as people became wealthier they would save a larger *proportion* of

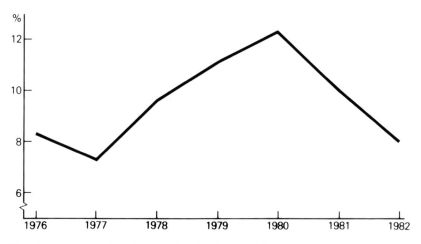

Fig. 3.7.: Personal savings ratio, 1976 to 1982.

their income. In the UK and Germany, for example, there has been a definite post-war increase in personal savings as a proportion of personal disposable income. This has been especially marked in the 1970s. But in the United States the average proportion of income saved has stayed roughly constant over a long period. The reason for this difference is not known.

The recession in 1981–82 coincided with a fall in UK personal savings as a proportion of personal disposable income, as Fig. 3.7 shows. In other words, consumer spending held up better in real terms than income. The change would be even more striking if we looked only at 'discretionary' savings, since most savings in the UK are 'contractual' (such as life assurance premiums, pension contributions, and mortgage repayments) and cannot be changed much in the short run.

3.3 Saving and Investment

3.3.1 Time Preference

One way of looking at how households divide their income between consumption and saving is to regard saving simply as a way of *postponing* consumption. The choice is then between consumption now and consumption *later*. The **rate of interest** is the 'price of time'. It allows people with low rates of **time preference** to *lend* on the capital markets, thus postponing consumption. It also permits those with high rates of time preference to *borrow* in order to bring forward consumption.

Lending or borrowing on the capital markets enables people to enjoy a time-pattern of *consumption* which differs from their time-pattern of *income*. The young and the old will normally consume more than they currently earn; while people of working age contribute out of current income towards children's upkeep or retirement pensions.

In modern economies, commercial interest rates usually comprise three component parts:

1. the price of *time*
2. an *inflation* premium
3. a *risk* premium.

There is not a *single* interest rate in the financial markets, but a whole range, depending on the length of the loan, the credit-worthiness of the borrower, and other factors. Because all these interest rates tend to be linked together, however, it is normal to refer to 'the' rate of interest. This may be thought of as the current yield on 3-month government Treasury bills. Government securities are regarded as 'risk-free', since they are virtually certain to be repaid in full on the due date. That does not, of course, rule out the risk of inflation, which is allowed for separately. And index-linked government securities are now available, yielding a 'real' rate of interest between 2½ per cent and 3½ per cent.

One intriguing question in political economy is whether *governments* have high or low rates of time preference. A government preoccupied with being re-elected in the near future might seem to have a high rate of time preference. On the other hand, a government concerned with the welfare of future generations may seem to have a very low rate of time preference. But 'government' is not a monolith. One suggestion is that in practice politicians may tend to think short-term while civil servants think long-term!

3.3.2 Classical Interest Theory

In the classical theory, a rise in the rate of interest was supposed to increase savings (the *supply* of funds for investment). It would also tend to reduce the *demand* for funds for investment, since marginal projects would no longer be profitable enough. An increase in the interest rate would increase the opportunity cost of funds committed to capital projects. Hence it would increase the **discount rate** applied to projects' expected cash inflows, and thus reduce their **present values** and make them seem less attractive than before.

The rate of interest would change fairly quickly, according to classical theory, to act as a 'market-clearing' price tending to keep savings equal to investment, as shown in Fig. 3.8. In this respect the market for investment funds was regarded as similar to any competitive market (see **1.1.2**).

Both assumptions of the classical theory of interest are open to question. In practice, capital seems *not* to be very responsive to short-term changes in the rate of interest (**'interest-elastic'**). Thus the demand curve may be more nearly vertical than shown in Fig. 3.8: this means it would need a *larger* change in the rate of interest to induce any given amount of change in the demand for investment funds. Moreover, for political and other reasons, the rate of interest may not be free to fluctuate in the required way.

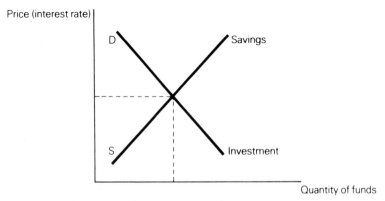

Fig. 3.8: The market for investment funds.

3.3.3 Keynesian Theory

In classical theory the *rate of interest* (price) fluctuates in order to bring savings and investment into balance. But Keynesian theory tends to focus on changes in the *quantity* of investment (or of output or of employment) in causing a move towards equilibrium. (This was described in more detail in Ch. 2.) There is another way to interpret this difference of emphasis. The classical theory stresses the *long-term* outcome, in which price changes are likely to be important. Keynes, however, was more concerned with the short-term, in which price changes may not occur, or (even if they do) may not have an immediate effect.

Part of Keynesian theory on investment (the **accelerator theory**) suggests that when national income is constant, investment will be limited to *replacing* capital assets as they wear out or become obsolete. If real national income is increasing, it will be necessary to invest in additional capital assets in order to expand existing productive capacity. The theory assumes a fixed **capital-output ratio**, and concludes that changes in the demand for consumer goods bring about more than proportionate changes in the demand for the *capital* goods used to make them.

As shown below, there are many factors which influence capital investment decisions. Hence it seems unlikely that aggregate investment spending would be related in any simple way to year-to-year changes in national income, as the accelerator theory implies. And the theory does seem, at least in its simple form, to be a poor predictor of observed changes in the level of investment.

3.3.4 What Determines Investment?

Figure 3.9 lists several possible factors which may affect an individual firm's capital investment decisions. It may also be more profitable to make better use of existing capital assets than to invest additional funds in new assets. That is, the *quality* of investment in, and use of, capital assets may be more important than the quantity.We must also remember that in the UK nearly a third of all fixed capital investment (excluding dwellings) is undertaken by the **public sector**. Central government, nationalised industries, and local authorities may not use quite the same criteria for investment as profit-seeking enterprises.

The items listed in Fig. 3.9 fall under four headings, each of which is briefly discussed below. The importance of the four topics covered in separate chapters in Part II will be evident: they are (4) Economic Growth, (5) International Business, (6) Money and Inflation, (7) Labour.

Demand for output. The expected future *volume* of demand is often critical in capital investment decisions, especially for expansion or new product projects. For many businesses volume comes from *exports* as well as from domestic sales. Hence the pound's exchange rate may be important, especially if demand is price-elastic.

It may not be easy to 'pass on' increased costs in higher selling prices in competitive markets; hence the perpetual pressure to minimise costs. Again the pound's exchange rate will affect the sterling cost of imported materials. The

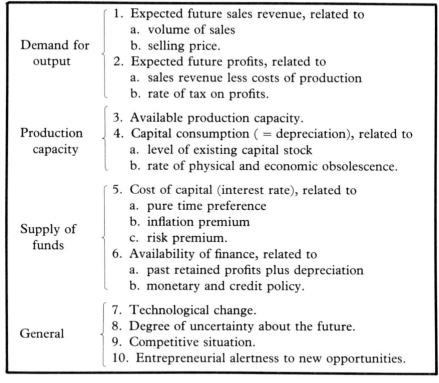

Fig. 3.9: Factors influencing capital investment by a profit-seeking enterprise.

other major component of costs is likely to be wages, so the climate in the labour market may also be critical.

Production capacity. New capacity may be needed either to reduce unit costs or else to increase the volume of output. Even in industries (such as steel) where total capacity outstrips supply, there may still be a need for new capital investment to modernise facilities. In today's international economy, an important question may be *where* to build new capacity, as well as *how much* to build.

Supply of funds. Shortage of funds restricts capital investment much less than does lack of profitable projects. But if real interest rates are high, firms may be reluctant to issue new equity shares or to borrow long-term. Thus if retained profits are low, new capital investment may be cut back.

General. Failure to keep up with technical change may reduce the competitive quality of products and reduce profit margins (through costs being too high). On the other hand, research and development can be expensive. Uncertainty may arise for many reasons: (a) political, especially just before a general election; (b) technical changes; (c) currency exchange rate changes; (d) input costs, for example oil or other raw materials; (e) competition; (f) other.

3.4 Capital Assets

The national income statistics include three kinds of capital assets:

1. Productive fixed assets, such as plant, machinery, vehicles, and factory and office buildings.
2. Stocks (inventories), which are sometimes called 'circulating' rather than 'fixed' assets.
3. Dwellings, which are included as 'capital assets', although they are really more like very long-lasting consumer durables.

In this section we look first at additions to productive fixed assets, then at deductions from them, and finally at stocks. Dwellings are dealt with in Chapter 10.

3.4.1 Gross Fixed Capital Formation

In considering productive fixed capital assets, we may look either at the total amount of capital goods in the economy, or at the rate of *change* in that amount. The total will rise (even after allowing for inflation) because of new additions to the stock of capital assets (**capital formation**). But the total will fall through 'capital consumption' as the assets gradually lose their value, either through physical wearing out or through economic obsolescence.

Figure 3.10 shows the stock of productive fixed capital assets in the UK at the end of 1981, together with the annual change in 1981. The net capital stock is stated at current **replacement cost**. This means the estimated amounts it would cost to replace the assets in their partly-used condition. The totals may be compared with UK gross domestic product in 1981 of about £250 b. (at market prices).

	Private	*Government*	*Total*
Net capital stock, end 1981:	*(£ b.)*	*(£ b.)*	*(£ b.)*
Plant, machinery, etc.	160	70	230
Buildings and works	140	170	310
	300	240	540
Fixed capital formation in 1981:			
Gross fixed capital formation	24	10	34
Less: capital consumption	17	10	27
Net fixed capital formation	7	–	7

Fig. 3.10: Net capital stock and net fixed capital formation 1981.

Figure 3.10 also shows the amount of investment in productive fixed capital assets in 1981, called **gross fixed capital formation**. It is 'gross' in being the *total* amount spent on capital assets, before deducting an allowance for **depreciation** of fixed assets ('capital consumption'), which is also shown. The difference between the two is 'net fixed capital formation'.

Gross fixed capital formation in the UK rose from about 10 per cent of gross domestic product just after the Second World War to about 15 per cent by the end of the 1960s. Apart from a brief spurt during the so-called 'Barber boom' of the early 1970s, the level has remained at about 15 per cent of GDP since then. The share of the government sector fell from just under a half in the late 1960s to less than a third of the total by 1981. This may seem surprising, in view of the nationalisation during the period of British Steel, British Leyland, and several other enterprises.

As noted earlier with the accelerator theory, there is some reason to expect capital investment to fluctuate more sharply than total output. But this has not happened recently in the UK: gross capital investment has fluctuated *less* than total output in most of the last dozen years.

Capital investment must depend on subjective views about the uncertain future, so it is understandable that different firms (let alone different industries) do not always take the same view. In practice, there are often differences of opinion even within individual enterprises! Capacity may still be needed for exported production even when the domestic market is in recession; governments may deliberately undertake **counter-cyclical** investment; different industries may not all move together; and some firms may choose to continue 'normal' capital investment programmes even in a slump, in view of favourable prices and delivery times, as long as they continue to expect ultimate recovery. Thus analysis in terms of aggregates is generally unsatisfactory.

3.4.2 Capital Consumption

Net fixed capital formation is the excess of gross fixed capital formation over capital consumption (depreciation). So if capital consumption were to *equal* gross fixed capital formation, then net fixed capital formation would be *zero*. In that case, real capital assets would only just be maintained.

Figure 3.3 showed that total capital consumption rose from 10 per cent of UK national income in 1970 to 16 per cent in 1980. Excluding dwellings, this amounts to a rise from $7\frac{1}{2}$ per cent to $10\frac{1}{2}$ per cent of GDP. The main reason is the rise in the stock of capital assets, not an increase in the rate of depreciation. In times of inflation, capital consumption needs to be stated at current replacement cost. It would be misleading to compare new capital investment at current prices with capital consumption based on *past* costs.

As noted earlier, gross fixed capital formation has been a fairly steady proportion of GDP in recent years, at around 15 per cent. Thus in Fig. 3.11 an increasing capital consumption percentage is deducted from a static gross fixed capital formation figure. This results in a noticeable *decline* in *net* capital formation, from $7\frac{1}{2}$ per cent of GDP in 1970 to only 3 per cent in 1981.

Figure 3.12 shows that the private sector's share of total net capital formation

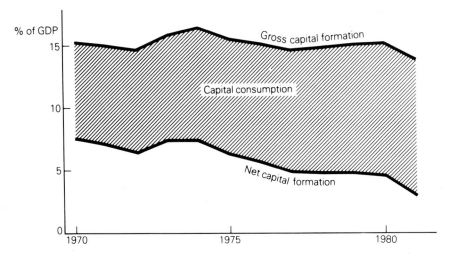

Fig. 3.11: Gross and net capital formation, 1970 to 1981.

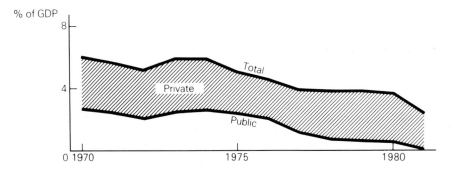

Fig. 3.12: Private and public net capital formation, 1970 to 1981.

has been fairly steady, at between $3\frac{1}{2}$ per cent and 4 per cent of GDP. But the public sector's net capital formation has fallen from $3\frac{1}{2}$ per cent of GDP in 1970 to virtually nothing in 1981. (This was also shown in Fig. 3.10 earlier.)

3.4.3 Stocks (Inventories)

We saw in section **3.4.1** that net capital assets (excluding dwellings) amounted to more than twice as much as annual GDP at the end of 1981. **Stocks** represent 'cushions' between different stages in the chain of production (less than one third of total stock in manufacturing industries represents **finished goods**). Figure 3.13 shows that in total stocks represent about one third of annual GDP: the proportion is some 75 per cent of annual output for agriculture and manufacturing, 90 per cent for distribution, and less than 10 per cent for all other industries together. At the end of 1981 the total value of stocks held was £72 b.

	Stocks (£ b.)	*Output* (£ b.)	(%)
Agriculture, forestry, mining	6	8	75
Manufacturing	38	50	76
Distribution	18	20	90
All other industries	10	133	7½
	72	211	34

Fig. 3.13: End-1981 stocks compared with 1981 output.

National income statistics include the value of the physical increase (or decrease) in stocks in a year as part of output. The real annual increase in stocks rarely exceeds 2 per cent of GDP, so it is much smaller than the annual gross investment in fixed assets, which is about 15 per cent of GDP (plus about 3 per cent for dwellings).

Gross fixed capital formation can never be *negative*; but in five post-war years (1946, 1950, 1975, 1980 and 1981) there has been a real *decrease* in the level of stocks held. The national income estimates show this as a negative amount (see Fig. 3.3) Stock levels declined for ten successive quarters from the beginning of 1980 to mid-1982 – easily the longest post-war run-down of stocks.

The current *money* value of stocks may rise sharply from one year to the next, but when inflation is rapid most of this money increase in value consists of 'stock appreciation' – the increase in *prices* of the same physical volume of stocks. Only a small part of the money increase in stock levels represents the value of the 'real' (physical) increase in the *volume* of stocks.

Changes in stock levels may aggravate economic cycles. For example, suppose that output has been rising at 4 per cent a year, in line with the rate of increase in demand by final customers. After three years of this, suppose that final customer demand happens to *fall* by 2 per cent in Year 4, but that output does not react immediately. Figure 3.14 shows that the level of stocks held will rise sharply by the end of Year 4, as production continues at the same level, but sales decline.

Suppose that in Year 5 final customer demand recovers to its Year 3 level. The appropriate stock relationship is assumed here to be 75 per cent of annual demand. In order to restore that ratio, the volume of output in Year 5 will need to fall by no less than 14 per cent. If final demand then resumes its 4 per cent annual growth rate, output will then need to increase in Year 6 by 16 per cent. Obviously such large variations can lead to serious business problems, especially as the relevant time-lags are likely to be hard to predict.

		Level of stock		*Final*
	Output	*Opening*	*Closing*	*demand*
Year 1	103	72	75	100
Year 2	107	75	78	104
Year 3	111	78	81	108
Year 4	115	81	90	106
Year 5	99	90	81	108
Year 6	115	81	84	112
Year 7	119	84	87	116

Fig. 3.14: Fluctuations in output and stocks.

The precise assumptions in this example may be open to question, but the principle remains valid. Stock changes may aggravate changes in output. This explains why businessmen take so much care to monitor the level of final demand, even if their own firms do not sell directly to the retail customers. Demand for their 'intermediate' products will ultimately be 'derived' from final retail sales. Thus the supplier of car components to car manufacturers will be very interested in the rate of sales of motor cars.

Forecasting changes in demand (both the amount and the timing) can be crucial. If a change in the rate of demand is temporary, businesses may not need to change their rate of production. The difference can be taken care of by temporary changes in the level of stocks. But if a change in demand is thought to be more permanent, then the rate of production may need to be changed very quickly. Otherwise there will be a danger either of running out of stocks, and thus losing sales (if demand is rising), or else of piling up unwanted stocks (if demand is falling). For similar reasons, changes observed in the levels of stocks held may be used as predictors of the level of future activity (see also **9.1.1**).

Work Section

A. Revision Questions

A1   What are 'bads'?
A2   Give four examples of 'economic' transactions that may be omitted from, or inadequately recorded in, national income estimates.
A3   What is the 'black economy'?
A4   Name three different ways to estimate national income.
A5   'Reliability gradings' are attached to items in national income estimates. (a) What are they? (b) Why are they necessary?
A6   Define 'stock appreciation'.
A7   Define 'capital consumption'.
A8   Why is domestic spending likely to differ, in total and in detail, from domestic production?
A9   How is domestic production at *market prices* converted into gross domestic product at *factor cost*?
A10 Why do 'output' estimates of national income use 'value added' rather than sales revenue?

A11 Define 'consumption'.
A12 Define 'disposable income'.
A13 Name three factors that affect consumption.
A14 How could government directly affect the personal savings ratio (= personal savings as a proportion of personal disposable income)?
A15 Is expenditure on durable consumer goods (a) consumption or (b) saving? Why?
A16 Why is it hard to tell how much of a consumer durable's services have been used up in a period?
A17 Name two consumer goods which could not be described as 'durable'.
A18 How do national income statistics treat dwelling houses?
A19 What is a 'second-hand market'?
A20 What is 'permanent income'?
A21 Give two examples of 'windfall' income.
A22 What is the difference between financial investment and 'real' investment?
A23 Define 'saving'.
A24 Why do consumers save?
A25 Give two examples of 'contractual' saving.

A26 Are you more likely (a) to borrow or (b) to lend, if you have a low rate of time preference?

A27 What are the three components of a commercial rate of interest?

A28 If interest rates rise, would you expect saving to (a) rise, (b) fall, or (c) stay the same? Why?

A29 Why would an increase in the real rate of interest tend to reduce the amount of fixed capital investment?

A30 Why is classical interest theory unsatisfactory?

A31 Name two differences between classical interest theory and Keynesian theory.

A32 What is the 'accelerator' theory? Why is it unsatisfactory?

A33 Name two factors which might affect (a) future sales revenue, (b) the availability of finance.

A34 Why might public sector authorities use different investment criteria from the private sector?

A35 Name three kinds of uncertainty that may affect business investment.

A36 How do national income statistics treat spending on (a) productive equipment, (b) houses, (c) stocks?

A37 Why does the stock of capital assets change over time?

A38 What is the difference between gross and net fixed capital formation?

A39 What proportion of UK fixed capital investment is undertaken by the public sector: (a) gross? (b) net?

A40 Name three reasons why capital investment may not fall in a slump.

A41 Why does capital consumption need to be estimated at current replacement cost?

A42 How can investment in stocks be negative?

A43 Roughly what percentage of annual output is represented by stocks: (a) in manufacturing? (b) in distribution?

A44 Define 'stock appreciation'.

A45 Why should a business manager in manufacturing industry take care to monitor final consumer demand?

B. Exercises and Case Studies

B1 What is a thousand million pounds (a 'billion' pounds, using the American terminology which is now common in the UK)? If some organisation had been spending a thousand pounds a day since the birth of Christ, it would not yet have spent a billion pounds!

   a. How much would the organisation have spent so far?
   b. To what level of accuracy should your answer to (a) be stated?
   c. Suggest *three* ways of expressing huge sums of money in a more understandable way.

B2   Special Steels Limited produced special high tensile steel for instrument making. In 1983 it bought its annual supply of imported ore for £1,000,000, and after processing it in an electric arc furnace sold its total output to Scitool Limited, a firm of precision engineers, for £2,500,000. From the steel bars Scitool made a wide range of precision instruments, mainly for the medical profession; Scitool sold them for £4,500,000 to wholesalers, who themselves disposed of their products for £7,000,000.
Calculate each firm's contribution to the GDP, and explain how you have avoided 'double counting'.

B3   Refer to Fig. 3.2 on page 51. Between 1960 and 1980, national income grew by 50 per cent in terms of constant 1975 pounds. Why did national income per head grow by a different proportion?

B4   Refer to Fig. 3.3 on page 52.
a. How much was net capital formation as a percentage of national income in 1960, 1970, and 1980 for (i) the private sector? (ii) the government ('public') sector?
b. In which of the three years shown was there a balance of payments deficit?

B5   Refer to Fig. 3.4 on page 53.
a. Why was the Primary sector's fall in share of output between 1960 and 1970 reversed between 1970 and 1980?
b. Between 1960 and 1980 which four industries show the largest declines in share of output? Rank them in order. What alternative method(s) of ranking might be possible?
c. Take any category of output other than manufacturing and, with the help of reference material, analyse the 1980 output share into as many sub-divisions as possible.

B6   Refer to Fig. 3.5 on page 54.
a. How much has the real amount spent on food changed between 1960 and 1980, in terms of 1975 £ billion?
b. On which category of consumer spending, if any, did real spending more than double between 1960 and 1980?
c. With the help of reference material, give as many sub-divisions as possible of the food category for 1980.

B7   In December 1982, ordinary government 'risk-free' securities yielded 10.75 per cent a year, while index-linked government securities yielded 2.75 per cent a year. What rate of inflation was being anticipated?

B8   Three capital investment products, each costing £36,000 and each using a discount rate of 10 per cent a year, each promise a net present value of + £1,345. Details are as follows:

i.   Annuity*   £15,016   Life   3 years
* see Glossary if necessary.

    ii.   Annuity   £ 7,000   Life   8 years

    iii. Annuity   £ 4,386   Life 20 years

    Show what happens in each case if the interest rate rises from 10 per cent a year to 12 per cent a year.

B9   Shown below in alphabetical order are various items of national expenditure for 1981. From the items listed, and referring also to Fig. 3.10 (on page 61), construct a statement of national income for the year.

	£ b.
1. Consumers' expenditure	151
2. Exports of goods and services	68
3. Expenditure taxes	43
4. Government consumption	55
5. Imports of goods and services	61
6. Private stockbuilding	(4)
7. Subsidies	5

B10 Refer to B9 above. Convert your statement into percentages, and compare with Fig. 3.3 (on page 52).

B11 Refer to Fig. 3.14 on page 65.

    a. Draw up a similar table on the same basic assumptions as those described in the text (4% per year underlying growth in real output and demand), except that:

       i . after only *two* years, final consumer demand falls by 3 per cent in Year 3; and

      ii. in Year 4 final demand recovers to its Year 2 level.

    b. What happens to closing stock in Year 3?

    c. What happens to output in Year 4?

B12 Refer to Fig. 3.14 on page 65.

    a. Draw up a similar table on the same basic assumptions as those described in the text (4% per year underlying growth in real output and demand), except that:

       i . after *three* years, final consumer demand rises by 7 per cent in Year 4; and

      ii. in Year 5, final consumer demand falls back to its expected 'trend' level.

    b. What happens to closing stock in Year 4?

    c. What happens to output in Year 5?

C. Essay Questions

C1   Why is national income calculated? Why is it subject to a significant margin of error?

C2   'People save for a rainy day, yet when it rains they go on saving.' Discuss.

C3   Why might real fixed capital investment not be very sensitive to short-term changes in the rate of interest?

C4   Under what circumstances might net fixed capital formation be negative? What would be the implications?

C5   How does the 'black economy' affect the national income? What do you see as its advantages and disadvantages?

C6   What are the dangers of using aggregates in economic analysis? How can they be overcome?

C7   Does it matter if a decline in real government capital investment is exactly offset by an equal increase in government consumption?

C8   Does it matter if the share of manufacturing industry in national output continues to decline? Why or why not?

C9   'In the long run we are all dead.' Keynes.
Should governments accept this view? Should individuals?

C10 Do different parts of the public sector have different rates of time preference? If so, does it matter?

C11 'Increasing specialisation may lead to high returns, but it involves high risks.' Discuss.

C12 Is capital investment a 'good thing'? How can you tell?

C13 Are profits too low a proportion of the national income?

C14 Why may 'national income' be an unreliable comparative measure of human welfare?

C15 What is the function of stocks (inventories)? Why might they be a higher proportion of national income in the UK than in most other countries?

Part II

Economic Topics

In the next four chapters we shall be discussing the four specific topics which for many years have been the most important 'national' objectives: economic growth, international trade, inflation, and unemployment. The general aim has been to maximise the rate of economic growth, without incurring large balance of payments deficits, and with rates of inflation and unemployment as low as possible.

The last three topics have varied in relative importance in the post-war period. In the mid-1960s the UK balance of payments problem was at the centre of the stage, the drama ending with the devaluation of sterling in November 1967. In the mid-1970s inflation, at levels unprecedented in the UK in peacetime, was the most serious economic problem. Now, in the mid-1980s, continuing very high unemployment in the face of major technological changes seems likely to be the major worry for all the developed countries.

First, however, we discuss economic growth, which is more important than any other topic. It seems by no means certain whether governments can in fact do much to promote economic growth; though no doubt they can obstruct it. (Adam Smith said of governments: 'If their own extravagance does not ruin the state, that of their subjects never will.') The various kinds of government intervention briefly noted in Chapter 1 were not directly aimed at affecting the rate of economic growth. The circular flow model in Chapter 2, with its suggestions of government action to restore 'equilibrium', relates mainly to short-run fluctuations in an assumed constant national income. It may be that investment is necessary for growth; if so, Chapter 3 showed that government net capital formation in the UK had fallen virtually to zero in 1981, implying a minimal government contribution to economic growth.

Economic growth is not synonymous with an increase in human happiness. As noted in 3.1.1, national income statistics are not precisely accurate, and they omit several kinds of economic transactions. Moreover, economic aspects form only a part of life, and arguably not the most important part. As Adam Smith says: 'The beggar who suns himself by the side of the highway possesses that security which kings are fighting for.' Nevertheless the massive long-term improvement in Western countries' standards of living over the last two centuries has stemmed mainly from the unprecedented cumulative high rates of economic growth.

Chapter 4

Economic Growth

Objective: *To define economic growth; to describe historical UK and other growth rates; to outline some of the causes of economic growth; and to consider future prospects for growth*

Synopsis: *Economic growth is the annual rate of increase in real national income per head. In making estimates, it is necessary to start and finish at the same stage of the trade cycle, especially for short-term calculations.*

For two centuries the UK growth rate has been about 2 per cent a year in peace-time; and about 1.3 per cent a year on average including periods of war. As a result real national income per head has risen about 13-fold since Adam Smith's day, after allowing for a 7-fold increase in population. Other developed countries have been growing faster than the UK since the war; their levels of income per head mostly now exceed the UK's.

The two ways to grow are to increase resources or to combine resources more effectively. It is not clear to what extent capital accumulation 'causes' growth: both quality and quantity of investment are required. Three important elements in combining resources more effectively are: (1) mobility, (2) specialisation, and (3) knowledge.

Even rather modest positive growth rates compound impressively over time. Less developed countries (LDCs) need to increase output even to maintain their rapidly increasing populations; but there are several reasons for long-term optimism about their prospects.

4.1 What is Economic Growth?

'Economic growth' may be defined as the annual percentage rate of increase in real national income per head. We have already seen three ways to estimate national income (**3.1.1**), by adding up everyone's (a) income, (b) expenditure, or (c) output ('value added'). These estimates are not precisely 'correct', so apparent rates of change in them over time may involve large margins of error.

Percentage rates of increase can be misleading unless we bear in mind the *size of the base*. An American growth rate of 1 per cent means an increase of $25 billion in national income, whereas a 10 per cent growth rate in Norway represents only $5 billion. We can guard against such confusion by dividing total national income by the number of people in the country. But even 'per head' figures can mislead: a country whose population is increasing fast (as in some less developed countries) will contain many children who are not yet productive.

To interpret *money* changes in national income over time, we also need

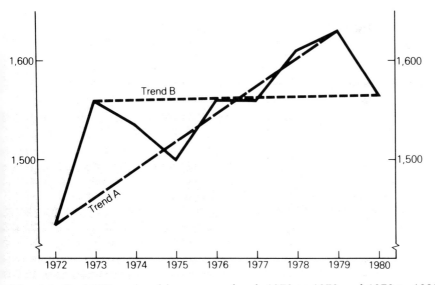

Fig. 4.1: Real UK national income per head, 1972 to 1979 and 1973 to 1980 (in constant 1975 pounds).

to allow for inflation. Using an index of the 'general price level' (see ch. 6) allows us to deflate national money income into 'real' terms.

In principle we might measure economic growth by rates of increase in 'full-employment' national income (see **2.1.1**). But in practice we tend to use 'actual' national income. In making short-term estimates of growth, however, we need to compare national income figures at the same stage of the trade cycle (see **9.1.1**). Otherwise the particular year one starts or finishes can make a big difference to the apparent growth rate.

For example, Fig. 4.1 shows an average UK growth rate from 1972 to 1979 of 1.7 per cent a year (Trend A). But from 1973 to 1980 (Trend B), the growth rate averages only 0.1 per cent a year. This large difference between seven-year periods only one year apart was caused by 1973's national income being abnormally high while 1980's was abnormally low.

4.2 Historical Growth Rates

4.2.1 United Kingdom

Figure 4.2 shows that real UK national income per head (in 1975 pounds) has multiplied roughly six-fold from £250 in 1855 to £1,500 in 1980. Despite two world wars, the average economic growth rate over the 125-year period has been about 1.5 per cent a year. It would obscure the long-run picture to include annual figures, but taking only every fifth year (as in Fig. 4.2) risks using years which are 'abnormal'.

The average real growth rate may have been 1.0 per cent a year between 1775 and 1855 (when more accurate statistics first became available). These years, of course, included the lengthy Napoleonic Wars. Thus the average UK growth rate has probably been about 1.3 per cent a year since Adam Smith's time. This may not sound much, but it means that real national income per head in 1980 was about *13 times* as large as 200 years ago. Moreover, the 1980 UK population of 56 million compares with an estimated 8 million population in 1775.

Clearly we need to regard these figures with caution. Two hundred years ago economic statistics were much less accurate than now; and even today there is still a significant margin of error. Moreover, the growth in national income is exaggerated due to an increase in the proportion of output being exchanged on the market. The national income figures now include some output which was previously consumed (unrecorded) within family households.

Even so, over the last two centuries there has been an increase in real national income per head which is completely unprecedented in history. Looking back now, we can easily come to regard this growth as if it were somehow 'inevitable': we tend to take it for granted. Indeed, throughout the long period there have

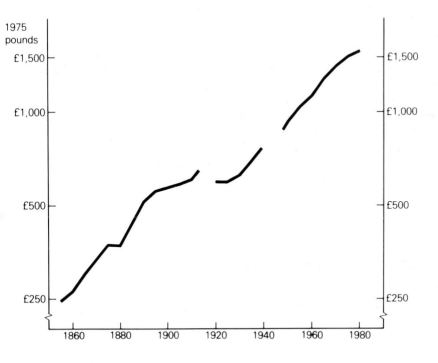

Fig. 4.2: UK national income per head, 1855 to 1980 (in constant 1975 pounds).

often been complaints that the rate of real growth has not been fast enough! For over a century the UK's peace-time rate of economic growth has been less than Germany's; and there were characteristic British grumbles about how far behind we were falling as long ago as the Great Exhibition of 1851!

Yet the early economists feared that population growth would always tend to bring the masses back to 'subsistence level'. Hence economics was called the 'dismal science'. During the century after Adam Smith (say from 1776 to 1870), the classical economists advocated *laissez-faire* as the best way to obtain economic growth. But even they never foresaw the immense productive potential of a market economy based on freedom, property ownership, and competition.

Simple arithmetic can prove that rates of economic growth in the last two centuries have been without precedent. For example, extrapolating backwards at a growth rate of 1.5 per cent a year from 1855 produces this incredible result: at about the date of the battle of Bosworth Field, average annual income would have been £1 per head! Since this is clearly absurd, growth rates between 1485 and 1855 must have been much *lower* than 1.5 per cent a year.

4.2.2 **Other Developed Countries**

Figure 4.3 shows levels of national income per head since 1875 for the United States and the four largest Western European nations. It shows that all five countries have enjoyed rapid rates of economic growth during the last 100 years.

The United States growth rate has been fairly steady since 1875. The post-war US growth rate has been similar to the UK's; so the US lead which opened up in the first quarter of the twentieth century has been maintained.

France and West Germany had lower levels of national income per head than the UK in 1900; and after two world wars, that was still so 50 years later. But since 1950 both countries have had faster economic growth, and their national income per head is now higher than the UK's.

Italy's post-war growth rate has also been faster than the UK's; but Italy still had a lower national income per head in 1975. For all the countries, problems in translating foreign currencies complicate the post-war estimates.

The European countries have also greatly increased their populations since 1800; with Italy and the British Isles also providing large numbers of emigrants

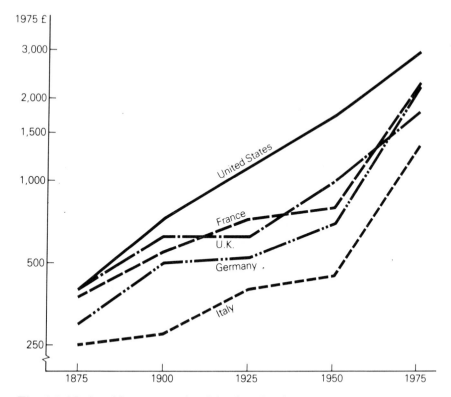

Fig. 4.3: National income per head for five developed countries, 1875 to 1975 (in constant 1975 pounds).

Millions	United States	France	Germany	Italy	United Kingdom
1800	6	27	20	17	9
1850	23	36	33	24	18
1900	76	39	56	32	32
1950	151	42	51 (+ 18*)	47	44
1980	228	54	62 (+ 17*)	57	56
* = East Germany					

Fig. 4.4: Population since 1800 for five countries.

to the Americas and elsewhere. Figure 4.4 sets out the numbers. But France's population increased only about 15 per cent in the century between 1850 and 1950, while that of the other countries doubled. The American population is now about the same as that of the four other countries combined.

4.3 Causes of Economic Growth

Several related factors underlie the last two centuries' growth in national income. It is not clear which are more important, nor even which are causes and which effects. But all serious scholars agree on one point: that the causes of economic growth are very complex. We cannot be sure what caused the **industrial revolution** to happen first in Britain. Even the period it is supposed to have spanned is a matter of dispute.

Several factors were probably important in Britain:

a. prestige of science, and the practice of observing facts rather than relying on theory;

b. social mobility, and political and religious tolerance;

c. increase in the labour force, both from population growth and from agriculture;

d. freedom of internal trade, with cheap sea and canal transport.

There are broadly two ways to increase economic well-being: to increase the quantity of resources, or to improve the ways of using given resources. We shall consider them in turn. Since the first way tends to be once-for-all, most long-term growth must depend on *combining* given resources more effectively.

4.3.1 Increasing Resources

a. *Land*. Much can be done to improve the quality of land, but as a rule little to increase the amount. (The best-known exception is the Dutch 'reclamation' of land from the sea.) Historically people gained new land by migrating into formerly empty areas; and particular nations have often acquired territory as a result of war or colonisation.

Minerals are classed as 'land', but strictly we should not reckon new discoveries as increasing the amount available. What changes is merely our *knowledge* of scarce resources that were already there. That is why the 'proved' reserves of certain minerals may seem rather small, if they are equivalent, say, to only 25 years' consumption at current rates. The market system provides no incentive to go on finding new reserves as long as existing supplies seem to be ample.

Improvements to the quality of land include irrigation, drainage, fencing, and the building of harbours and roads. Constant maintenance is also required. It is surprising how quickly a well-kept garden will revert to wilderness once it is abandoned.

b. Labour. Extra labour resources stem mainly from increases in population: we saw in **4.2.2** the growth in developed countries since 1800. Better food, housing, sanitation, and medicine have sharply reduced death rates, especially for children. Medical improvements include vaccination to prevent smallpox, and the discovery of anaesthetics and antiseptics in the nineteenth century and of antibiotics in the twentieth.

In the last 100 years the death rate for babies under one year old has fallen in Europe from 200 per thousand to 20. Overall death rates have fallen steadily too, with the birth rate following after an interval. During the interim period, the excess of births over deaths has caused large increases in population.

There have also been important social changes affecting the size of the productive work force in developed countries (see Ch. 7). Children have tended to stay at school longer and start work later than before, and more married women now go out to work. The quality of the labour force is also affected by education and training, as well as by experience and innate aptitudes.

c. Capital. We saw in Chapter 3 that capital stock grows by saving the excess of income over consumption, and investing in capital goods such as land improvement, buildings, and machinery. But it is not easy to establish any direct link between the proportion of GDP invested and the rate of economic growth.

Figure 4.5 shows growth rates and capital formation as a proportion of GDP for five developed countries over a 20 year period. The average (unweighted) growth rates fell from 4½ per cent in the 1960s to 3 per cent in the 1970s; while average capital formation remained unchanged at 21 per cent of GDP. (The Japanese figures are not shown: the growth rate fell from 11 per cent to 5 per cent, with capital formation unchanged at 33 per cent of GDP.)

It is not 'investment' as such that is desirable, but *profitable* investment. There is plenty of evidence that capital investment can be misdirected. British Steel's 1982 accounts, for example, wrote off £3,500 million of capital as lost; but in the early 1970s this was proudly pointed to as massive modernisation. In other words, as with land and labour, it is *quality* of capital as well as quantity that counts.

Education is sometimes regarded as an 'investment' in **human capital**. (Though national income statistics, perhaps sensibly, treat the cost of a child's dozen years at school as 'consumption'.) But it probably costs no more to get children to learn useful skills, knowledge, and attitudes than to fill their heads with nonsense. Teaching science, mathematics, and English might well cost no more than teaching flower-arranging, astrology, and Sanskrit.

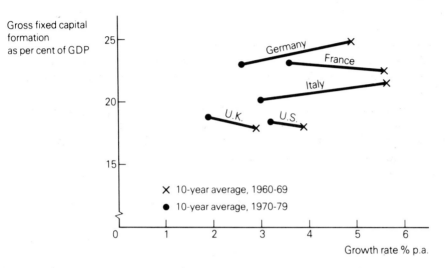

Fig. 4.5: Growth rates and capital formation, 1960 to 1979 in five developed countries.

4.3.2 Combining Resources Effectively

We noted above that combining resources better is likely to be the main source of continuing economic growth. In this section we discuss three ways to do it: mobility, specialisation, and knowledge.

a. Mobility. In the market system, resources must be able to move from existing uses to more profitable ones. Thus labour moved from the land to the towns as employment switched from agriculture to manufacturing.

In several developed countries agriculture now employs less than 10 per cent of workers. In Germany, France, and Italy the proportions have fallen from 25, 35, and 48 per cent respectively in 1939 to 6, 9, and 14 per cent by 1980. These are massive changes in a period of 40 years. The United Kingdom, now down to 2½ per cent, led other countries, having fewer than 10 per cent of workers in agriculture even before 1914.

'Post-industrial' society will probably see a continuing shift from manu-

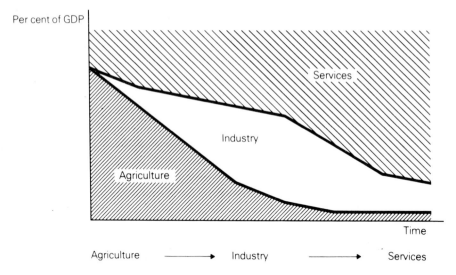

Fig. 4.6: The movement between sectors over time.

facturing to services. Figure 4.6 portrays the changes between sectors of the economy as development proceeds. People may move out of cities back to rural areas as improved communications obviate the need to keep large groups of workers close together. The 'place of work' may switch from factories or offices back to the home.

The spread of motor vehicles has helped physical mobility even more than the railways did. Private passenger road mileage has multiplied 10-fold since the war, while the railway's route miles have halved. And there has also been a vast world-wide growth in air travel.

There may also be major changes in the kinds of skills workers will need. The idea of someone having only a single 'job' from leaving school to retirement may also need revision. Part-time work and continual retraining may be features of a more flexible labour market in future. In a long-term perspective, the way that developed economies have worked in the last 100 years may turn out to have been quite exceptional.

An 'affluent' society must be free to adapt; but some parts of the modern economy may be too rigid. Thus tax laws can obstruct the mobility of capital or labour; pension plans may make it costly to change jobs in mid-career; council housing rules may hinder movement of workers; trade union rules may reduce flexibility at work; and foreign exchange controls may restrict the transfer of capital funds. The systems that are least rigid are likely to cope best with any structural changes that may be required in future.

b. Specialisation. Adam Smith pointed out the importance of the **division of labour** in increasing output. The spreading of the money market economy (see **6.1.1**) together with major improvements in transport and communication has led to much greater specialisation. Indeed, the growth of international trade (see **5.1.2**) has enabled countries, as well as family households, to become less self-sufficient and more productive.

Specialisation produces higher returns, but in a sense it may be seen as involving more 'risk'. In a developed economy people are 'interdependent'. Hence war – with its pressures for self-sufficiency – is utterly alien to the market system. The century of *laissez-faire* was a century of *peace*. In modern conditions it is the centrally planned economies that are more likely to be aggressive. Napoleon, Hitler, and the post-war Russian imperialism share a centrally planned domestic economy.

Technical conditions may be such that a few large firms can produce at much lower cost than many small ones. We noted earlier the possible dangers of monopolies (see **1.3.2**), but large producers may be able to benefit from **economies of scale**. As long as there is effective competition, however, these will tend to be passed on to consumers.

c. Knowledge. We discussed earlier the extent to which capital formation may be responsible for economic growth. We also saw that the *quality* of any investment is probably more important than the quantity. For example new methods of teaching might allow large increases in the value of the output of schools without *any* additional capital investment.

The many technical and scientific inventions of the past 200 years have enormously improved our standard of living, and advances in communication have helped knowledge to spread rapidly. ('Knowledge' as a product has some features similar to those of public goods.) The full impact of recent discoveries in biology and micro-electronics lies in the future: hence the need for continuing adaptability to change.

Economic 'profit' may be regarded as possible only because of ignorance. If people dealing on markets knew everything there was to be known, the prices of products would already fully reflect consumers' valuations. This would leave no potential margin of profit for entrepreneurs. But in acting on the basis of uncertainty, businessmen inevitably have to take *risks*. That is why the market system is a profit *and loss* system. The profits on successful

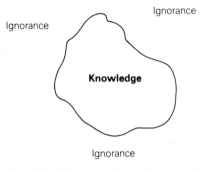

Fig. 4.7: The frontiers of knowledge.

products may need to be large to finance all the losses on unsuccessful products. (A large majority of all new products *fail*.) As Fig. 4.7 suggests, the frontiers of knowledge are also the frontiers of ignorance!

4.3.3 Why Do Growth Rates Vary?

a. Over time. The war years were omitted from Fig. 4.2, not because they somehow 'don't count', but because the national income statistics in those years are exceptionally unreliable. Though it is somewhat obscured in Fig. 4.2 by using only one year's figures out of every five, it is clear that even in peace-time there have been exceptions to the 'normal' upward trend in national income. In some years the growth rate flattens out or becomes negative, and in others growth has seemed especially rapid, as Fig. 4.1 shows between 1972 and 1980.

There are several reasons why economic factors may change and lead to fluctuations in national income. In a primitive society, for example, a crop failure in a particular year could lead to famine and a severe downturn in economic activity. Other natural disasters, such as floods, earthquakes or plagues, might also cause major fluctuations from one year to another.

In a developed society, variations in the rate of new inventions, or in their application, might lead to fluctuations in national income over periods of years. So might severe industrial disputes in particular years. And major wars, which history suggests can occur in societies at all stages of economic development, can seriously affect the 'normal' trend of economic growth. There are currently fears that 'protectionism' might cause a serious reduction in the rate of growth of international trade (see 5.1.2), which would be likely to reduce national rates of economic growth.

b. Between countries. Different countries are not all at the same stage of development, and their cultural and political backgrounds may also differ. So perhaps it is not surprising that economic growth rates vary. But why do some poor countries embark on rapid rates of growth while others do not? Why have growth rates in many African countries been much lower than in many Asian countries at apparently about the same level of national income per head? Why has Argentina's economic performance been worse than Brazil's?

If we cannot adequately explain what causes economic growth, it is not surprising that we find it hard to account for differences in rates of growth between countries. All that we can probably say, however, is that causes and effects may change over time. It would thus be risky to extrapolate far into the future on the basis of the recent past. Trends go on until they stop!

4.4 Future Prospects

The cumulative effects of compound interest can be impressive. We saw in 4.2.1 that an average rate of increase of 1.3 per cent a year in the UK in the last 200 years has led to a 13-fold increase in real income per head. An increase of 2 per cent a year amounts to a quadrupling of real income per head over a lifetime of 70 years. Over 200 years it amounts to a *50-fold* increase! Keynes pointed out: 'This means that the economic problem is not – if we look into the future – the permanent problem of the human race.'

For millions of people in the **less developed countries** (LDCs) such talk may seem fantastic. In the next generation or two they desperately need economic growth to escape grinding poverty for their rapidly increasing populations. The rate of increase in world population seems likely to flatten out soon, as it already has in the developed countries. Even so, world population is projected to increase from more than $4\frac{1}{2}$ billion in 1980 to more than 6 billion by 2000. This requires a considerable increase in economic growth simply to *maintain* the average real income per head, let alone increase it.

Yet there are good reasons for optimism. Birth rates in the LDCs are likely to decline in future, following the decline in death rates. This will in time improve the proportion of directly productive members of the population. In the last 20 years life expectancy in LDCs has increased by about nine years, due to significant improvements in health and nutrition. Adult literacy rates too have improved sharply, and will probably continue to do so. A better educated population is more likely to be able and willing to adapt to new events, which will assist the process of economic growth.

A recent World Bank report says: 'The rise in agricultural output over the past two decades has confounded the predictions of widespread famine which were common in the 1950s and 1960s.' Dramatic improvements in the yields from wheat and rice crops have been called the Green Revolution. The growth performance of most LDCs has improved markedly over the past three decades; and as population increases slow down, if such growth rates can be maintained they will translate into sharp increases in income per head.

Figure 4.8 shows annual rates of increase in population, real GNP, and GNP per head for the periods 1955–70 and 1970–80 for five main groups of countries. Real growth in GNP per head averaged at least $1\frac{1}{2}$ per cent a year in each group, with the single exception of low-income countries other than China and India for 1970–80. The exception was mainly due to many poor economic performances in African countries, where, however, the proportion of the population of working age actually fell between 1970 and 1980.

Annual percentage rates of increase	Population 1955–70 (%)	1970–80 (%)	Real GNP 1955–70 (%)	1970–80 (%)	GNP per head 1955–70 (%)	1970–80 (%)
China	2	2	$3\frac{1}{2}$	6	$1\frac{1}{2}$	4
India	2	2	4	$3\frac{1}{2}$	2	$1\frac{1}{2}$
Other low-income countries	$2\frac{1}{2}$	$2\frac{1}{2}$	$4\frac{1}{2}$	$2\frac{1}{2}$	2	–
Middle-income countries	$2\frac{1}{2}$	$2\frac{1}{2}$	6	$5\frac{1}{2}$	$3\frac{1}{2}$	3
Industrial market economies	1	1	$4\frac{1}{2}$	$3\frac{1}{2}$	$3\frac{1}{2}$	$2\frac{1}{2}$
World	2	2	5	4	3	2

Fig. 4.8: World increases in GNP per head, 1955 to 1980.

Work Section

A. Revision Questions

A1 Define 'economic growth'.

A2 Name three different ways to estimate national income.

A3 Why may different age-patterns within a population cause misleading comparisons of economic growth rates?

A4 How can inflation be allowed for in calculating 'real' rates of increase in national income?

A5 Why may starting or finishing dates be critical for short-term calculations of economic growth rates?

A6 What has been the average annual rate of increase in real national income per head in the UK over the past 200 years?

A7 Since Adam Smith's day (200 years ago), how many-fold has (a) UK population and (b) UK real income per head risen?

A8 Why might the UK statistics exaggerate the real rate of economic growth over the past 200 years?

A9 How can we tell that UK economic growth rates must on average have been higher in the last 200 years than in the preceding four centuries?

A10 In what respects have the economic growth experiences of France, Germany and Italy been (a) similar to, (b) different from, that of the UK?

A11 Name two different ways to increase economic well-being.

A12 Why have European populations increased so much in the last 200 years?

A13 Why was Economics called the 'dismal science'?

A14 Why might economic growth be expected not to be related directly to the amount of real capital formation?

A15 What is 'human capital'?

A16 What three factors were identified as contributing to more effective combination of economic resources?

A17 Why is mobility important for economic growth?

A18 What kind of mobility other than geographical may be important?

A19 Name two possible causes of fluctuations in a country's economic growth rate over time.

A20 Name two possible causes for different rates of economic growth in different countries.

A21 How many years does it take for a 2 per cent annual rate of increase to quadruple real income per head?

A22 Why is a considerable increase in national income needed in many LDCs over the next 20 years simply to maintain the existing levels of real income per head?

A23 Why does an improvement in adult literacy rates help economic growth?

A24 What changes in the size and distribution of population in many LDCs can be expected over the next generation?

A25 Name two reasons why growth in national income may not mean an increase in human happiness.

B. Exercises and Case Studies

B1 Refer to Fig. 4.2 on page 75. Rank the following three 30-year periods in order or rate of growth (fastest first):
   a. 1860 to 1890
   b. 1900 to 1930
   c. 1950 to 1980

B2 Refer to Fig. 4.2 on page 75. How many years did it take real UK national income per head (in terms of 1975 pounds):
   a. to double from £250 to £500?
   b. to double from £500 to £1,000?
   c. to double to its 1980 level?

B3 Refer to Fig. 4.3 on page 76.
   a. Which 25-year period for the UK seems different from the others?
   b. What seems to be the main difference between the UK pattern and those for France, Germany and Italy?
   c. What feature of the United States pattern stands out?

B4 Refer to Fig. 4.1 on page 73.
   a. Use reference material to estimate real UK national income per head for 1981.
   b. Estimate the average annual growth rate for the seven-year period 1974 to 1981.
   c. Compare your estimate of the 1974–81 real growth rate with the two other seven-year average growth rates noted in the text.

B5 Reported UK national income figures are as follows (in £ b.):
   1950: 10.8   1960: 20.8   1970: 39.7   1980: 167.0
   It looks as if national income roughly doubled in the decade between 1950 and 1960, and roughly doubled again in the decade between 1960 and 1970. Yet national income seems to have *more than quadrupled* in the decade between 1970 and 1980.
   a. What adjustments, if any, are needed to the above figures in order to make a realistic comparison?

   b. How would you set about making any necessary adjustments?
   c. Do so.
B6 **The Economic Marathon**
   A hundred years ago Britain led the world. Now we're lagging behind.
   Why? What, if anything, can be done about it? And does it really matter?
   In overall average national income per head, the UK is now worse off
   than most other developed countries of comparable size, apart from Italy
   (see Fig. 4.3 on page 76). But since the Second World War, average
   real incomes in the UK have been going up at least as fast as over any
   other long period. So we don't seem to have been doing worse than in
   the *past* – what has changed is that *other countries* have mostly been doing
   better.
   Four theories are put forward below to try to explain the problem.
   Money Which? carried out a survey to discover to what extent each of the
   theories met with the support of particular groups: economists, in-
   dustrialists, MPs, trade union leaders. The extent of support for each
   theory was classified as being: strong; fairly strong; weak; very little; or
   divided.
   a. You are asked *individually* to decide for *each* of the four theories to
      what extent you support it as a significant explanation of why the UK
      economy has been growing slowly compared with most other de-
      veloped countries of comparable size.
   b. You are then asked to discuss within your group to what extent *as a
      group* you support each of the four theories. Groups need not be
      unanimous, but please use the 'divided' category only where there
      really is no possible alternative. Choose one member of the group who
      can report your combined view at the full class discussion.
   1. *Not Enough Investment*
   The UK has been investing too little of its output in new and better
   factories and machines. So the average amount of capital employed per
   worker is lower in the UK than in many other countries, and the average
   age of capital equipment may be higher. Investment in the UK has also
   been *misdirected*, and has been spent in the wrong industries or on the
   wrong developments. Because of the low level of investment, the average
   level of productivity (output per worker) is lower in the UK than elsewhere.
   2. *Bad Government*
   Successive governments – of both parties – have aimed at providing fair
   shares for all, rather than at increasing the size of the cake. Governments
   have created uncertainty about the future of the economy by frequently
   reversing previous policies. This has led to defensive reactions – such as
   cutting down on investment by firms, and less flexibility on the part of
   trade unions. It's expensive for tax payers to have to prop up outdated
   industries which employ a lot of people. It would clearly be better for
   the UK in the long run if the people employed in such industries were to

move to jobs where their productivity would be higher. But the system of subsidised council housing, together with harassment of private landlords, makes it hard for people who don't own their own homes to find anywhere to live if they move to a job in a different part of the country.

3. *Bad Management*

UK industry has bad management. One study found that in three very large firms the top management seemed incapable of taking decisions to adapt to changing conditions. Another study found that UK companies were less profitable than the subsidiaries of US companies operating in the UK in the same industries. Bad management has been blamed for being unwilling to take risks, making bad investment decisions, producing poor-quality products, conducting bad industrial relations, and a hatful of other mistakes. Bad management could be the result of the brightest and most highly-educated people not going into industrial management, but into the City, the Civil Service, the professions, etc.

4. *Trouble with the Unions*

UK industry has problems with trade unions. It's not just strikes: trade unions hamper firms in other ways too; for example, by making rules about what jobs their members may and may not do; by their reluctance to accept reorganisation and change which might result in some of their members' jobs being lost; and by insisting on the over-manning of new machinery. The problem is made worse by the way in which UK unions are organised – i.e. the union you join depends, in the main, not on the firm you work for, or the industry you work in, but on the particular skill you've got. This means that the management of one particular factory may have to negotiate with shop stewards from a large number of different unions – who won't necessarily agree amongst themselves on what they want. This may be a cumbersome and lengthy process.

C. Essay Questions

C1   Does it matter if the real income per head in Ruritania is higher than in the UK?

C2   Why, if at all, is it useful for government and for business firms to know what a national economy's rate of growth has been over, say, the last five years?

C3   Bertrand Russell wrote: 'The Industrial Revolution caused unspeakable misery both in England and in America. I do not think any student of economic history can doubt that the average happiness in England in the early nineteenth century was lower than it had been 100 years earlier.' Discuss.

C4   Should the cost of education be regarded as 'capital formation' in national income statistics, or should it continue to be treated as 'consumption' expenditure? Why?

C5   What are the main arguments for and against fast economic growth?

C6   What are the main arguments for and against zero economic growth?

C7   Which one of the following average annual rates of economic growth would you predict for the UK over the next 20 years?
a. + 4 per cent   b. + 2 per cent   c. zero   d. − 2 per cent.
Or would you predict some different rate? Try to give reasons.

C8   Do you agree with Keynes that 'the economic problem is not ... the permanent problem of the human race'?

C9   'In a long-term perspective, the way that developed economies have worked in the last 100 years may turn out to have been quite exceptional.' Discuss.

C10 How can governments promote economic growth?

C11 Would most of the less developed countries be economically better off today if they were still colonies?

C12 Why are calculated rates of growth in real income per head over long periods of time probably overstated?

C13 Should we be worrying about 'Spaceship Earth' running out of resources?

C14 Adam Smith wrote: 'It is in the progressive state, while the society is advancing to the further acquisition ... of riches, that the condition ... of the great body of the people seems to be the happiest and the most comfortable. It is hard in the stationary, and miserable in the declining state.' Discuss.

C15 John Stuart Mill wrote: 'I am not charmed with the ideal of life held out by those who think that the normal state of human beings is that of struggling to get on; that the trampling, crushing, elbowing, and treading on each other's heels ... are the most desirable lot of human kind ... It is only in the backward countries of the world that increased production is still an important object.' Discuss.

Chapter 5

International Business

Objective: *To explore the benefits of international trade and the results of protection; to explain how fixed exchange rates worked and why they came to an end; to distinguish between fixed and floating exchange rate systems; to outline the components of the 'balance of payments'; and to discuss the effects of changes in exchange rates.*

Synopsis: *International trade is an extension of domestic trade which permits further specialisation. It takes place mainly between firms and individuals, not between governments. Protection tends to benefit domestic producers, but at the expense of consumers or taxpayers.*

The gold standard, like the Bretton Woods 'dollar exchange' standard, was a fixed exchange rate system. Both required domestic price adjustments in the long run to correct balance of payments deficits. Since 1971 'floating' has been accompanied by sharp fluctuations in currency exchange rates.

The overall balance of payments consists of the current account (trade in goods and services) and the capital account. The effect of changes in exchange rates depends on the price-elasticity of demand for imports and exports. UK visible trade with EEC countries has increased considerably since 1960.

5.1 International Trade

5.1.1 Comparative Advantage

If there were no market exchanges, every household would have to be 'self-sufficient'. But the division of labour aids specialisation and leads to increased output (see **4.3.2**). Trade which crosses national boundaries is just an extension of domestic trade. But it takes place between individuals or firms who happen to reside in different countries.

Both parties normally expect to benefit from a voluntary deal. The theory of **comparative advantage** means that even if Cloudia can produce *everything* more cheaply than Sunland both countries can gain from mutual trade. This is the basic argument for **free trade**.

The firms in Cloudia should produce those goods where they have the *greater* advantage, and the firms in Sunland should concentrate on making those goods where they have the *smaller disadvantage*. The theory refers to a producer's *relative* advantage in making *one product rather than another*. It does *not* compare two producers' *absolute* cost of making particular goods.

The same principle applies to more mundane examples. I may be a better typist than my secretary, but she more closely approaches my superior standard in *typing* than she does in teaching! Hence I have a *comparative* advantage in teaching (though I have an absolute advantage in both teaching and typing); *and my secretary has a comparative advantage in typing even though she is a worse typist than I am!*

In practice a country's comparative advantage is established multilaterally, vis-à-vis *all* other countries, rather than **bilaterally**, with only one other country at a time. There is still plenty of international **barter** trade, but trading for *money* has great advantages abroad as it does at home (see **6.1.1**).

The theory of comparative advantage assumes that factors of production cannot move between countries, but some factors are fairly mobile over time. Under completely free trade, factors such as **raw materials**, capital, labour and knowledge should flow to wherever they can best be used. Despite great improvements in transport and communications, however, many factors of production are still rather immobile in the short run. Many countries still restrict the free movement abroad of materials and capital, as well as of people.

The theory also assumes that within a country factors are mobile between industries, but in practice this too requires time. Indeed, we saw earlier (**1.3.2**) that government intervention may be able to help move immobile factors of production.

5.1.2 **Post-war World Trade**

International trade increases the effective use of resources in the world as a whole. Between 1920 and 1939 widespread peacetime restrictions on trade caused severe problems. So after the Second World War there was a General Agreement on Tariffs and Trade (GATT), which applied to goods but not to services. The underlying GATT principle was that a country should treat all its trading partners alike. There were four main features:

1 Condemnation of **dumping** (selling abroad at less than domestic prices or production costs).
2 Forbidding quantitative restrictions on imports, *except*:
    a. to maintain 'standards';
    b. to stabilise agricultural or fisheries markets;
    c. temporarily to protect currency reserves.
3 Forbidding subsidies on exports or on 'import substitutes'.
4 Recognising the special needs of developing countries:
    a. providing non-reciprocal access to more prosperous markets;
    b. protecting infant industries;
    c. allowing import quotas during the early stages of development.

Since the war there have been three major 'rounds' of negotiated world

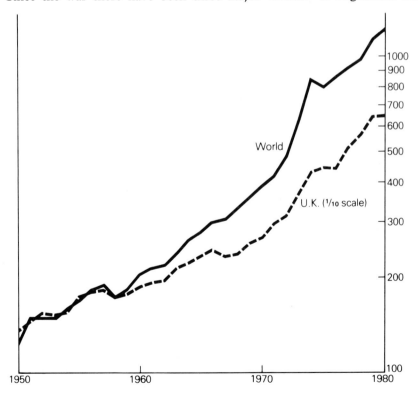

Fig. 5.1: World exports and UK exports, 1950 to 1980 (in 1975 $billions).

tariff reductions: in Geneva (1947), the 'Kennedy Round' (1964–67), and the 'Tokyo Round' (1973–79). In between agreed reductions in levels, tariffs and other barriers to trade may tend to creep up again in response to domestic political pressures in various countries.

Partly as a result of GATT, world trade has expanded at an average rate of about 7½ per cent a year since 1950, much faster than total growth of output. Hence imports and exports account for a rising share of most countries' gross domestic products. They represented nearly 30 per cent of the UK's GDP in 1980.

Figure 5.1 shows that in the post-war years UK exports have increased about five-fold in real terms, while total world trade has increased nearly 10-fold. Hence UK exports have fallen from about 11 per cent of world exports to about 6 per cent. This fall is not surprising, since the UK had a very large share of world trade in 1950.

Small countries, such as Belgium or the Netherlands, tend to 'depend' more on world trade than larger countries, which are naturally more nearly self-sufficient. Hence smaller countries may export about half their total output, while Japan exports only about 10 per cent of her output and the United States only about 7½ per cent.

To some extent the calculation of 'world trade' is arbitrary. If the 10 EEC countries were counted as 'one', intra-EEC trade would become 'domestic' instead of 'international'. This would reduce the percentage of EEC output 'exported' from 24 per cent to 12 per cent, and 'world' trade would appear to fall by about 20 per cent.

One sometimes sees lists comparing sales of multinational companies (MNCs) with the gross domestic products of nation-states. But GDPs consist of 'value added' (see **3.1.4**), so it overstates the relative size of MNCs to compare their *sales*. Using their value added instead of sales revenue would probably halve the apparent size of most MNCs. Most of the 'genuine' multinational companies (say with more than half their total sales outside their home countries) are European. This is because world markets tend to be much more important to them than to American companies, which have a large domestic market.

5.1.3 Protection versus Free Trade

Protection means government measures designed to 'protect' domestic producers against the competition of foreign producers. **Import tariffs** are taxes on foreign products, which may be overcome by a sufficiently large foreign cost advantage. **Import quotas** are legal limits on the quantity of particular foreign products which may be imported in a period. Open subsidies for domestic producers do not raise consumer prices (as tariffs and quotas do), and they explicitly reveal the *cost* of protection. But many government subsidies are 'hidden'.

Recent use of **non-tariff barriers** has also been significant. A blatant example was the French government's 1982 requirement for all Japanese video-recorders to be routed through a very small customs post at Poitiers, many kilometres along poor roads. Other forms of non-tariff barriers might be unreasonably complicated regulations concerning safety testing or certification. They are designed to achieve protection without technically breaching international trading agreements.

Protection tends to insulate domestic producers from the pressures of competing foreign firms; hence it reduces their incentive to be efficient. A policy of widespread protection could retain resources in uncompetitive industries at the expense of potentially profitable new industries. It is thus essentially a conservative doctrine. In contrast, free trade in the market system would lead to *change*: it would gradually eliminate the weakest firms, and channel capital into other industries.

Protection benefits domestic producers, but at the expense of domestic consumers or taxpayers. Those who favour protection implicitly believe the welfare of producers matters more than that of consumers. Certainly the **vested interests** of well-organised producers may be *politically* important. Their per capita benefit from protection greatly exceeds the cost to individual consumers or taxpayers.

Restricting imports will not help the **balance of payments** in the long run, since exports will tend to fall to the same extent. Nor does protection increase domestic employment in the long run. The issue is not whether to employ domestic workers or foreign workers; but *in which industries* to employ domestic workers.

There may be exceptions to the general presumption in favour of free trade:
1. *Gradual* removal of existing protection, to avoid sudden domestic unemployment.
2. *Temporary* protection for declining domestic industries, to prevent or mitigate **structural unemployment**. (But 'temporary' protection often tends to last a long time.)
3. Threats of protection as a means of international bargaining, to induce other countries to reduce *their* protective barriers to trade.
4. Protection for defence-related industries, on security grounds. But Adam Smith's view that 'defence ... is of much more importance than opulence' does not mean that protection *increases* opulence!
5. Many writers also think the **infant industry** argument (outlined below) may sometimes justify temporary protection.

A new domestic industry may be unable to compete with an established foreign industry which enjoys economies of scale. It may then be argued that the 'infant industry' needs temporary protection to help it survive until it can gain similar economies of scale and stand on its own feet. But from a world viewpoint it may be more efficient to establish the industry in only a few countries, in order to gain full benefit from economies of scale. Does Zaire really need its own steel industry?

In theory, if large enough subsequent benefits are expected, they should induce domestic investment in an infant industry even without any assistance from the government (paid for by taxpayers). But *unless* the later benefits will repay the earlier costs, protection cannot be justified on *economic* grounds. In other words, either a domestic infant industry doesn't *need* protection, or else it doesn't *deserve* it.

Of course if a country's producers are absolutely inefficient at producing everything, then that country's people are likely to end up rather poor compared with people in other countries, under free trade as under any other system. *But protection will not make them richer.*

5.1.4 Trading Blocs

In a **free trade area**, member countries have no trading barriers between each other, but each has its own trading policy with other countries. A **customs union** is a group of countries with no trading barriers between each other and with a *common* external tariff and trading policy.

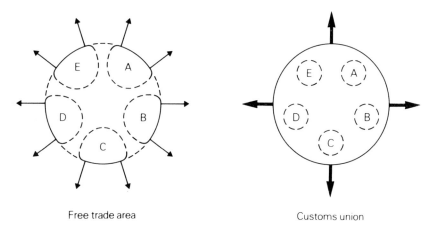

Free trade area   Customs union

Fig. 5.2: Free trade area and customs union.

Customs unions can increase efficiency through **trade creation**, if consumers now buy from abroad something previously bought at home. By enlarging the market, customs unions make possible product variety, international specialisation and economies of scale. Competition within the enlarged market counters monopoly and leads to an increase in welfare. But customs unions may *reduce* welfare through **trade diversion**, if consumers buy from within it something they would otherwise buy from outside. This might happen if a common external tariff exceeded the average prior level of tariffs of member countries.

The best-known customs union is the European Economic Community (EEC). The original 'six' members of the EEC were: France, Germany, Italy,

Belgium, Netherlands and Luxembourg. Denmark, Ireland, and the United Kingdom joined in 1973, and Greece in 1981. Portugal and Spain will probably join by 1986. EEC integration provides for free movement of labour and capital, and harmonising social security and regional policies. The EEC's Common Agricultural Policy (CAP) may cause trade diversion. It provides for tariffs on imported foodstuffs to bring prices up to the levels of EEC production costs – which may be higher than in some non-EEC countries.

If the external tariff of a customs union is similar to that of an individual country before joining, the effect of joining on particular firms is evident. Exporters now face access to a much larger market, as do importers. But domestic firms now face much more competition than before.

5.2 International Money

5.2.1 The Gold Standard

Precious metals have served as money since ancient times. In many countries silver fulfilled this role, but from about 1870 the main countries of the world all used gold as money. The local currency units were expressed in terms of gold, and local paper currency could be exchanged freely into gold at a fixed stated rate.

What happened if a country's receipts from abroad exceeded its payments? No country wanted to receive another country's paper currency: it wanted gold. So if it had a balance of payments *surplus* (see **5.3**) its **gold reserves** would increase. Since gold was money, this meant an increase in the domestic money supply. The result (after a time) would be a general tendency for domestic prices to rise (see Ch. 6). Hence imports (becoming relatively cheaper than domestically-produced goods) would tend to increase, and exports (become relatively more expensive than foreign-produced goods) would tend to decline. Thus the balance of payments surplus would tend to disappear.

The reverse would apply to a balance of payments deficit. If a country's payments exceeded its receipts, its gold reserves would fall. The resulting fall in the money supply would cause a tendency for domestic prices to fall. Hence imports (now becoming relatively more expensive than domestically-produced goods) would tend to decline, while exports (becoming relatively cheaper than foreign-produced goods) would tend to increase. Thus the balance of payments deficit would tend to disappear, as set out in Fig. 5.3 (see also **5.3.2**).

The **gold standard** worked as long as countries were prepared to abide by its 'automatic' rules and exchange gold for banknotes at par. But after the First World War, national governments felt it desirable to intervene in their domestic economies before the gold standard's mechanisms had *time* to work. So economic nationalism in the 1920s and 1930s destroyed the gold standard.

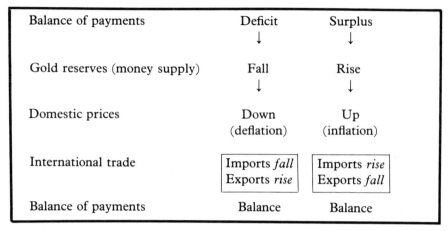

Fig. 5.3: Automatic gold standard mechanism.

Gold is not a perfect money: there is no such thing. The quantity of gold in existence varies over time, so the 'value of money' is not entirely stable. (Annual production of gold is about 3 per cent of the total stock of monetary gold.) If the increase in the stock of gold failed to keep pace with the increase in total world output, prices in general would move gradually lower.

Changes in the supply of money depended on random discoveries of new gold and technical changes in the process of gold mining and refining. But the extent of uncontrolled fluctuations can easily be exaggerated. For example, the notorious inflow of precious metals from the New World to Europe between 1500 and 1650 accounted for price increases in England averaging less than ½ per cent a year!

More important than technical details was the fundamental *political* implication of the gold standard. As Schumpeter wrote: 'The "automatic" gold currency is ... extremely sensitive to ... all those policies that violate the principles of economic liberalism. ... It imposes restrictions on governments or bureaucracies that are much more powerful than is parliamentary criticism.'

The main virtue of the gold standard was that it prevented deliberate inflation by governments (see Ch. 6). Paper currency could always be converted on demand into a known amount of gold, and the quantity of gold could not be rapidly increased. Experience, both ancient and modern, raises doubts whether politicians can be trusted to exercise monetary discretion with both honesty and competence.

5.2.2 The Bretton Woods System

After the Second World War the **Bretton Woods system** amounted to a dollar exchange standard. All other countries' currencies were linked at a **fixed exchange rate** to the US dollar, which was the only currency directly linked to gold (at $35 an ounce). Gold was no longer money, and in many countries, including the UK, people were legally forbidden to own it. Often people were not allowed to hold foreign currencies either, but had to sell them to the government at **official exchange rates**.

Short-term balance of payments imbalances were to be corrected by demand management (see **2.2.5**). An **International Monetary Fund** (IMF) was set up to act as a source of short-term borrowing for countries with temporary balance of payments deficits. Changes in the dollar exchange rate (and thus indirectly with gold) were allowed only if a country's balance of payments was in **fundamental disequilibrium**. Trade restrictions, such as import tariffs or quotas, were not officially allowed, though in fact they were fairly common. Government intervention implied use of national reserves of gold and convertible currencies, together (possibly) with various **exchange controls** (see **8.5.1**).

Apart from the 1949 **devaluation** of sterling from $4.03 to $2.80 (which was followed by many countries), the system worked quite well for many years. But from the late 1960s ever more frequent and severe problems finally caused the Bretton Woods system to break down in 1971. One problem was that the volume of world trade rose faster than the volume of gold and currency reserves: they amounted to 85 per cent of annual world trade in 1950 and only 30 per cent in 1970.

Even more important, continued debasement of the US dollar eventually made it impossible to maintain the fixed exchange rate into gold at $35 per ounce. If the dollar had been stable, the Bretton Woods system could have continued, but that was thought to produce intolerable strains for the domestic US economy. As a result several European countries (particularly France under de Gaulle) lost confidence in successive American governments' **monetary** and **fiscal policies** (see Ch. 9). In order to provide some flexibility in domestic economic management, each country wanted to maintain or build reserves. But they preferred to hold their reserves either (like the French and Swiss) in gold or in 'strong' currencies such as the German deutschmark. They were no longer prepared to treat the dollar as being 'as good as gold'.

The result was that US balance of payments deficits caused US gold reserves to fall; but for strategic reasons the US government was unwilling to see its gold reserves fall below 300 million ounces. The solution – 'devaluation' – effectively raised the dollar price of gold; but it was not possible simply to move to another, higher, 'fixed' gold price. Once the possibility of changing the gold price was admitted, the system of fixed exchange rates lost credibility. Instead, national currencies were left free to float against each other.

5.2.3 Fixed versus Floating Exchange Rates

Figure 5.4 sets out possible international monetary systems.

Milton Friedman has suggested: 'The ultimate objective is a world in which exchange rates, while *free* to vary, are in fact highly stable.' He identified four possible ways for a country to deal with a 'permanent' balance of payments deficit or surplus:

1. FIXED RATES

   a. Gold Standard

   b. Commodity Basket Standard

   c. Some other single world currency.

2. 'FIXED' (BUT ADJUSTABLE) EXCHANGE RATES

   a. Bretton Woods system

   b. Some variant of Bretton Woods.

3. FLOATING EXCHANGE RATES

   a. 'Crawling Pegs' – regular small changes

   b. 'Dirty Floats' – with government intervention

   c. Freely floating exchange rates.

Fig. 5.4: Possible international monetary systems.

Deficit	*Surplus*
1. Devalue currency	1. Revalue currency
2. Domestic deflation	2. Domestic inflation
3. Direct exchange controls	3. Direct exchange controls
4. Let reserves fall	4. Let reserves rise.

1. Devaluations or revaluations can be either adjustments to a nominally 'fixed' exchange rate, or simply events in a flexible **(floating)** rate system. The trouble with 'fixed' rates is that needed adjustments tend to be delayed too long, and then made in large jumps. This naturally attracts one-way speculation – which can lead to large short-term capital flows of **hot money**.

2. Domestic deflation is likely to be politically unpopular in deficit countries; and if many prices (especially wage-rates – see Ch. 7) are 'sticky' downwards, it may not work, or not quickly enough. To a lesser extent, domestic inflation may also be unpopular in surplus countries.

3. Exchange controls (including import controls) can be difficult to enforce. They are likely to lead to a misallocation of resources, since officials may not know which are the 'correct' items to control. They may also be counter-productive in deficit countries, in that their very existence makes the currency less desirable to hold.

4. Reserve changes will probably not be needed if a balance of payments imbalance is small and temporary; and will not work if it is large and permanent. With a deficit, the national reserves will eventually run out; and with a surplus, no country will be prepared for ever to pile up reserves of gold and foreign currencies in exchange for supplying real goods and services.

5.2.4 **Floating Exchange Rates**

After the 1971 breakdown of the Bretton Woods fixed exchange rate system, the major countries let their currencies fluctuate ('float') against each other. Governments continued to intervene in currency markets (**dirty floats**), but ostensibly only to 'smooth out' changes in exchange rates, not to try to counteract trends.

A country whose transactions would, with fixed exchange rates, give rise to a balance of payments surplus finds its currency, under floating exchange rates, appreciating relative to others. Similarly a country which, with fixed exchange rates, would have a deficit finds its currency **depreciating** against others, when it is allowed to float.

An immediate result of **floating exchange rates** was a very sharp rise in the dollar price of gold. But Fig. 5.5 shows that the gold price has fluctuated quite widely. It declined throughout 1975 and 1976, and from late 1980 to mid-1982. But the end-1982 gold price of $450 an ounce is more than 12 times the official $35 an ounce maintained under Bretton Woods.

The 1970s were years of rapid and fluctuating rates of inflation in most

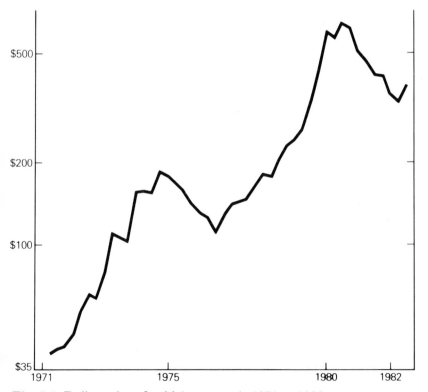

Fig. 5.5: Dollar price of gold (per ounce), 1971 to 1982.

countries (see Ch. 6). These naturally led to continued sharp fluctuations in currency exchange rates, which have caused major problems for many businesses. It has been difficult to know how to price goods for export, amounts due from foreign customers have been liable to fluctuate in terms of domestic currency, and there have been serious accounting problems.

Foreign exchange rates reflect the *relative* value of one currency against another. One theory says that changes in exchange rates will depend on the relative rates of inflation in the two countries. This **purchasing power parity** theory may seem plausible in the long run, but it cannot account for the short-term volatility of exchange rates in recent years. Another theory allows for capital flows by relating changes in exchange rates both to interest rate differentials and to expectations about the future. But nobody has been able to explain very well some of the unexpected movements in exchange rates in the last few years.

Figure 5.6 shows the 'effective exchange rates' since 1975 of the pound and the US dollar, each against a weighted average of other currencies. It is no longer very useful to measure the pound solely against the dollar, for an obvious reason. The pound may appear 'strong' against the dollar either because the pound really is strong (against most other currencies) or because the *dollar* is *weak*. Thus using weighted averages gives a more reliable picture.

The weakness of the US dollar in the 1970s prompted the EEC countries to develop the **European Monetary System** (EMS), which could potentially

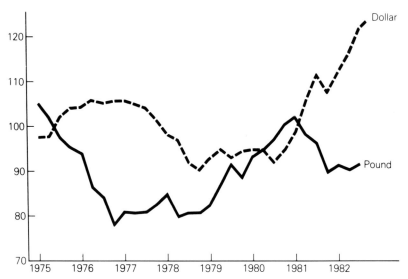

Fig. 5.6: Sterling and US dollar effective exchange rates, 1975 to 1982 (1975 = 100).

form the basis for a new fixed exchange rate system. All member countries' currencies (except the pound sterling) were linked within a limited band of fluctuation (the **snake**). The EEC countries together account for some 40 per cent of world trade, and (with Switzerland) hold about 50 per cent of official world reserves of gold.

5.3. Balance of Payments

5.3.1 Components of the 'Balance of Payments'

Balance of payments statistics show money transactions for a period between one country and the rest of the world. In fact the 'balance' of payments is a small difference, usually less than 5 per cent, between two much larger totals. The initial estimates often have to be revised later, due to the large margins of error in estimates of foreign transactions. Figure 5.7 outlines the component items in 'balance of payments' figures. It highlights two headings: the **current balance** and the **overall balance**.

Current account	Visible balance Imports and exports of goods *Invisibles* Imports and exports of services Interest, profits, and dividends Current transfers
	CURRENT BALANCE
Capital account	Direct investment Portfolio investment Banking liabilities Balancing item (errors, omissions, etc.)
	OVERALL BALANCE
Official financing	Official borrowing Changes in reserves

Fig. 5.7: Outline of the balance of payments.

The balance of payments current account consists of the **visible balance** plus invisibles. The visible balance is the difference between imports and exports of goods (**visible trade**). The UK normally has a deficit on visible trade, offset by a surplus on **invisible trade** (services). Exports of services, including transport and financial services, are about 25 per cent of total UK exports, while imports of services are about 20 per cent of total UK imports. 'Invisibles' also include interest, profits and dividends; and current transfers, which include military items as part of the government's current transactions.

Capital account transactions represent direct and portfolio investment, and changes in banking liabilities; together with a **balancing item** to cover errors, omissions, and unidentified items (which are sometimes large). **Direct investment** means that the investor *controls* a foreign business, while **portfolio investment** implies only a passive financial interest, usually amounting to only a small proportion of the total capital of a business.

The overall balance on current and capital accounts together is the amount which has to be covered by official financial transactions. These comprise official borrowing (or repayment), from the IMF or from foreign governments, and/or movements on official reserves of gold and foreign currency holdings.

5.3.2 The Effect of Exchange Rate Changes

The main way to clear balance of payments imbalances is *price* changes, either domestic prices or foreign exchange rates. But these may be delayed by allowing reserves to take the initial strain. Technical accounting expressions should not connote emotional meaning. Thus a balance of payments 'surplus' *is in no sense a sort of national 'profit'*. It just means that a country is exporting more value in goods and services than it is getting back in imports.

Fig. 5.8: UK terms of trade, 1970 to 1982 (1975 = 100).

Given suitable financing arrangements (such as permanent credit from suppliers), each country would ideally like to have a permanent *deficit* on current trading. That would enable its citizens to import (and consume) more than they exported (and produced). For developed countries, however, *in the long run imports of goods and services must roughly equal exports.* (Thus import controls are likely in the end to reduce *exports* too.)

Depreciation of a country's currency may increase the *volume* of its subsequent exports. But if demand for the goods concerned is not **price-elastic**, the foreign currency *value* of exports may not increase. Product quality and design, prompt and reliable delivery and servicing, etc., may often be more important than price in increasing export sales. Export markets may take *time* to respond to price changes, while imports (which may also be **price-inelastic** in the short run) will *immediately* become more expensive in terms of domestic currency. This can lead to the '**J-curve effect**': devaluation may actually *increase* a current balance of payments deficit in the short run, even if it may reduce it in the long run.

	Before	*After*
Currency depreciation (e.g. of £1 from 4DM to 3DM) *UK imports*		
Makes them dearer in £s, e.g. imports from Germany costing 240DM	£60	£80
UK exports		
i. Makes them cheaper in DMs, e.g. exports to Germany priced at 600DM	£150/600DM	£150/450DM
ii. Increases profit margin in £s or,	£150/600DM	£200/600DM
iii. Some combination of above, e.g.:	£150/600DM	£175/525DM
Currency appreciation (e.g. of £1 from $1.50 to $2.00) *UK imports*	*Before*	*After*
Makes them cheaper in £s, e.g. imports from US costing $300	£200	£150
UK exports		
i. Makes them dearer in $s, e.g. exports to US priced at $600	£400/$600	£400/$800
ii. Reduces profit margin in £s or,	£400/$600	£300/$600
iii. Some combination of above, e.g.:	£400/$600	£350/$700

Fig. 5.9: How exchange rate changes affect imports and exports.

Devaluation of a currency will tend to reduce export prices and to increase import prices. Thus the *ratio* of export prices divided by import prices, known as the **terms of trade**, will tend to fall. Figure 5.8 shows the UK terms of trade since 1970, revealing a sharp fall between 1972 and 1974.

Figure 5.9 shows how exchange rate changes might affect the balance of payments current account. The arithmetic deals only with price, but it is worth re-emphasising that in foreign trade – as in domestic – *price may not be the most important aspect.*

5.3.3 Changing UK Visible Trade Patterns

Figure 5.10 analyses UK visible exports and imports by product group since 1960. The recent increase in fuel exports has been offset by the decline in the share of manufactures. The fall in imports of food, beverages and tobacco has been balanced by an even sharper increase in the share of imports of finished manufactures. Thus both sides of the international trade account illustrate the decline in competitiveness of UK manufacturing.

The geographical pattern of UK visible trade has also changed since 1960. The proportion of trade with the EEC has increased from about 15 per cent in 1960 to more than 40 per cent by 1980.

	1960 (%)	1970 (%)	1980 (%)
Exports			
Food, beverages and tobacco	6	7	7
Fuels	4	3	13
Manufactures	84	84	74
Miscellaneous	6	6	6
	100	100	100
Imports			
Food, beverages and tobacco	33	23	12
Fuels	10	10	14
Basic industrial materials	30	22	15
Semi-manufactures	16	22	18
Finished Manufactures	11	23	41
	100	100	100

Fig. 5.10: UK visible exports and imports, by product group, 1960, 1970 and 1980.

Work Section

A. Revision Questions

A1 What precisely is 'comparative advantage'?

A2 What was suggested as the basic argument for free trade?

A3 Why should I teach, if I can type better than my secretary?

A4 What is the difference between bilateral and multilateral trade?

A5 What does the theory of comparative advantage assume about the mobility of factors of production?

A6 What is protection? Name four different forms that it may take.

A7 What is the difference between import tariffs and import quotas?

A8 What are non-tariff barriers?

A9 Who gains from protection? Who loses?

A10 Name as many arguments in favour of protection as you can.

A11 What is the 'infant industry' argument? Is is economically justified? Why or why not?

A12 Why do small countries tend to export a larger proportion of their domestic output than large countries?

A13 What is the difference between a Free Trade Area and a Customs Union?

A14 Define and distinguish 'trade creation' and 'trade diversion'.

A15 Why may the EEC's Common Agricultural Policy cause trade diversion?

A16 What was meant by the 'gold standard'?

A17 Explain fully the 'automatic' balancing mechanism under the gold standard for a country (a) in deficit and (b) in surplus.

A18 What was claimed to be the main virtue of the gold standard?

A19 Why did the gold standard come to an end?

A20 How did the Bretton Woods system work from 1945 to 1971?

A21 What was the IMF's role under the Bretton Woods system?

A22 How was a country supposed to deal with a temporary balance of payments deficit under the Bretton Woods system?

A23 Under what circumstances could a 'fixed' exchange rate be changed?

A24 Why did the Bretton Woods system come to an end?

A25 Why was it not practicable simply to continue with a fixed-rate system after 1971, but with a higher gold price?

A26 What happens with floating exchange rates to the currency of a country which, with fixed exchange rates, would have had a balance of payments deficit?

A27 What happened to the dollar price of gold after 1971, following nearly 40 years at $35 an ounce? Why?

A28 What problems do fluctuating exchange rates cause for businesses?

A29 Why is the 'strength' or 'weakness' of the pound sterling measured against a weighted average of currencies, not solely the US dollar?

A30 What is the European Monetary System?

A31 What does the balance of payments 'current account' consist of?

A32 What is the difference between visible and invisible trade?

A33 What does the balance of payments 'capital account' consist of?

A34 What is official financing?

A35 How are balance of payments deficits or surpluses adjusted?

A36 Why isn't a balance of payments surplus equivalent to a sort of national 'profit'?

A37 Why won't restricting imports help the balance of payments in the long run?

A38 Why is the price-elasticity of demand for imports and exports relevant in connection with devaluation of a currency?

A39 What are the 'terms of trade'?

A40 With which region of the world has UK trade increased most sharply over the past 20 years? Why? Will the trend continue?

B. Exercises and Case Studies

B1 In Cloudia the opportunity cost of making one ship is *a* cars, while in Sunland it is *b* cars (assume that $a > b$)
   a. What is the opportunity cost of making cars
      i. in Cloudia?   ii. in Sunland?
   b. In which product has Cloudia a comparative advantage? In which product has Sunland a comparative advantage?
   c. What happens to *total* car production if Sunland produces one more ship while Cloudia makes one less ship?
   d. What happens to total ship production if Cloudia makes one more car while Sunland makes one less car?

B2 Refer to Figs. 5.5 (page 99), 5.6 (page 100) and 5.8 (page 102). From reference material, find out the latest:
   a. $ price of gold per ounce
   b. Sterling Effective Exchange Rate
   c. UK Terms of Trade

B3 Given the following information about the production capabilities of France and Italy, which country will export wine to the other? Give an example of a mutually beneficial exchange rate between wine and bread.

	Wine	*Bread*
France	40 units or	60 units
Italy	10 units or	5 units

B4 Extract from Bastiat's Petition to the French Chamber of Deputies on behalf of the Candlemakers:

'We are suffering from the ruinous competition of a foreign rival who apparently works under conditions so far superior to our own for the production of light that he is flooding the domestic market with it at an incredibly low price. The moment he appears, our sales cease, all the consumers turn to him, and a branch of French industry whose ramifications are innumerable is all at once reduced to complete stagnation. This rival, which is none other than the sun, is waging war on us so mercilessly that we suspect he is being stirred up against us by perfidious Albion.

'In order to encourage industry and increase employment, we ask you to be so good as to pass a law requiring the closing of all windows, dormers, skylights, inside and outside shutters, curtains, casements, and blinds – in short, all openings, holes, chinks, and fissures through which the light of the sun is wont to enter houses to the detriment of our industry.'

To what extent is this 1845 request justified?

B5 Since the mid-1970s there have been arguments in favour of import controls by economists at Cambridge. Four of their points are listed below, and you are asked to explain (with reasons) to what extent you agree or disagree with each of them:

a. If the EEC rules against tariffs continue to be applied, Britain will probably become, within 10 years, a derelict industrial area, with many factories closed down, industrial employment drastically reduced, and no alternatives in prospect but emigration.

b. Since the EEC was created in the mid-1950s it has become manifest that British industry has become progressively less able to stand up to competition from the industries of other countries.

c. Devaluation is not a real alternative to industrial protection. Except in conditions very favourable to wage stability, the stimulus it provides tends quickly to be eroded away by the inflation it generates.

d. The main difference between devaluation and a tariff on manufactures is that devaluation raises the price of foodstuffs and raw materials as well as manufactures, whereas the tariff raises the price of imported manufactures only.

B6 Examine the following statements about devaluation of a currency and explain briefly why each is either true or false:

a. A devaluation of the pound by 10 per cent requires an increase in the volume of exports (priced in pounds sterling) of *over* 10 per cent if the value of exports in foreign exchange terms is to rise.

b. Provided that the price-elasticity of demand for imports exceeds zero, the value of imports in terms of foreign exchange will decline following a devaluation.

   c. Devaluation will only 'work' if it is accompanied by measures to reduce domestic demand.

B7   Refer to Fig. 5.9 on page 103. Draw up a similar table showing the effects of:

   a. depreciation from £1 = 540 Japanese yen to £1 = 400 yen;

   b. appreciation from £1 = 9 French francs to £1 = 12 francs.

B8   In which part of the UK balance of payments account (if any) would you place the following activities? Why?

   a. German tourists spending money in London hotels;

   b. purchases of British turbo-generators by Middle East countries;

   c. American capital invested in North Sea oil rigs;

   d. the sales of Volvo cars in Britain;

   e. Saudi Arabia's increased bank deposits in London clearing banks;

   f. insurance premiums for sea and air freight between Africa and Latin America, taken at Lloyd's of London;

   g. acquisition of American military equipment by the UK government;

   h. the purchase by EEC countries of crude oil from OPEC countries;

   i. the cost of UK companies' acquisitions of subsidiary companies in the United States;

   j. dividends paid by UK subsidiaries to their French parents.

B9   The following items (listed in alphabetical order) comprise the main headings for the UK balance of payments in 1980. You are asked to construct the balance of payments account in suitable format, showing in particular:

   a. Visible trade balance

   b. Current balance

   c. Overall balance.

	£ b.
1. Balancing item	1
2. Exports of goods	47
3. Exports of services	16
4. Government transfers abroad (net)	2
5. Imports of goods	46
6. Imports of services	12
7. Official financing (addition to reserves)	1
8. Other capital items (net)	1
9. Overseas investment in UK'	5
10. Private investment overseas	7
11. Property income from abroad	8
12. Property income paid to abroad	8

B10 Home and Overseas Trolleys Ltd.

Home and Overseas Trolleys Limited sold a heated food trolley (to serve

8 to 12 people). The HOT trolley had two important advantages: it kept food hot between cooking and serving, and it could be wheeled round the table, making the process of serving much easier. A new design had greatly increased its safety and reliability, thus reducing after-sales care to a negligible level. In February 1982, the trolley sold at £100 in the home market and at $225 in the American market.

Home sales were running at about 150,000 units a year. When the company had begun, two years earlier, to try selling in the American market at $225 per unit, the trolley's success had surprised HOT's management. Export sales volume amounted to 60,000 units in the year ending March 1981, and was expected to reach 100,000 units in 1982. In view of the success of their exporting effort, HOT decided to try to expand their American export sales further for the year ending March 1983.

Two factors bothered them. They had not been impressed with their American marketing agency, and planned to improve this aspect of the business. Secondly, the company's cost structure needed careful watching. The present breakdown of trolley costs and profit was: Selling price £100; variable costs £60; contribution margin £40. The contribution had to cover fixed costs as well as provide a net profit margin after allocation of all expenses. Of the variable costs, 25 per cent consisted of a German heating element. If this part increased in price, the overall gross margin could be greatly affected, as there was no obvious alternative product.

In planning its 1983 budget, HOT decided to work on the basis of keeping its price the same all through the year to March 1983. For various reasons it was difficult to change the quoted price in mid-year. Meanwhile, Mr Andrew Rolls, the Finance Director, was studying movements in foreign exchange rates over the recent past. When the company had first started exporting to the United States, in April 1981, £1 = $2.25. Since then the £ had depreciated by almost 20 per cent, to about £1 = $1.80.

Mr Rolls decided to begin his 1983 planning by assuming that the exchange rate would remain at £1 = $1.80 throughout the year to March 1983. If anything he felt that the £ was more likely to appreciate against the dollar, rather than to fall further. The question was, what dollar selling price per unit should be charged in 1983? At $180 per unit (the dollar equivalent of the current pound selling price), the trolley would seem underpriced compared with US competitors. On the other hand, it might be hard to increase sales volume much if the price were kept at its present level of $225 per unit. There was also a danger, if sales volume expanded too far, that domestic production capacity of 300,000 would be reached.

The latest sales forecast for the home market was for sales of 150,000 units in 1983. As far as the American market was concerned, HOT had less confidence in the accuracy of their sales forecasts. Their best guess was that export sales volume in 1983 would be as follows at various prices:

     At $180 ...   150,000 units
     At $200 ...   135,000 units
     At $225 ...   120,000 units.

The exchange rate between the pound and the Deutschmark was currently about 4.50DM = £1 in February 1982. Mr Rolls felt that American interest rates might fall soon (like other people, he had been feeling this for some months now), which would weaken the dollar. If the £/$ exchange rate stayed fairly stable at £1 = $1.80, then the pound might fall against the German DM. Mr Rolls thought he ought to consider the effect of a fall over the next year to an average of, say, 4.00DM = £1 on the profitability of the trolley's export sales. Alternatively, the £/DM exchange rate might stay the same; but the pound might strengthen against the dollar, say to £1 = $2.00.

On the basis of the information given, what $ price do you think Mr Rolls should recommend for the American export market in 1983, assuming foreign exchange rates as follows:

a. £1 = $1.80, 4.50DM.
b. £1 = $2.00, 4.50DM.
c. £1 = $1.80, 4.00DM.

C. Essay Questions

C1 Should imports of Japanese cars into the UK be restricted?

C2 Will international trade continue to increase faster than output?

C3 'The free traders win the debates, but the protectionists win the elections' (Frank Knight). To what extent is this true, and why?

C4 'If infant industries will eventually be successful, they don't need government protection; if not, they don't deserve it.' Discuss.

C5 Explain why a British exporting firm might be concerned by:
   a. rising prices at home;
   b. a 15 per cent surcharge on all imports;
   c. a low price-elasticity of demand for their exports.

C6 If the sterling exchange rate depreciated by 15 per cent and the UK government placed a six-month quota restriction on imported luxury manufactures (50 per cent of the previous 12 months' sales), how might this affect:
   a. the British Steel Corporation's raw material supplies?
   b. the main Nissan car agency in Britain?
   c. a wine importer?

C7 How might a London tour operator arranging holidays in the United States deal with the possibility of fluctuations in the external value of the US dollar?

C8 In what ways might a 20 per cent downward float of the pound sterling affect the business operations of:
   a. UK importers?
   b. UK exporters?

C9 Professor Paul Samuelson says reintroducing the gold standard is not a good idea, because it would help South Africa and Russia (which he objects to on political grounds). Are there any *economic* arguments against the gold standard?

C10 What would be the main likely consequences of a single European currency covering all the EEC countries?

C11 What would be the main likely consequences of four *separate* currencies for England, Scotland, Wales, and Northern Ireland?

C12 Should exchange controls be reintroduced? Why or why not?

C13 Early in 1983 the Cambridge Econometrics Group produced a forecast suggesting that much of the expected recovery in consumer demand would be dissipated in imports. The implication was that the UK economy would not gain much benefit. Comment.

C14 How, if at all, over the next 15 years is the UK's pattern of goods and services imported and exported likely to change, by product and/or by geographical region?

C15 'Now that the pound is floating, governments no longer need worry about the balance of payments.' Discuss.

Chapter 6

Money and Inflation

Objective: *To describe the functions and evolution of money; to outline the Quantity Theory, and its interpretation; to explain how inflation is measured, and its post-war extent; to discuss two main theories as to the cause of inflation; and to explore some of the problems it creates.*

Synopsis: *Money is a medium of exchange, a unit of account, and a store of wealth. It has evolved from gold to paper, but still depends on public confidence. Most of the 'money supply' consists of bank accounts. The Quantity Theory suggests that increasing the money supply too much in the long run will cause inflation; but in the short run the velocity of circulation may vary.*

Inflation means generally rising prices: it is measured by the Retail Price Index.

Inflation has averaged more than 10 per cent a year in the UK since 1967, causing the pound's purchasing power to fall by more than 80 per cent.

The two main suggested explanations of inflation are demand-pull and cost-push; the distinction relates to active causation versus passive accommodation by the money supply. Possible sources of cost-push inflation include wages, import costs, taxes, or price 'stickiness' downwards.

Inflation obscures economic calculations, leading to a need for some form of 'inflation accounting'. It also causes extra transactions costs and uncertainty, which can seriously affect business firms. And inflation can have important political implications.

6.1 Money

6.1.1 Historical Evolution

Money is any generally accepted **medium of exchange**. Its main function is acting as a means of payment. Money can also represent a **unit of account**, for purposes of economic calculation, if its purchasing power is reasonably stable. A stable money can also be a **store of wealth**, enabling people to separate the timing of purchases from that of income.

If there were no money, people would have to exchange goods and services by means of barter. This is a cumbersome process, where two people must each want precisely what the other has got to offer, thus depending on a 'double coincidence of wants'. By *unlinking* purchases from sales, money allows specialisation and the division of labour to develop.

For centuries precious metals like gold or silver were used as money, being scarce, durable, divisible, and easily recognised. The ruler's seal on a 'coin' guaranteed its weight and fineness. This avoided the need to weigh the metal at each payment and made coins acceptable 'at face value'. Rulers themselves often 'debased' their coinage by adding base metal to the precious metal; though eventually milled edges prevented coin-clipping.

Bankers held money (gold) in safe-keeping, and issued paper notes (receipts) to the owners. They represented a promise by the banker to pay the holder, on demand, a certain amount of gold. Most people found paper notes more convenient than gold for day-to-day payments. Soon, therefore, bankers saw no need to 'back' each paper note with equivalent gold in their vaults. In practice banks could normally lend out at interest about ten times more 'paper money' than the gold they held.

Some bank loans were for long periods. So if all holders of paper banknotes had demanded instant repayment in gold, banks could not have met their legal obligations in time. Thus prudent banks had to take great care to avoid any loss of public confidence in their solvency. But paper notes of a reliable bank were reckoned to be 'as good as gold'.

In time **central banks** evolved, to act as banker to the government as well as to the commercial banks. Within a country they often became the sole issuer of paper notes. Eventually most governments nationalised their country's central bank, and withdrew the legal right to convert paper banknotes into gold. The lack of convertibility into a scarce commodity such as gold makes it easy for modern governments to print more notes and inflate the supply of paper currency.

6.1.2 The Money Supply

There are two main definitions of the **money supply**, 'M1' and '£M3'. M1 consists of notes and coins together with bank current accounts (which are withdrawable on demand). M3 includes not only the very 'liquid' items contained in M1, but also bank deposit accounts (which require a period of notice – often seven days – before they can be withdrawn). Figure 6.1 shows the size of the various items in February 1983 in £ billions seasonably adjusted.

£M3 = 93

M1 = 38		Deposit accounts	
Notes and coins	11	with banks	53
Current accounts with banks	27	Public sector deposits	2

Fig. 6.1: The money supply: M1 and £M3, in February 1983 (£ b.).

It can be seen that *bank accounts* comprise about 85 per cent of the £M3 money supply. Under the gold standard bankers were able to lend out about ten times as much money as they had gold in their vaults. In modern conditions, too, the banks can 'create money' by expanding *credit*: they lend out more money than has been deposited with them. What limits the amount that banks lend out? Commercial prudence, based on experience; and, until recently, government regulations. The banks were required to hold 12½ per cent of their liabilities (representing customers' **current** and **deposit accounts**) in the form of 'reserve assets', which were highly liquid. Recent changes have removed this as a formal requirement, but it remains as an unofficial 'norm' for the banks.

6.1.3 The Quantity Theory

The **Quantity Theory** of money is best known in the form of Irving Fisher's equation:

$$MV = PT$$

where: M = Money supply
V = Velocity of circulation

P = general level of Prices
T = volume of Trade.

In its simplest form, the Quantity Theory says that, at any given level of output, the purchasing power of each unit of money varies inversely with the supply of money. The more pound notes are printed, the less each pound note is worth (will buy). But this plausible proposition is misleading. Figure 6.2 summarises, in their extreme forms, three different views of what effect a change in M (say an increase) will have on the Quantity Theory equation.

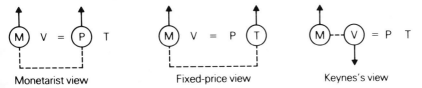

Monetarist view   Fixed-price view   Keynes's view

Fig. 6.2: Increasing the money supply: three views.

1. The 'monetarist' view assumes that V is more less constant, and that T is not much affected, in the long run, by changes in the money supply. (This may be because 'full employment' of factors of production is assumed.) Then increasing M will tend, after a time lag, to cause a proportionate increase in P (i.e. inflation). Not all *specific* prices, however, will necessarily rise in the same proportion as the increase in the general *average* level of prices.
2. A second (fixed-price) view, while also assuming that V is constant, focusses on a different assumption: that P is virtually constant. Then increasing M will tend, at *less* than full employment, to cause after a time a proportionate increase *in* T.
3. A third view, held by Keynes, is that V is *not* constant: in the extreme, it will vary *inversely* with M. Thus an increase in M may be exactly balanced by a fall in V, with *no* effect on either P or T.

The three views have been stated in their extreme forms above in order to distinguish them clearly. In practice, combinations are also possible. Attempts to choose between these different views have centred on two aspects: trying to establish what causes inflation (see **6.**3), and trying to establish whether or not V is constant.

6.1.4 Velocity of Circulation

The **velocity of circulation** may be defined as 'the ratio of annual **gross national product** at market prices to the money supply M3'. In the 1960s, velocity seemed to be fairly stable, not varying more than 5 per cent from a value of 2.9. But, as Fig. 6.3 shows, since 1970 velocity has varied considerably, as low as 2.25 in 1974, and as high as 3.5 in 1980.

The record since 1970 casts doubt on the view that V is stable, at least in

Fig. 6.3: UK velocity of circulation (M3), 1970 to 1982.

the short run. But the increase between 1974 and 1980 does not suggest that *V* varies *inversely* with M3, which nearly doubled in those six years. (The basis of calculating money supply M3 was changed in the 4th quarter of 1981.)

6.1.5 Cigarettes as Money[1]

In a prisoner of war camp there is little production of goods, though some of services: the economic emphasis lies on *exchange*. In the camp being described there were about 2,000 people. Everyone received a roughly equal share of essentials, and there were also private parcels from time to time. Consumer preferences were expressed by means of exchange, and most trading between individuals was for food against cigarettes or other foodstuffs.

Within a week or so, rough scales of exchange values had emerged. By the end of the month there was a lively trade in all commodities, with their relative values well known. These were expressed in terms of *cigarettes*, which had quickly risen to the status of a currency. Exchange and Mart noticeboards in every bungalow published cigarette prices for each commodity, which tended to equality throughout the camp. Though barter was never extinguished, everyone (including non-smokers) was willing to sell for cigarettes, using them to buy something else later.

Cigarettes performed all the functions of a metallic currency: medium of exchange, unit of account, and store of wealth. They were homogeneous, reasonably durable, and of convenient size for the smallest (or, in the case of

---

[1] Taken from R. A. Radford, Economic Organisation of a P.O.W. Camp. *Economica*, Vol. XII, 1945.

packets, largest) transactions. Hand-rolled cigarettes could be rolled between the fingers so that tobacco fell out. With the currency thus 'debased', prices could no longer safely be quoted in them. Instead people examined each hand-rolled cigarette before accepting it; and rejected thin ones, or valued them at a discount.

Certain brands were popular to smoke: hence buyers used the poorer brands as currency. Machine-made cigarettes were always acceptable; but their main drawback was a strong demand for non-monetary purposes. Thus the economy was continually subjected to deflationary pressures as smoking reduced the 'money supply'. But periods of monetary stringency were ended when a large new delivery of cigarettes suddenly arrived, increasing the supply of money.

At first prices used to fluctuate weekly, falling towards Sunday, and rising sharply on Monday morning with the weekly issue of food and cigarette parcels. Later, when many people held reserves, the weekly issue had no such effect, being too small a proportion of the total stock. *Credit* entered into many transactions: a treacle ration might cost four cigarettes now or five next week – the difference representing 'interest'.

In August 1944 the supplies of parcels and cigarettes were both halved. Since this affected both sides of the equation equally, changes in prices were not anticipated. But the non-monetary demand for cigarettes was less elastic than the demand for food, and food prices fell a little.

The general price level was affected by inflationary expectations. One morning a rumour circulated before breakfast of the arrival of parcels and cigarettes. Within 10 minutes a treacle ration (hitherto offered in vain for three cigarettes) could be sold for four. By 10 o'clock the rumour was denied, and treacle found no more buyers that day, even at two cigarettes.

There were often fluctuations in relative prices; for example, due to a change in the supply of a particular commodity. In hot weather demand for cocoa fell and that for soap rose. New inventions also affected prices: the discovery that raisins and sugar could be turned into a potent alcoholic liquor permanently affected the dried fruit market.

The remainder of the article describes:

a. *the introduction of a paper currency (the Bully Mark), 100 per cent backed by food; and the flight from it when confidence waned;*

b. *official attempts at price-fixing, undermined by a black market when official prices didn't fall quickly enough during the occasional deflations;*

c. *general public hostility to the middleman, whose function in bringing buyer and seller together was ignored. He was regarded as being redundant, even though his very existence was proof to the contrary.*

6.2   Inflation

6.2.1   Measuring Inflation

Laymen define **inflation** as 'generally rising prices' or 'too much money chasing too few goods'. In fact, experts find it hard to do better, though there may be dispute over whether there is 'too much money' or 'too few goods'. In a competitive market with productivity gradually increasing over time, prices in general will *fall* gradually, unless the money supply increases. To keep the general level of prices stable, the money supply would need to rise in line with the increase in output.

Perhaps even more than most economic statistics, the measurement of inflation is only approximate. For practical purposes the index of inflation which is published most quickly and most often is likely to be the most useful. Hence the normal measure of the general rise in prices in the UK is the **Retail Price Index** (RPI). This appears monthly about five weeks after the middle of the month to which it refers.

The modern UK Retail Price Index series goes back to June 1947, recent figures being based on January 1974 = 100. On that basis, June 1947 = 29 and January 1983 = 326. Thus prices in general have increased more than 11-fold in 35 years. Average annual rates of increase have been:

$$1947 \text{ to } 1952: \quad 6\tfrac{1}{2} \text{ per cent}$$
$$1952 \text{ to } 1967: \quad 3 \quad \text{per cent}$$
$$1967 \text{ to } 1982: \quad 11\tfrac{1}{2} \text{ per cent.}$$

Figure 6.4 shows annual percentage increases in the Retail Price Index since 1970. There were very rapid increases between 1972 and 1975, and between

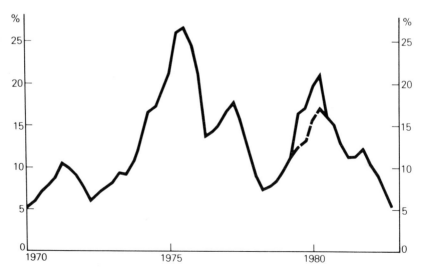

Fig. 6.4: Annual rates of increase in Retail Price Index, 1970 to 1982.

1978 and 1980. The 1979 switch from direct to indirect taxation (see Ch. 8) increased Value Added Tax and added about 4 per cent to the RPI. The broken line allows for this.

The rate of increase in the money supply is *not* usually taken as a direct measure of the rate of inflation. There are problems in defining the 'money supply' (see **6.1.2**). There are also time-lags of varying and uncertain length between an increase in the money supply and its ultimate effect on retail prices. If there is existing widespread unemployment prices may not rise, or not for some time. In any event, as noted above, if productivity is rising, some increase in the money supply would be consistent with *stable* prices in general.

An alternative measure of domestic inflation might be the exchange rate of the currency against foreign currencies. But this is subject to time-lags, and to other distortions, such as capital flows; and it also assumes no foreign inflation. It might be suitable if poor statistics or political manipulation affected internal price indices, or if the rate of inflation were extremely rapid, as in a **hyper-inflation**. This may be defined as being when prices in general are rising by at least 50 per cent *per month*. In Weimar Germany between August 1922 and November 1923, prices rose by ten thousand million times! (The price of a cup of coffee would apparently increase between the time one ordered it and the time one paid for it!)

6.2.2 UK Experience Since 1914

By modern standards, apart from the period around the Napoleonic Wars, the UK experienced virtually no inflation between 1660 and 1914. Prices rose from time to time – but they *fell* too. So there was no persistent *cumulative* increase in the general level of prices. Thus on the outbreak of the First World War, the general price level was about the same as it had been at the Restoration of Charles II in 1660.

Figure 6.5 shows the internal purchasing power of the pound since 1914. On the basis that 1914 = 100, then 1935 = 70, 1965 = 20, and 1982 = $3\frac{1}{2}$.

The First World War brought very rapid inflation, averaging about 14 per cent a year between 1914 and 1920. It was followed by a severe **deflation**, which averaged 4 per cent a year between 1920 and 1934. The UK has experienced inflation in every year since 1934. Only people now aged over 50 can remember a single year without inflation.

Between 1934 and 1939 the rate of inflation was fairly mild; then very rapid during the Second World War; then much reduced again between 1946 and 1967. But after 1967 the UK rate of inflation accelerated fiercely, amounting on average to *more than 10 per cent a year* between 1967 and 1982. This was truly a sensational rate by British standards in peacetime over the previous millennium.

The pound's purchasing power halved between 1945 and 1965; it halved again between 1965 and 1975; and it halved *again* between 1975 and 1980. Thus the historical 'half-life' of the pound was 20 years in 1965, 10 years in 1975, and

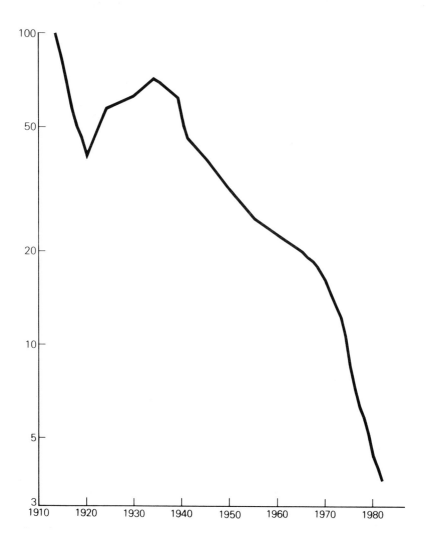

Fig. 6.5: The internal purchasing power of the pound, 1914 to 1982.

a mere *5 years* in 1980. By 1982 the pound had lost *more than 80 per cent* of its purchasing power in 1967, only 15 years earlier.

Rather than 'inflation' it may be preferable to use the term **currency debasement**. This makes it clear that the value of *money* is falling, which is why prices expressed in terms of money are generally rising. And it implies, probably correctly, that the phenomenon results from deliberate government policy.

6.2.3 The World-wide Post-war Inflation

Figure 6.6 shows average inflation rates for three post-war decades for selected countries from among the larger Latin American and OECD countries.

	1950–60 (%)	1960–70 (%)	1970–80 (%)	1950–80 (%)
Latin America				
Chile	34	27	130	58
Argentina	22	21	119	48
Uruguay	14	45	63	39
Brazil	17	45	35	32
OECD				
France	6	7	10	7
United Kingdom	4	4	14	7
Italy	3	4	14	7
Japan	4	6	9	6
United States	2	3	8	4
Germany	2	3	5	3

Fig. 6.6: Annual inflation rates, 1950–80, selected Latin American and OECD countries.

The Latin American countries show easily the highest inflation rates throughout the period. Chile's 30-year average rate of 58 per cent a year is the highest; but in the decade 1970–80 Argentina has also suffered from inflation exceeding 100 per cent a year!

Of the OECD countries, Germany, closely followed by the United States, is lowest; and Japan, Italy, the United Kingdom and France follow in that order over the 30 years. In the last 10 years, Italy and the UK are highest (with annual rates of inflation averaging 14 per cent), while the United States has been nearly as high as Japan and France. Germany's inflation rate since 1970 has been easily the lowest of the major countries.

6.3 Causes of Inflation

It may be helpful to recall the Quantity Theory of money (see **6.1.3.**):

$$MV = PT$$

where: M = Money supply
     V = Velocity of circulation
     P = general level of Prices
     T = volume of Trade.

If the velocity of circulation is roughly constant in the long run (but see **6.1.4**), then unless there is a substantial fall in the volume of trade, a substantial inflation in prices must be accompanied by an increase in the money supply.

But does the increase in the money supply come first and *cause* the inflation? Or is it 'passive' ('accommodating' or 'validating'), merely allowing the occurrence of an inflation originally caused by something else? There are two main explanations of the causes of inflation – **cost-push** and **demand-pull** – but they are not entirely separate.

6.3.1 Cost-push Inflation

Many firms probably set their selling prices by adding a constant percentage 'mark-up' to input costs. Maintaining the *volume* of trade at higher prices then requires an 'accommodating' increase in the money supply. An initiating 'cost-push' may come from several causes without any *prior* increase in monetary demand:

1. *Trade unions* may negotiate rises in wage-rates (see Ch. 7) higher than justified by market conditions. This suggests an element of monopoly power, at least in the short run, to allow employers to pass on increases in wage-costs in higher selling prices. But do coal miners, for example, really have the power to 'create inflation'? Or will unduly high wage-rates for miners produce other results?
   a. closure of loss-making pits, leading to lower employment for miners;
   b. cheap imports from abroad, with the same result for UK miners;
   c. higher taxes to subsidise the National Coal Board's losses.
2. There may be a rise in the *cost of imports* with no short-run substitutes. This is why there are worries if the pound's exchange rate falls (see Ch. 5). The OPEC oil price increases in the 1970s probably led to 'imported' inflation in many countries; though in the 1980s the OPEC cartel is having difficulty in maintaining its high prices.
3. *Tax changes* may increase costs. The 1979 switch from personal income tax to Value Added Tax added about 4 per cent to the Retail Price Index. For a year this increased the quoted 'rate of inflation', and may well have affected inflationary expectations and increased 'cost-push' pressure.
4. Some prices, especially wage-rates, may be 'sticky' downwards. This aggravates unemployment in declining industries and price inflation in expanding ones. If some prices can readily rise but others don't fall, then the *average* ('general') level of prices must increase.

In responding to such 'cost-push' pressures, the government must either increase the money supply to 'accommodate' the price rises, or else find some way to offset the potential price rises. Structural reforms to increase *competition* in the economy might encourage downward pressure on some prices; for example, reforming trade union practices (see Ch. 7) or denationalising some major public services (see Ch. 8). Another possible solution – prices and incomes policies – is discussed in Chapter 7.

6.3.2 Demand-pull Inflation

People may be consistent in the amount of *purchasing power* they want to hold in the form of cash or liquid assets. So if the total supply of money increases, households may not be content merely to hold larger cash balances than before (*someone* has to hold the extra money). Instead, they use the surplus to buy real goods and services. Thus they bid up money prices of goods until the amount of cash they hold (although still more than at first) again represents the *same* amount of purchasing power (since the general level of prices will have risen).

Given full employment, a rise in aggregate monetary demand will create *excess* demand in many markets. When prices in those markets are bid up, first prices of factors of production will rise, and then retail prices throughout the whole economy. Even aggregate figures of unemployment may conceal a combination of heavy unemployment in some industries or regions of the country and virtually full employment in others. If the money supply is increased, *some* prices will then rise (and increase the average level of prices) even if employment also increases in certain industries or regions.

How far prices will rise depends on many factors, including the price-**elasticity of demand** and the state of competition. For example, the coal industry is clearly helped by the quadrupling of the price of oil (a competitive fuel). On the other hand, the steel industry is not helped by substantial European over-capacity.

Increases in government spending in the UK have not been fully financed either by tax increases or by borrowing from the public. In effect, governments have paid for part of their increased spending by 'printing money' (see Ch. 9). Fiscal action to *reduce* aggregate monetary demand, either by increasing taxes or by reducing government spending, may be thought politically unpopular. Hence inflation as a deliberate policy, or at least tolerating it, may be tempting for governments, at least in the short run.

6.4 Effects of Inflation

There are four main reasons why inflation matters: accounting complications, extra transaction costs, uncertainty, and political aspects.

6.4.1 Accounting Complications

Having to allow for significant rates of inflation *complicates* economic calculations. It makes budgets hard to monitor, since they may in effect measure merely the accuracy of inflation forecasts. It can distort appraisal of capital investment projects. And firms require **inflation accounting** in reporting or forecasting financial results in order to tell to what extent their money profits are 'real'.

In the early 1980s many large UK companies are using **current cost accounting** (CCA) on a trial basis. CCA is not strictly a system of accounting for general 'inflation': it uses current replacement costs of specific assets in accounts, instead of original money costs as in 'conventional' accounting. But CCA continues to use money as the unit of measurement.

In contrast, **constant purchasing power** (CPP) accounting applies the Retail Price Index to translate the money costs of past transactions into up-to-date **purchasing power**. By using such 'indexed' units of account, CPP allows proper comparison of financial results over a number of years.

Figure 6.7 outlines the main differences between CCA and CPP. CCA uses current costs instead of historical costs as the basis of valuation, while CPP uses indexed units instead of monetary units as the units of accounting measurement. Because CCA and CPP are trying to achieve different aims, there is no logical inconsistency in proposing a combination of the two, as in the bottom right-hand corner.

| | Basis of 'valuation' | |
Unit of measurement	*Past cost*	*Current cost*
Money	(conventional) Historical Cost (HC)	Current Cost Accounting (CCA) Replacement Cost
Unit of constant purchasing power ('indexed unit')	Constant Purchasing Power (CPP)	CCA/CPP combination

Fig. 6.7: Different kinds of inflation accounting.

6.4.2 Extra Transactions Costs

Inflation causes numerous extra costs in everyday transactions, both for businesses and for individual consumers. For example, fares increase, postage stamp denominations change, new coins and notes are introduced, slot machines keep having to be altered. Businesses find it necessary to increase selling prices frequently, which is expensive. Workers have to negotiate new wage-rates at least once a year, tax-rates and thresholds are altered, pensions have to be changed, and so on.

Relative prices of goods represent important *signals* in the market system. Inflation is therefore a major problem, since it *obscures* the meaning of price signals. To give just one irritating example, it is extremely hard to interpret any money amounts mentioned in books or newspapers of the last 30 years, since one needs to work out the equivalent purchasing power. (Of course most people do so only very roughly.) Hardly anyone these days is unaware of the *existence* of inflation, but it remains a very costly business to make full allowance for it.

It would be very confusing for everyone if measures of distance or of time kept changing their real meaning every month. So it is with economic values: past money values are in effect like 'foreign' currencies!

6.4.3 Uncertainty

The rate of inflation *varies* sharply. If it remained constant and predictable, say at a fairly steady 10 per cent each year, much of the *uncertainty* would disappear; though other problems, such as those noted above, would remain. Many industrial relations problems are no doubt caused or exacerbated by workers being understandably anxious to protect their standards of living against an *unknown* future rate of inflation.

If prices in general are not fairly stable, people may become less willing to make long-term commitments, for fear of significant unanticipated inflation. Given the importance of capital investment in creating **wealth** (see Ch. 3), inflation which adds to uncertainty seems likely to damage standards of living. Indeed, if it persists it may even undermine the whole structure of society.

Inflation can distort economic decisions. Most of its supposed 'advantages' probably stem from the assumption that people will *not* anticipate inflation correctly. Interest rates provide a striking example. Figure 6.8 shows 'real' interest rates from 1970 to 1982, calculated by deducting actual inflation rates from nominal (money) interest rates.

The chart reveals very large swings in 'real' interest rates. (In fact the tax system often complicates things even more.) In a single decade real interest

Fig. 6.8: 'Real' interest rates, 1970 to 1982.

rates have swung from plus 3 per cent in 1972 to minus 12 per cent in 1975 to plus 5 per cent in 1978 to minus 9 per cent in 1980. Contrast this with the nineteenth century: in the *whole* of Queen Victoria's 64-year reign, interest on government securities hardly ever moved outside the range $2\frac{1}{2}$ per cent to 4 per cent. In real terms *10 times* that range may now be spanned in two or three years! No businessman can help being seriously affected by such devastating volatility in a crucial financial cost.

6.4.4 Political Aspects

People on *fixed incomes* are likely to suffer from inflation. Those groups which the government chooses to protect, or which are in strong bargaining positions, do better than others. But the results are fortuitous. This may be one important reason for some politicians to *welcome* inflation: it increases the government's power to redistribute incomes among different groups.

Keynes saw advantages in inflation, which he referred to as 'flexible money'. He thought that inflation 'benefitted *new* wealth at the expense of old, armed enterprise against accumulation, and emancipated new men from the dead hand of the past'. Clearly these are political as much as economic issues. Inflation exceeding 10 per cent a year seems to be regarded as undesirable. But it is not clear whether the difficulties of reducing it much below that level will outweigh the disadvantages of inflation.

Work Section

A. Revision Questions

A1 What are three functions of money?

A2 What are the main advantages of money over barter?

A3 Why were banks vulnerable, under a fractionally-backed gold currency, to a 'run on the bank' by holders of paper banknotes?

A4 What makes it easy for modern monetary authorities to inflate the supply of paper currency?

A5 What is the difference between M1 and M3?

A6 What is the largest component in the money supply?

A7 In Irving Fisher's version of the Quantity Theory of Money, $MV = PT$, what does each letter stand for?

A8 What are the three different extreme views about the effect of increasing the money supply on the Quantity Theory equation?

A9 Define the 'velocity of circulation'.

A10 How has V behaved in the UK since 1970?

A11 Why were even non-smokers in a POW camp prepared to exchange food for cigarettes?

A12 How could hand-rolled cigarettes be 'debased'?

A13 What caused *deflation* in a POW camp using cigarettes as money?

A14 Why did weekly prices in a POW camp originally fluctuate about the time of the weekly issue of cigarettes, but not later?

A15 What were the main disadvantages of cigarettes as money in a POW camp?

A16 If the money supply were constant, what would happen to the general level of prices? Why?

A17 Why is the measurement of inflation only approximate?

A18 What has happened to UK prices-in-general since 1947?

A19 Why is the rate of increase in the money supply not usually taken as a direct measure of the rate of inflation?

A20 Why is the sterling exchange rate against foreign currencies not taken as a measure of UK inflation?

A21 What proportion of its 1913–14 purchasing power had been lost by the pound by 1982?

A22 Define the term 'the half-life of the pound'.

A23 What proportion of its purchasing power did the pound lose in the 15 years between 1967 and 1982?

A24 Why was it suggested that the term 'currency debasement' might be preferable to 'inflation'?

A25 Which major European country's inflation rate has been lowest since 1950?

A26 What are the main differences between 'cost-push' and 'demand-pull' inflation?

A27 Name three different possible sources of cost-push inflation.

A28 What three possible consequences were suggested if coal miners negotiated 'excessive' rises in wage-rates?

A29 How does 'price-stickiness' affect cost-push inflation?

A30 Name two ways in which it was suggested that governments might seek to offset cost-push pressures.

A31 How might the size of people's desired holdings of cash be affected by an increase in the money supply?

A32 If there is demand-pull inflation, why don't all prices rise at the same time and in the same proportion?

A33 Define 'price-elasticity of demand'.

A34 Why was it suggested that the coal industry's position on raising selling prices might differ from that of the steel industry?

A35 Why was it suggested that governments might be tempted, at least in the short term, towards a deliberate policy of inflation?

A36 Name three different reasons why inflation matters.

A37 What are the main differences between CCA and CPP accounting?

A38 Give three examples of transactions costs affected by inflation.

A39 How may uncertainty about inflation affect economic behaviour?

A40 Why is the *average* annual rate of inflation not the only important aspect?

B. Exercises and Case Studies

B1 The following two pairs of figures relate to the Quantity Theory:

	A	B	C	D
M (£ b.)	35	60	60	90
V	3.0	3.5	3.5	3.0
P	100	—	100	150
T (£ b.)	100	107½	105	—

a. What must P have been in Year B?

b. What must T have been in Year D?

B2 Refer to Fig. 6.5 on page 120.

Roughly by what percentage did the pound's value change between:

a. 1913–14 and 1920?

b. 1920 and 1934?

c. 1913–14 and 1934?

d. If the 'half-life' of the pound is defined as the number of years it has taken for the pound to fall to one half of its starting value, what was the 'third-life' of the pound in 1982?

e. The pound's value in 1965 may be taken as 20, and in 1980 as 5. If the pound continues to lose value at the same annual average rate, by what year will the pound have lost 95 per cent of its 1965 value?

B3 With an average inflation rate of 5 per cent a year, in 15 years prices 'in general' rise by 108 per cent. How much do prices 'in general' rise in 15 years if the average inflation rate is:

a. 10 per cent a year;

b. 15 per cent a year.

B4 In April 1950 (RPI = 33), the top graduated rate of income tax started at a taxable income level of £20,000. At what level would the top rate need to start in April 1982 (RPI = 320) in order to be starting at the same purchasing power level? (The actual starting point was a taxable income of £31,500 in April 1982.)

B5 A record 'high' level for the Financial Times-Actuaries 500 Share Index was reached in April 1983 (RPI = 330), when the Index touched 461. In August 1972, the date of a previous peak, the Index had reached 228 (with the RPI then at 86).

a. Roughly what proportion of the August 1972 level did the Index reach in April 1983, in terms of constant purchasing power?

b. How much of its 'real' value had the 500 Share Index then lost since it was started at 100 in April 1962 (RPI = 53)?

B6 Figure 6.9 shows details of the money supply (M1) for the second quarter of 1975 and 1981:

£ m.	1975	1981
Notes and coins	5,370	10,256
UK private sector sight Deposits:		
Non-interest-bearing	8,819	17,524
Interest-bearing	1,712	5,007
	15,901	32,787

Fig. 6.9: UK money supply (M1), 1975 and 1981.

a. By what percentage has each category risen between 1975 and 1981?

b. What proportion of the total is each category:
   i. in 1975?   ii. in 1981?

c. From reference material, find the necessary information to determine M3   i. in 1975;   ii. in 1981.

d. Compare the rate of increase between 1975 and 1981 of M1 and M3.

e. What factors would you consider in choosing between M1 and M3 as your definition of the 'money supply'? Why wouldn't you simply take 'Notes and coins' to represent the money supply?

B7   Figure 6.10 shows underlying data for an index of retail prices:

	Weights		Prices	
	1974	*1982*	*1974*	*1982*
Food	25	20	100	300
Drink and tobacco	12½	12½	100	400
Housing	12½	15	100	360
Clothes	10	7½	100	200
Transport	10	15	100	350
Other goods	30	30	100	
	100	100	100	325

Fig. 6.10: Data for price index, 1974 and 1982.

a. What is the price index for 'Other Goods' in 1982?
b. What would the overall price index be in 1982 using 1974 weights?
c. What would the overall price index be in 1982 if food prices stood at 400 instead of at 300?

B8   Refer to Fig. 6.4 on page 118. Roughly how much did retail prices in general change between:
a. 1972 and 1975?
b. 1975 and 1978?

B9   Use appropriate reference material to update:
a. Figure 6.4 on page 118;
b. Figure 6.8 on page 125.

B10   In the year ended December 1981, the Retail Price Index rose from 276 to 309 (January 1974 = 100). In the year ended December 1982 the RPI rose from 309 to 328. The average interest yield on 2½ per cent Consolidated Stock was 12.4 per cent in 1981 and 11.5 per cent in 1982.
a. Estimate the 'real' interest rate, net of inflation, in 1981 and 1982. How do you account for the difference?
b. Assume that a taxpayer has to pay income tax at 30 per cent on his gross interest. What is his 'real' interest rate, net of inflation *and tax*, in 1981 and 1982?

B11   Give a numerical example to show that the 'rate of inflation' is not the same as the 'rate of currency debasement'. (Hint: think of the Latin American countries.)

C. Essay Questions

C1 'The non-monetary demand for cigarettes was less elastic than the demand for food' (**6.1.5**). Explain precisely and fully what this statement means.

C2 Explain the connection between changes in the money supply and changes in the general price level as measured by the Retail Price Index.

C3 Can increasing the money supply lead to inflation even at less than 'full employment'? Why or why not?

C4 'The Quantity Theory includes everything but explains nothing.' Discuss.

C5 'In determining a change in the "purchasing power" of money it is necessary to know on what it is spent ... a general index of the "purchasing power" of money is unlikely to be helpful.' (The Report of the Inflation Accounting Committee, 1975.) Discuss.

C6 'Post-war inflation has come about simply because there has been too much money chasing too few goods.' Discuss.

C7 What factors have caused the massive inflation of the past 15 years in the UK?

C8 Discuss the view that demand inflation may be good for business but cost inflation is not.

C9 'It doesn't matter what our country's rate of inflation is, as long as it's about the same as the inflation rate in most other countries.' Do you agree? Why or why not?

C10 How can high rates of inflation seriously affect business firms? How, if at all, can its damaging effects be mitigated?

C11 Is the ideal rate of inflation zero?

C12 If a firm expected the rate of inflation to fall steadily from its present level to zero over the next three years, what actions would you recommend it to take? Why?

C13 Explain the principle behind fractional reserve banking. Why is it important in relation to controlling the money supply?

C14 Why does it matter whether the velocity of circulation is stable or not?

C15 Are wage-rates 'sticky' downwards? If so, why? Does it matter? If so, what can be done about it?

Chapter 7

Labour

Objective: *To discuss the volume of 'employment', and ways to analyse the work force; to describe the extent and structure of unemployment and some of its causes; to explain some effects of trade unions; and to outline the relationship between inflation and unemployment.*

Synopsis: *'Labour' is not homogeneous, hence it is hard to measure the 'volume' of labour services. Demographic and social changes can affect the structure of the work force over time. Wage-rates are not the only important influence on employment; people also value leisure and other aspects of work. Ultimately it is consumers who pay for workers' wages.*

The 'pool' of unemployed is not stagnant: every month there is both a large inflow and a large outflow. But a growing number of people have been without work for many months. Increased oil prices, relocation abroad of traditional manufacturing industries, and the 'shaking out' of UK over-manning have caused unemployment on the demand side. On the supply side, a major cause of persistent long-term unemployment on a large scale is that wage-rates are too high. In addition there are a number of obstacles to labour mobility.

Trade union monopolies may be able to increase their members' wage-rates; but the cost is likely to be to reduce competition and increase unemployment of non-members. Cutting wage-rates may help to increase employment, and may also increase the total *amount of wages paid. The key question is whether* competition *will be allowed in the labour market.*

Changing rates of inflation may have a short-term effect on unemployment, but no long-run effect on its 'natural' level. Prices and incomes policies may help reduce inflationary expectations, but do not themselves constitute required longer-term structural changes.

7.1 Employment

7.1.1 Volume of Employment

The total 'volume' of employment of labour is difficult to measure, partly because labour hours vary in quality, and partly because of the many informal or part-time arrangements in a free society. The total number of labour hours in a year depends on:
1. The total population.
2. The proportion in the 'work-force'.
3. The average number of hours worked per year.

1. Total population. The total population may change because of births and deaths, immigration and emigration. During the 150 years from 1800 to 1950, the UK population grew by about 1 per cent a year on average, from 10 m. to 50 m. In addition the UK provided some 20 m. emigrants, mostly to America

	Millions			*Percentages*		
	Male	*Female*	*Total*	*Male*	*Female*	*Total*
Under 16	6.6	6.2	12.8	*24*	*22*	*23*
16 to 59/64*	17.5	15.9	33.4	*64*	*55*	*60*
60–65* and over	3.2	6.6	9.8	*12*	*23*	*17*
Total	27.3	28.7	56.0			
Work force	16.0	10.1	26.1			
Work force as per cent of people of working age:				*91*	*64*	*78*

*Females/males

Fig. 7.1: UK population by age and sex, 1981.

and the colonies. Between 1950 and 2000 the increase is expected to average only about $\frac{1}{4}$ per cent a year, from 50 m. to 58 m. Figure 7.1 gives details of population by age and sex in 1981.

2. *Proportion in work force.* The proportion of males between 16 and 64 in the 'work force' seems to have fallen from 100 per cent in 1961 to 91 per cent in 1981. The reasons for this are not clear. In contrast, the female work force has risen from 54 per cent of people of 'working age' in 1961 to 64 per cent in 1981, with a large increase (from 35 per cent to 60 per cent) for married females. There are several possible reasons:

a. industries employing a high proportion of females may have expanded more rapidly;
b. sex discrimination in the labour market may have fallen;
c. mechanised household appliances may have increased housewives' 'productivity', making more time available for outside work;
d. reductions in family size may have released more married women for work;
e. social attitudes may have become more tolerant of wives and/or mothers going out to work.

The actual work force does not consist only of people of official 'working age'. Child-actors, paper-boys, and so on, may be under 16; while some people over 65, such as writers, judges, and politicians, may be perfectly able to go on working. Conversely, people may stay at school beyond 16, or retire 'early'. Others may simply have no occupation describable as 'work'. The modern notion of a universal 'school-leaving age' and 'retirement age' may be needed to run inflexible compulsory state systems of schooling and pensions. But in fact people's aptitudes and preferences differ widely.

Varying social conditions may affect the ages of schooling, marriage, and retirement. A higher proportion of the total UK population is in the work force than in many other European countries, though many women are part-time. The UK figure of 44 per cent compares with Germany 41, France 39, Italy 36, and Spain 30 per cent.

3 *Number of hours worked per year.* A work force of 26 m., working 235 days per year, provides 6,100 m. working days a year. About 5 per cent of this total is lost through certified sickness, some 300 m. days. This is about *25 times* as many as the average number of days a year (about 12 m.) lost as a result of strikes. But the number of days actually lost may not fully reflect the overall cost of strikes. Firms may take expensive precautions to guard against the chance of *potential* strikes, such as holding extra stocks or arranging for dual suppliers.

In some occupations the number of hours worked may fluctuate as business conditions change. But in general the number of overtime hours has been fairly stable for people working overtime; though the number of people doing so has fallen. Overtime seems to be used more as a way to increase workers' pay than to increase output. This can be done by continuing to work the same total number of hours, reducing the 'basic' number of hours per week, and paying for more hours of time at the higher 'overtime' rate.

The average number of hours worked in the UK has fallen by about 7 per cent between 1960 and 1980. As noted in **3.1.1**, choosing to work fewer hours (enjoy more **leisure**) is one way to improve standards of living not recorded by national income statistics.

7.1.2 Structure of Employment

Hours of labour represent an 'input' to the economy. The corresponding 'output' depends on the *quality* of work as well as the quantity. (We could probably all benefit from Drucker's advice: 'Work smarter, not work harder.') Two key questions are whether work is *efficient*, in maximising the output from a given volume of inputs; and (even more important) whether it is *effective* in producing what people want. One can be highly efficient in producing something worthless.

Total employment numbers can conceal structural changes over time. Figure 7.2 shows the percentages of employees in different productive sectors between 1960 and 1980.

	1960 (%)	1970 (%)	1980 (%)
Primary	6	4	3
Secondary	46	43	36
Tertiary	48	53	61
	100	100	100
Government sector employees	n/a	29	33

Fig. 7.2: Employees by sector, 1960 to 1980.

There was a sharp fall in the primary sector between 1960 and 1970, and in the secondary (manufacturing) sector between 1970 and 1980. These match the changes in the shares of output which we saw in Fig. 3.4 on page 53. But there has been a continuing increase in (tertiary) employment in service industries, which in the main have been the expanding areas of the economy. The proportion of government employees has also increased between 1970 and 1980, matching the increase in government spending (see Ch. 8).

There have also been regional shifts in the UK population since the war, away from London and the North and towards the East Midlands, the South East and the South West.

7.1.3 **Price of Employment**

In **1.1.2** we discussed supply and demand in a competitive market. Although 'labour' has some peculiar features, it is still in principle open to the same kind of economic analysis as any other commodity. Many people regard the Bible as a sacred book, but it is subject to the 'laws' of supply and demand no less than to the law of gravity.

The 'price' of labour services is called the 'wage-rate'. If we look at average wage rates after allowing for inflation, we see that conditions have changed since 1975. Up till then real wage rates were regularly increasing at about 3 per cent a year, slightly more than the rate of increase in GDP per head. But since 1975 there has been very little real increase in average wage rates, only about $\frac{1}{2}$ per cent a year. Thus the climate in the labour market has clearly changed.

The labour market deals with the services of human beings, and wage-rates (prices) alone do not determine the volume of employment. People also care about conditions of work, geographical location, their fellow-workers, and so on. Few people could be induced to change jobs *merely* by being offered higher wages, without regard to possible changes in these other factors.

People also value *leisure*. If wage-rates go up, will people work more hours or less? The **price effect** suggests they may work more hours, since the rate of reward for *substituting* work for leisure has increased. On the other hand, the **income effect** may lead them to work fewer hours: they can now earn the same money as before in less time. We cannot be sure in advance which effect will prevail. (The same ambiguity applies to changing the rate of *tax* on incomes, which in effect alters the 'after-tax wage-rate' – see **8.2.1**.)

Ultimately it is *consumers* who pay for workers' wages; hence the amount a worker is paid is related in the long run to the value (to consumers) of what is produced. The employer estimates how productive workers will be (as 'factors of production') and how much consumers will pay for the goods or services concerned. Acting as 'entrepreneur', he then estimates how much he can 'afford' to pay in wages. But this is not an arbitrary judgement by the employer: it represents an estimate of market conditions. The 'two sides' of industry are not really employers and employees – as sometimes portrayed – but *producers and consumers* (see Fig. 1.5 on page 8).

'Labour' is not homogeneous: some labour hours are more valuable than others. Wages are paid, not for 'labour in general', but for *specific* labour services. Failure to recognise this can lead to bafflement at the 'paradox' that there can be situations vacant and people unemployed at the same time. But it is hardly surprising if a semi-skilled unemployed plumber in Durham fails to apply for a job which he doesn't want and couldn't do, in a different part of the country, at a wage-rate less than he seeks, and (not least important) of which he is not even *aware*.

7.2 Unemployment

7.2.1 Volume of Unemployment

At the end of the Second World War Beveridge expected a minimum of 3 per cent 'frictional' **unemployment,** to allow for movement between jobs, and seasonal and world trade fluctuations. With a work force of 25 m., that would imply 750,000 unemployed even at **full employment.** Moreover, a small part of the work force may be unsuited for normal work, and another small percentage may represent 'false' unemployment.

Between 1949 and 1974 total unemployment exceeded 750,000 only in one year (1972) when it touched 4 per cent. For a quarter of a century this was full – or even 'overfull' – employment. It represented a sharp contrast with the very high pre-war rates of unemployment. But since 1974, and especially in the early 1980s, total unemployment has increased very rapidly in the UK, as in most other developed countries.

Figure 7.3 shows UK unemployment as a percentage of the work force between 1970 and 1982. From about 4 per cent in 1975, it rose to nearly 6 per cent between 1976 and 1979. Then there were very sharp increases

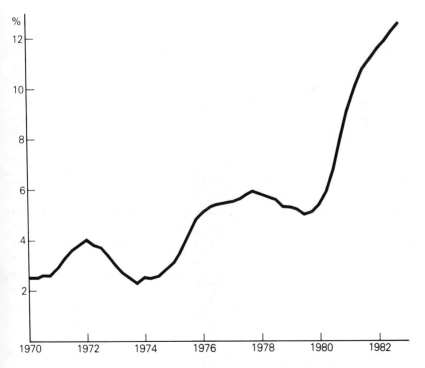

Fig. 7.3: Percentage of UK work force unemployed, 1970 to 1982.

in 1980 and 1981, and by 1982 the level of unemployment exceeded 12 pe
cent. This was certainly extremely high by post-war standards.

There is no stagnant pool of 'unemployed': there is a large inflow joinin
– *and a large outflow leaving* – the unemployment register each month. I
a changing world people change jobs from time to time. Out of a total Uk
work force of about 26 m. there are probably at least 6 m. changes of employe
each year, as well as many 'invisible' job changes *within* firms.

Over the five years 1978 to 1982 the outflow averaged nearly 300,000 pe
month (roughly one third female), or $3\frac{1}{2}$ m. a year. But in 1980 and 198
the *inflow* to the unemployed total was even higher, nearly 350,000 per month
Hence the total number of unemployed in 1980 and 1981 increased by som
50,000 per month, that is by 600,000 in each of those two years.

7.2.2 Structure of Unemployment

Fig. 7.4 shows the total of 3.2 m. unemployed at January 1983, analysed b
age and past duration of unemployment. Short-term unemployment i
especially heavy for younger people, and longer-term unemployment for male
over 55 years old.

Thousands	*Under 25* (M)	(F)	*25 to 54* (M)	(F)	*55 and over* (M)	(F)	*Total* (M)	(F)
Up to 6 months	400	300	475	175	125	25	1000	500
6 to 12 months	150	100	200	75	75	—	425	175
Over 12 months	200	75	475	100	250	25	925	200
Total	750	475	1,150	350	450	50	2,350	875
Work force (m.)	$3\frac{1}{2}$	$2\frac{1}{4}$	10	6	3	$1\frac{1}{4}$	$16\frac{1}{2}$	$9\frac{1}{2}$
Unemployed as %	*21*	*21*	*11*	*6*	*15*	*4*	*14*	*9*

Fig. 7.4: UK unemployment by age, sex and past duration, January 1983.

Unemployment rates tend to be higher for young people. This may be partl
because their relative pay (compared with older workers) is high compare
to the value of their output. It takes time to train new young workers to b
fully productive. Moreover, in a recession firms tend to economise on labou
and reduce recruitment. Apart from the younger age groups, the female rate
of unemployment appear to be less than the male rates; but some marrie
women may fail to register as unemployed if no social security benefits ar
available for them.

Two main kinds of unemployment are usually distinguished: frictional an
structural. Frictional unemployment lasts for a fairly short time for individu

workers: it represents the 'normal' turnover of labour, where a young person does not always precisely replace an old retiring worker. Structural unemployment is longer-term: it relates to shifts in the economy away from certain industries and areas and towards others.

Some people may take a few weeks to look around for a new job, or they may even welcome a holiday between jobs. So one must distinguish between 'short-term' unemployed and people who are without work for a long period. The social consequences are likely to be very different. Someone who is unemployed for, say, two months probably loses earnings equivalent to about 1 per cent of the 'capital value' of his future lifetime earnings. This is less than the cost of transferring most capital assets.

Long-term unemployment, however, is a much more serious matter. For older workers it may mean they will never work again. For young people it may mean no job for a year or more after leaving school, with a soul-destroying impact on life and motivation. There is a fear that some of the younger people with no jobs for long periods may actually become unemployable. While the macro-economic consequences of that may be tolerable, the individual results are obviously tragic. Again we must be careful to look below the surface of the aggregate figures.

Figure 7.5 shows the sharp increase in longer-term unemployment between the end of 1980 and the end of 1982. The total number of people unemployed for over 6 months reached $1\frac{3}{4}$ m., with over 1 m. unemployed for more than 12 months.

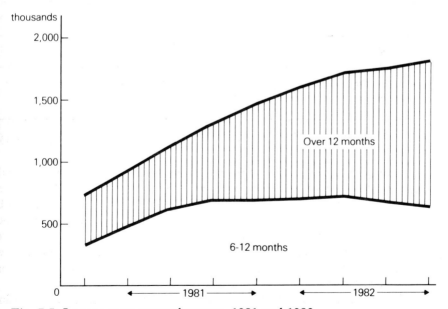

Fig. 7.5: Longer-term unemployment, 1981 and 1982.

Unemployment has consistently been higher than the UK national average in certain regions: Northern Ireland, Scotland, Wales, and the North and North-West of England. It has been lower than average in the South-East, East Midlands and East Anglia. Other regions have usually been close to the national average; though in the last few years unemployment has increased disproportionately in the West Midlands. As levels of unemployment have more than doubled all over the country, the rise has tended to be proportionately higher in the South East and lower in the North. Thus the disparity between regions has been somewhat reduced.

7.2.3 Causes of Unemployment

If many people are without jobs for long periods against their will, something must have gone wrong with the market-clearing mechanisms in the labour market. The problems may arise either from the 'demand' side or from the 'supply' side.

a. Demand. Two factors have caused rising rates of 'structural' unemployment in other industrial countries besides the UK:

1. The large increase in energy prices, which has made many processes and products obsolete.
2. The drift in the most efficient location for many traditional manufacturing industries to the **newly industrialising countries** (NICs).

In addition, a third factor is special to the UK: the long-delayed attack on **overmanning**. This was triggered by the sharp rise in the sterling exchange rate in 1979–80 (see Fig. 5.6 on page 100), with its consequent pressure on profit margins (see Fig. 5.9 on page 103). Comparisons with other countries although not precise, suggest substantial UK overmanning in a number of industries. In terms of lost output, overmanning may be more expensive than explicit unemployment.

Certain 'employment protection' laws may have the unintended result of hindering the employment of new workers. Employers may be reluctant to risk later having to compensate workers for 'unfair dismissal', and they may also fear trade union resistance to any such dismissals.

b. Supply. A persistent surplus of any commodity suggests that its market *price* may be too high to 'clear' the market. That applies to labour as much as to tomatoes. (The butter mountains and wine lakes in the EEC are caused by fixing the prices of those commodities above the world market-clearing prices.)

Keynes proposed deliberate inflation because he thought it was politically impossible to reduce money wage-rates. So he wanted to reduce 'real' wage-rates by leaving money wage-rates the same, or even a little higher than before but reducing the value of *money*. The trouble is that even if the 'money illusion' does deceive workers (which seems unlikely for long), *general* inflation may not produce the necessary changes in *relative* wage-rates.

'Minimum wage' practices may overprice some labour services, so that anyone whose work is worth *less* than the minimum will not be employed at all. This may especially hurt younger workers, if trade unions insist on employers paying them the same wage-rates as adult workers. 'Equal pay' laws may have a similar effect. They aim to help female workers who are currently receiving less than supposedly equivalent male workers. But they may result in some females being priced out of employment, if there is some reason why their services in a competitive market are worth less to employers.

Lack of worker mobility may cause unemployment, if declining industries in certain regions are not balanced by suitable new employment opportunities for the same workers in the same regions. Regional policy has tended to encourage firms to invest *capital* in such areas, but this may not directly result in many new jobs. Moreover there may be obstructions to labour mobility, such as stamp duty on moving house, the council house system, or rules about transferring pensions.

7.3 Trade Unions

Figure 7.6 shows supply and demand curves as in Fig. 1.2 on page 4. In a fully competitive labour market the diagonal supply and demand curves intersect at X, at a wage rate OB and a quantity of labour employed OM.

But now suppose there is a single (monopoly) trade union supplier of labour, and many competing employers (buyers of labour). Assume the union can set 'the' wage-rate higher than the competitive level, say at OC (> OB). This

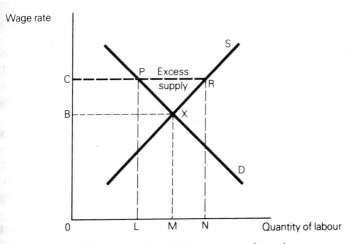

Fig. 7.6: The labour market with a monopoly union.

means that, up to point R, the wage-rate will be the same OC for each work(
however much labour is employed (up to ON). Thus the new supply cur
CRS is *horizontal* from C to R; and the new equilibrium is at P, where
cuts the demand curve.

The trade union has raised the wage-rate from OB to OC, but at the expen
of *reducing the amount of employment* from OM to OL. So the excess supp
of labour, the amount of unemployment, is PR (= LN). Although sor
workers would be willing to work for *less* than OC, they cannot get job
Trade unions would like to raise the wage-rates of their own members abo
the competitive level, by restricting competition. It is not their concern
non-members are unemployed as a result. But to do so, a union must be ab
to resist wage-cutting pressure (competition) from unemployed workers. Th
may be difficult if they are union members.

Cutting wage-rates may tend to restore full employment, though it m
reduce the total wages of union members. It may also increase the *total amou*
paid in wages, if the demand for labour is price-elastic. We must be caref
not to confuse wage-rates with total wages. For example, suppose 90 peop
work for the 'going wage-rate' of £100 a week. *Reducing* the wage-rate (pa
to everyone employed) to £98 may induce employers to hire five more peop
Then total weekly wages will increase from £9,000 to £9,310. Thus cutti
wage-rates need not result in any deficiency of aggregate demand.

Most professions, like trade unions, aim to benefit their members even
the expense of the public. Their ideal is to achieve some sort of governme
protection for a monopoly. They are very nervous about competition bei
allowed.

Professional bodies often claim to protect the public from 'unqualifi
suppliers, though their own entrance examinations and rules by no mea
guarantee career-long competence. Nor is it clear why allegedly 'incompete
people should not offer the public their services. After all, should or
'competent' politicians be allowed to stand for Parliament? Or only 'goo
books be published? And even if so, should the judges of quality be *exist*
politicians or authors? That would hardly invite 'creative destruction' (s
1.1.3) from competitors!

It is often not clear why 'protecting consumers' is so necessary (see a.
8.5.4). The public is usually not in much danger. A mistake will rarely
disastrous, and if they are not satisfied with suppliers of professional servi
then people can shop elsewhere next time. A professional person's *reputat*
is his most important business asset. Nor is it usually the *consumers* w
demand 'protection'. The *producer* unions/professions demand a monop
in order to provide unwanted 'protection', which just happens to raise t
incomes of their own members!

There are now many laws providing protection for *employees*. Much of t
legislation does not prescribe what kind of employment contracts are f
bidden, though some does. The general thrust is to require *disclosure* of k
aspects of employment. The provisions cover many topics: (i) on joinin

firm: the terms of job advertisements; racial or sex discrimination in recruitment; probation periods; disclosing the terms of the employment contract;
(ii) at work: health and safety in factories, offices or shops; methods of payment; strikes; (iii) on leaving a firm: wrongful or unfair dismissal; priority
of wages in insolvency.

In a free market, subject to honouring agreements already made, any workers
may choose to reject particular job offers if they don't like the pay or conditions.
But the key question is whether competition will be allowed in the labour
market. Will other competing workers be permitted to undertake those same
jobs on the same conditions that the original workers refused? Nowadays the
answer is clearly not. Trade unions have shown again and again that they
are prepared to use physical force ('picketing') to prevent competition, even
though this is illegal.

More than a hundred years ago there were complaints that some trade unions
opposed the introduction of more efficient methods of production in order
to protect existing employment. But the ultra-conservative Luddites were
wrong! Introducing more efficient machines greatly *increased* the numbers
employed in the textile industry. Newspapers and railways provide blatant
modern examples of this mistaken attitude. Too many British trade unions
have tended to worship the status quo. They have tried to guard jobs and
maintain existing methods and living standards, rather than allow (let alone
encourage) efficient firms to grow and become more profitable.

Labour-saving equipment need not reduce total employment. Indeed the
improvements in quality and cost-reduction that it allows may maintain or
increase both output and employment in the face of competition. Insisting
that a firm remains uncompetitive is hardly the way to guarantee life-long
employment for its workers. And in the long run the only way to increase
average real wage-rates is to increase the value of output per person, which
restricting competition seems unlikely to do.

The organisation of unions has also been a problem. There is a large number
of small unions, about half of them with under 1,000 members. This has
led to many petty demarcation disputes, understandable but expensive and
futile. And the heterogeneous mixture of craft, industrial, general and staff
unions means that many large organisations have to deal with a complex variety
of bargaining groups with different aims.

7.4 Inflation and Unemployment

7.4.1 The Phillips Curve

It used to be thought that there was a straightforward trade-off between inflation and unemployment. A government could reduce unemployment at the
cost of higher inflation, or vice versa. But the UK data suggesting this relation-

ship between 1861 and 1957 (known as the **Phillips curve**) was hard t
duplicate in other countries; and the emergence of **stagflation** in the 196(
cast doubt even on the UK Phillips curve.

The modern 'monetarist' view distinguishes short-term from long-term
changes in the level of unemployment. Increasing inflation may reduce un
employment at first, as the *unanticipated* increase in inflation reduces rea
wage-rates for a time. But as the market comes to expect higher inflation
the final result is only a higher rate of inflation. There will be no long-ru
change in the ('natural') rate of unemployment.

Figure 7.7 contains curves showing short-run outcomes for different rate
of inflation. Starting at point A, a rise in the inflation rate from L to M cause
a move along curve (1) to B; and to begin with unemployment falls from
W to Y. But as people come to *expect* higher inflation, the relevant curv
moves outward from (1) to (2); real wage-rates tend to move back to the
former level; and unemployment moves back to C (= W), its 'natural' leve
At a higher rate of inflation, the same process causes a move from C to D
and then back to E. Thus as inflation increases from L to M to N, monetarist
believe that long-run unemployment *remains* at its 'natural' level W (movin
from A to C to E); and the long-run Phillips curve is *vertical*.

Figure 7.8 relates UK inflation rates to unemployment rates from 197
to 1982. Interpretation is not easy, partly because of uncertain time-lags. C

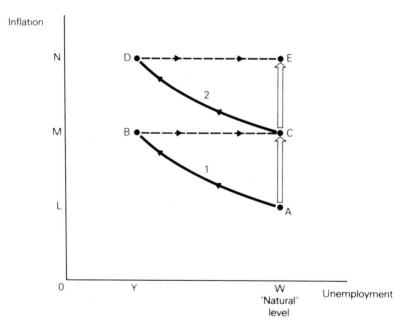

Fig. 7.7: The vertical long-run Phillips curve.

the 12 years, two (1970–72) seem doubtful, three (1972–3 and 1980–82) seem to support the traditional Phillips curve, sloping from north-west to south-east, and seven (1973–80) seem consistent with the vertical 'curve'. Even apart from the 1980–82 pattern, if one accepts the 'vertical' Phillips curve view there is a difficulty to explain away. It appears that since 1974 the 'natural' level of UK unemployment has increased substantially.

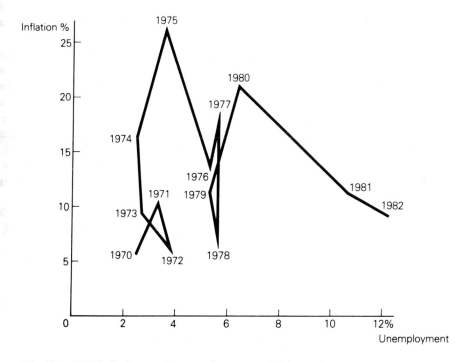

Fig. 7.8: UK inflation and unemployment, 1970 to 1982.

7.4.2 Prices and Incomes Policies

Government policies for paying public sector employees merely represent what every employer must have. **Prices and incomes policies** mean that the government also tells *private sector* employers what they may pay workers or charge customers. Most such policies have in fact been compulsory, even if nominally 'voluntary' (under threat of compulsion).

The main aim of such policies is to persuade powerful groups of workers to restrain their wage demands, by preventing other groups from thereby gaining an 'unfair' advantage. The groups concerned are often public sector unions which not only have a monopoly of *labour* in their industry, but whose industry itself enjoys a monopoly. Persuasion depends on some sort of 'code' setting out rules about permitted wage increases over a specified period, with agreed exceptions. The policies usually apply to prices other than wage-rates, and often even to **dividends**.

Relative prices must continually change to reflect changing technical production conditions and consumer demand. But bureaucratic time-lags are notorious. Hence some people argue that *open* inflation would be less damaging than trying to use a prices and incomes policy to conceal an inflation caused by inappropriate monetary policies.

The market system rewards the production of *value* (output) as judged by customers, not some arbitrary notion of *merit* (input). There is little incentive to produce what the customers want if 'fairness' determines wages regardless of consumer demand. Trade unions aim to 'preserve differentials' in the labour market even when relative wage-rates need to adapt to changed conditions. But it would be absurd to 'preserve differentials' between the prices of, say, tea and coffee without reference to market forces!

Experience has shown that a compulsory policy cannot last long. Anomalies and rigidities soon become intolerable. Thus the only long-term solution, according to advocates of prices and incomes policies, must be an agreed voluntary policy. At the same time, a permanent policy must allow for necessary shifts in the economy. So it must allow for genuine improvements in productivity, which may cause problems in many *service* industries. For example, how could an orchestra measure productivity? (To quote Morgenstern: 'Is a productively played quintet first played by 5, then by 4, then by 3 ... artists? Or do they play louder, faster ...?')

Many countries have introduced prices and incomes policies, but most of them have failed. As a rule temporary restrictions merely *defer* subsequent pay increases, and may induce *quality* deterioration. The case for prices and incomes policies rests more on short-term political expediency than on long-term economic theory. Practical statesmen must be concerned with the short-term as well as the long-term. Such policies may form part of a short-term plan to 'buy time' pending necessary long-term structural reforms. The problem, of course, is managing the long-term reforms.

Prices and incomes policies won't work for long unless accompanied by appropriate monetary measures; but given those measures and required structural reforms, prices and incomes policies may not be necessary. They may, however, help to reduce inflationary expectations, if 'cost-push' inflation is a danger.

Work Section

A. Revision Questions

A1 Why is it difficult to measure the total 'volume' of employment?

A2 What factors may cause total population to change over time?

A3 Given a stable total population, what factors may cause the size of the work force to change over time?

A4 Name three possible reasons for married females' increased rate of participation in the work force.

A5 Name two possible reasons why the proportion of males employed between the ages of 16 and 65 has been declining.

A6 Name three reasons why the work force does not simply consist of everyone aged between school-leaving age and retirement age.

A7 How does the proportion of the UK population in the work force compare with other European countries?

A8 How does the number of days lost in strikes compare with the number lost through illness?

A9 Why may the number of days lost in strikes not fully reflect their 'real' cost?

A10 How can overtime increase workers' pay without increasing output?

A11 How may working fewer hours improve one's standard of living?

A12 What is the difference between 'efficiency' and 'effectiveness'?

A13 Roughly what proportion of the employed population in 1980 worked in each of the primary, secondary, and tertiary sectors?

A14 What was the main employment shift between sectors from 1970 to 1980?

A15 Roughly what proportion of the work force did the government sector employ in 1980?

A16 Name three factors apart from wage-rates which may affect someone's decision about taking a particular job.

A17 How has the trend of average real wage-rates changed since 1975?

A18 What is (a) the 'price effect'? (b) the 'income effect'?

A19 Explain how an increase in the rate of income tax may either (a) increase or (b) decrease the quantity of labour services provided.

A20 What were suggested as the 'two sides' of industry? Why?

A21 What three factors did Beveridge reckon would lead to a minimum of 3 per cent unemployment even at 'full employment'?

A22 Why could the 25 years between 1949 and 1974 be described as a period of 'overfull' employment?

A23 What happened to UK unemployment between 1979 and 1982?

A24 Why may it be misleading to talk about a 'pool' of unemployed?

A25 What was suggested as the 'cost' of being unemployed for two months?

A26 For which age group is short-term unemployment highest? Why?

A27 Distinguish between 'frictional' and 'structural' unemployment?

A28 Which region showed an especially large proportionate increase in unemployment between 1979 and 1982?

A29 Which two demand factors apart from overmanning have caused recent increases in unemployment in many industrial countries?

A30 How may 'employment protection' laws increase unemployment?

A31 What is the most likely reason for long-term unemployment?

A32 Why did Keynes propose inflation as a way to reduce unemployment?

A33 How may 'minimum wage' levels cause unemployment?

A34 How may 'equal pay' laws cause female unemployment?

A35 How might improving labour mobility affect unemployment? Why?

A36 What is the likely result of a monopoly trade union setting 'the' wage-rate above the competitive market price?

A37 How may cutting wage-rates increase total wages paid?

A38 What does it mean for the demand for labour to be 'price-elastic'?

A39 Why was it argued that 'consumer protection' may be unnecessary?

A40 Why were the Luddites wrong?

A41 What is a Phillips curve? What is the argument which suggests that in the long run it is vertical?

A42 What is the 'natural' level of unemployment?

A43 What is a 'prices and incomes policy'?

A44 Why might 'open' inflation be preferable to 'concealing' it?

A45 Why do prices and incomes policies soon tend to break down?

B. Exercises and Case Studies

B1 Refer to Fig. 7.1 (page 133).
   a. From reference material construct a similar population table using latest estimated figures for (i) 1991, (ii) 2001.
   b. What are the most important differences from the 1981 table?

B2 Refer to Fig. 7.2 (page 135). From reference material, analyse the decline in manufacturing employment between 1970 and 1980 by industries.

B3 Refer to Fig. 7.3 (page 137).
   a. In which years were the last *two* peaks and troughs in the rate of unemployment?

b. What was the overall unemployment rate on each of the four occasions?

B4 An unemployed man expects to find a job again soon; and thereafter to maintain the same real wage-rate of £6,500 a year until he retires at 65. He thinks a real discount rate of 3 per cent a year is appropriate.

    a. Calculate the 'present value' of his future lifetime earnings:

        i. if he is 25; ii. if he is 35.

    b. For each of the above ages, calculate the percentage of the present value of future earnings he will lose (ignoring any social security benefits) if the man is without a job for:

        i. one month; ii. two months; iii. six months.

B5 Refer to Fig. 7.4 (page 138).

    a. From reference material, produce a similar table at the most recent date possible.

    b. Comment on the main differences from the January 1983 percentages.

B6 a. From reference material, produce a table showing regional unemployment percentages for the most recent date possible.

    b. Try to account for the difference between the North West and East Anglia.

B7 Refer to Fig. 7.6 (page 141).

    a. Why is the 'excess supply' of labour LN (= PR), not LM?

    b. Suppose a monopoly employer, negotiating with competing suppliers of labour, were able to force down the wage-rate (paid to all employees) to OA (at the level where the vertical line from R cuts the present demand curve, say at Q).

        i. What would be the new demand curve?

        ii. What amount of labour would be employed?

        iii. What would be the result in terms of surplus or shortage of labour?

B8 Refer to Fig. 7.8 (page 145).

    a. The more recent years (1980–82) seem to support the traditional Phillips curve. What prediction do you think a supporter of the 'vertical long-run Phillips curve' would make about the likely position on the chart for 1983 and 1984?

    b. If the 'natural' level of unemployment is allowed to shift from time to time, what remains of the argument for a vertical Phillips curve?

    c. From reference material,

        i. Try to confirm the positions shown on the chart for 1980, 1981, and 1982 (mid-year).

        ii. Update the chart by filling in positions for each year after 1982.

B9 A university is thinking of hiring a 25-year-old worker who will have 'academic tenure' (can't be sacked) until he retires at 65 – or until the university goes bust. His salary will be £10,000 a year to start with, and is unlikely to go down in 'real' terms. The university's finance officer reckons the long-term 'real' interest rate is 2 per cent a year. What is the 'capital commitment' (in present value terms) of hiring the worker?

B10 In 1974 the 'three-day week' lost two days out of five (40 per cent), but industrial production fell by only 6 per cent. Taking the size of the work force as 25 million:
  a. How much 'overmanning' do these figures suggest?
  b. If, in the longer-run, industrial production might have fallen by as much as 20 per cent during the continuation of a three-day week, how much overmanning would that suggest?
  c. Why might you expect industrial production to fall by more in the long run than the 6 per cent it actually fell in the short run?

B11 A Shorter Working Week?

One solution to the unemployment problem would be for everyone to work fewer hours. Reducing average weekly hours for all workers to 36 hours from the present level of about 40 hours could create jobs equivalent to 11 per cent of current employment, and thus virtually eliminate unemployment.

In the short run this means offering workers not more purchasing power, but more leisure time with the *same* purchasing power. But in the longer run, faster economic growth should result. And while individual people work fewer hours, ideally the phasing could allow *machines* to work for more hours and working floor-space to be used more intensively.

An essential part of the idea is for profits to increase. Since labour costs per hour will rise, other costs per hour need to fall – probably, in many cases, by spreading 'fixed' costs over more hours. The need to increase profits will impose pressure on managements and trade unions to find ways of increasing efficiency, such as ending restrictive practices, on introducing new capital-intensive working methods or new shift arrangements.

Detailed example. An existing factory is working 80 hours a week as normal time, in two 40-hour shifts, plus 10 hours a week overtime. Each worker receives average income of £162.50 per week, made up of (a) £3.00 per hour basic wage-rate, (b) 50 per cent premium for overtime, and (c) one-third premium over basic wage for night-shift.

Existing annual costs include labour costs of £1,380,000, consisting of £1,200,000 gross wages plus £180,000 social security taxes.

Labour-saving machinery with a life of 10 years would cost £1.0 m. on the basis of existing utilisation, and could reduce labour requirements by one-third. To reduce possible trade union objections, however, it is proposed to make only one sixth of the labour force redundant. This would reduce total annual labour costs by £230,000, but redundancy payments with average compensation of three months' pay would represent an initial extra cost of £50,000.

It is proposed to operate four shifts of 36 hours each. In effect this would reduce the initial outlay for equipment substantially for any given level of output. Overtime would be completely eliminated, but each retained worker would continue to receive average wages of £147.50 per week.

The estimated financial result of producing the same output as now is set out below:

Initial outlay £'000

Machinery: £1,000,000 $\times \dfrac{90}{144}$ = 625

Redundancy payments 50

Annual savings

Total labour costs 230

Under this scheme, the company makes an Internal Rate of Return (before tax) of about 32 per cent a year, the remaining workers get the same weekly pay for 80 per cent of their previous hours, and the redundant workers receive full compensation.

On the macro-economic level, demand for investment goods will rise, and lower unit costs of production may, in the longer term, lead to greater sales at home and abroad, and greater stability of employment.

a. Evaluate the proposal. Would it work? Why or why not?

b. What do you see as the main advantages and disadvantages of the scheme?

c. What reaction would you expect to this kind of proposal:

    i. From employers? ii. From trade unions? iii. From government?

C. Essay Questions

C1 'If we wish to increase the employment of labour in a depressed region, we should not subsidise the employment of capital there.' Discuss.

C2 Would reducing unemployment benefit reduce unemployment?

C3 Is labour-saving automation bound to increase unemployment?

C4 'A minimum wage-rate is either damaging or unnecessary.' Discuss.

C5 'The cure for unemployment is a shorter working week.' Discuss.

C6 Is it possible to have too little unemployment?

C7 What does 'equal pay for women' mean? What are the likely consequences of legislation to enforce it?

C8 Why is unemployment higher in Scotland than in southern England?

C9 'The cure for unemployment is earlier retirement.' Discuss.

C10 Firms try to reduce their labour needs to improve productivity; governments try to reduce unemployment to increase their popularity. Do their objectives conflict?

C11 Write an essay agreeing or disagreeing with Keynes's preference for 'flexible money' over 'flexible wages'.

C12 Is labour a scarce resource?

C13 Does the division of labour have more advantages for the firm than for the individual worker?

C14 'Many people now regard themselves as owning property rights in their jobs, which makes the labour market less mobile.' Discuss.

C15 'If workers owned the firms they work for, most of the "problems" of the labour market would no longer be significant.' Discuss.

Part III   Government

Chapter 8

Government Economic Activity

8.1. Government Spending
8.1.1 Extent
8.1.2 Cutting Government Spending

8.2 Taxation
8.2.1 Raising Revenue
8.2.2 Redistributing Income

8.3 Local Authorities
8.3.1 Receipts
8.3.2 Spending

8.4 Nationalised Industries
8.4.1 Extent
8.4.2 Reasons
8.4.3 Results
8.4.4 Privatisation

8.5 Miscellaneous Intervention
8.5.1 Foreign Exchange Controls
8.5.2 Price Controls
8.5.3 Capital Market Controls
8.5.4 Consumer Protection

Objective: *To give details of government spending and how it might be cut; to outline details of taxation and its two main aims; to describe local authorities' sources of revenue and main kinds of spending; to discuss the extent of nationalisation, the reasons for it, the results, and possible methods of privatisation; and to mention briefly some other kinds of government controls.*

Synopsis: *Between 1960 and 1980 government spending has risen from 45 to 60 per cent of national income, most of the increase occurring in the welfare state. Three ways to reduce government spending might be: (a) to stop pro-*

viding certain services; (b) to cut out waste; (c) to 'privatise' some government services.

Tax revenue has risen from 35 per cent of national income in 1960 to 50 per cent in 1980. The tax system as a whole is nearly proportional; redistribution comes mainly through government spending.

Local authorities get income from: local rates, housing rents, and central government grants. Their main spending is on education.

Three reasons for nationalisation have been: to promote greater efficiency, to regulate natural monopolies, and to save lame ducks. The results cannot be judged solely in accounting terms. There are several possible approaches to privatisation.

8.1 Government Spending

8.1.1 Extent

Government spending has increased from about 10 per cent of national income at the beginning of the twentieth century to about 50 per cent after the Second World War. Section 1.3 described some of the reasons. Figure 8.1 gives details of the main headings of government spending for 1960, 1970, and 1980, showing each item as a percentage of national income.

Over the 20 years from 1960 to 1980, in terms of constant 1975 pounds, national income increased by £29.1 b., government spending by £28.3 b. Much the largest share of the increase was on the welfare state. Between 1960 and 1980, while all other government spending rose from 28.7 per cent to 33.3 per cent of national income, welfare state spending increased from 16.3 per cent to 29.0 per cent.

Part of the reason for increased government spending was demographic. Total population rose by 6 per cent between 1960 and 1980, people of retirement age by 29 per cent. Clearly this affected how much the government spent on retirement pensions. Similarly, increasing the school-leaving age to 16 in 1970 increased the school population by about 10 per cent, which affected government spending on education. And the number of unemployed, entitled to government benefits, rose from 0.6 m. in 1960 to 1.8 m. by 1980.

Accurate comparisons over long periods of time are difficult, but the increase in government spending has clearly been substantial. It matches a similar large increase in tax revenues (see **8.2.1**). Most other developed countries have experienced the same kind of growth of government since the war. Another way to measure its growth in the UK is to show government current spending on goods and services (excluding transfer payments) as a percentage of personal consumption expenditure. Figure 8.2 shows the proportion rising from under 30 per cent in 1960 to 32 per cent in 1970, and over 40 per cent by 1981 – the highest level in any post-war year.

Percentages	1960 (%)	1970 (%)	1980 (%)
Welfare services	9.2	12.4	15.6
Education	4.4	6.4	7.1
Health	4.1	5.0	6.9
Other	0.7	1.0	1.6
Social security	7.1	9.9	13.4
Pensions	3.2	4.5	6.2
Other	3.9	5.4	7.2
= 'Welfare state'	16.3	22.3	29.0
Housing, environment, roads	5.1	7.5	8.0
Trade and industry	7.2	7.1	5.6
Defence	7.8	6.2	6.8
Debt interest	5.6	5.1	6.8
Miscellaneous	3.0	4.4	6.1
= Total government spending	45.0	52.6	62.3
	(%)	(%)	(%)
Economic category			
Current goods and services	20.4	22.7	29.2
Transfer Payments	16.7	21.5	27.6
Capital goods (inc. dwellings)	7.9	8.4	5.5
= Total	45.0	52.6	62.3
In constant 1975 £ b.	£ b.	£ b.	£ b.
Total government spending	26.4	40.8	54.7
National income	58.7	77.6	87.8

Fig. 8.1: Government spending as per cent of national income, 1960, 1970 1980.

8.1.2 Cutting Government Spending

Balancing the costs and benefits of government spending is not easy: it depend on political as well as economic judgements. The pressures for increasin government spending are strong, as indicated by the large rise over the 2 years from 1960 to 1980.

The most obvious 'cost' of government spending is the need to increas

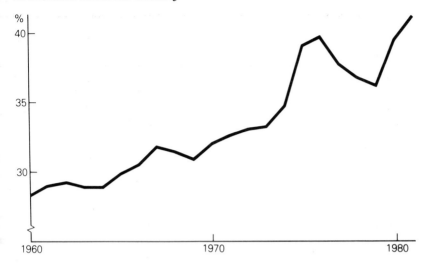

Fig. 8.2: Government spending on current goods and services as a percentage of personal consumer expenditure, at factor cost, 1960 to 1981.

taxes (discussed in **8.**2) to cover most of it. Taxes are compulsory levies by governments on individuals, and as a rule they are not popular. Hence governments would like to avoid increasing them if possible. To the extent that taxes do *not* cover government spending, there is a **Public Sector Borrowing Requirement** (PSBR) (discussed in **9.**1). If the PSBR grows too high, it can lead to inflation, depending on how it is financed (see **9.**3).

Government spending often lacks competitive pressures, so a good deal of it may be 'wasted'. And government spending depends on collective political choice instead of (as in the market) on individual consumer choice. So it may not satisfy consumers as much as spending their own money as they themselves choose. This does not apply to government transfer payments, which allow people to spend the cash they receive as they choose.

Whether to cut government spending, and if so by how much, is a political decision. But if that were the aim, there seem to be three main ways to do it:

1. The government could stop providing some services and performing some functions that it now undertakes. But those who used to benefit might complain. And since the government presumably tries to do only things that seem worthwhile, it is not clear that large amounts could be saved.
2. The government could try to cut out waste. The scope may be large, but:
   a. it is not easy to *identify* 'waste' in a system which deliberately separates costs from benefits, and thus prevents any estimate of profit or loss;
   b. there is bound to be resistance to cutting out waste: it may imply prior incompetence or sloth, and it may risk the jobs of some of those the government currently employs;

c. as long as the same general system continues, any waste cut out will probably tend to creep back in. Thus it might only be a temporary solution.

3. The government could 'privatise' some of its activities, by transferring them to the **private sector**. This could enable such services to be provided more cheaply, in the face of competition, and it could better satisfy consumers' wishes, if they are allowed choice. Moreover it need not cause much unemployment.

Since easily the largest part of government spending is on the welfare state, a substantial part of any cuts in government spending would probably need to be made in that area for any real impact. (For instance, even *halving* spending on defence would reduce government spending by only about 5 per cent.) There are three possible stages for the provision of welfare services:

1. The government is now responsible for *providing*, as well as paying for certain services, such as education and health. This probably incorporates an element of paternalism, as well as desire to redistribute incomes so that even the poor can 'afford' what is reckoned to be a decent level of provision. As we have seen, those two welfare services alone involve government spending amounting to 14 per cent of the national income.

2. The so-called **voucher system** would work rather like book-tokens, which must be spent on a definite category of consumer expenditure, but allow choice within that category. The government would continue to *finance* the services so they would still be part of government spending, but would no longer be *providing* them. Everyone would receive vouchers earmarked for 'education' or 'health', depending on the number of children, age, or other criteria. People could then 'spend' these vouchers on the named welfare service, in a market with competing producers. This would introduce competition into the supply of these services, and consumer choice into the demand for them. Thus it might be hoped that people would end up getting more value for their money.

3. Finally, another proposal would be simply to reduce taxes and let people pay for themselves. (In effect this would give them cash, rather than earmarked

	Present system	Voucher scheme	Pay for oneself
Competition?	NO	YES	YES
Consumer choice?	NO	YES	YES
Cut government spending?	NO	NO	YES
Cut taxes?	NO	NO	YES
Redistribution?	YES	YES★	NO★
Paternalism?	YES	YES	NO
★Possibly			

Fig. 8.3: Three kinds of welfare service provision

vouchers.) If the problem is thought to be some people's *poverty*, cash transfer payments out of tax revenue could continue the existing level of redistribution. But most people already pay for their own welfare services. At present they do so indirectly, by way of the tax system which finances the welfare state: the proposal is that they should be allowed to do so *directly* in future. This would allow a substantial fall in government spending, and in total taxes.

Figure 8.3 summarises the effect of the three stages.

8.2 Taxation

Taxation is a compulsory levy by the government. It has two main purposes: to raise revenue to finance government spending, and to redistribute incomes. A third possible aim of tax policy, demand management, will be considered in Chapter 9.

8.2.1 Raising Revenue

We have seen how government spending between 1960 and 1980 rose from 45 per cent to more than 60 per cent of national income. Over the same period total tax revenue rose from 35 per cent to 50 per cent of the national income. Part of the 'gap' between tax revenue and government spending is covered by miscellaneous revenue, and the balance is the Public Sector Borrowing Requirement (see Ch. 9).

Figure 8.4 shows a significant increase in most kinds of tax between 1960 and 1970. Between 1960 and 1980 national income rose by 50 per cent in real terms, but total taxes more than doubled.

Percentages	*1960* %	*1970* %	*1980* %
Expenditure taxes	11.9	14.1	15.0
Income taxes	13.0	19.3	19.1
Social Security taxes	4.4	8.9	10.4
Property and Capital Transfer taxes	5.3	5.9	5.6
Total tax revenue	34.6	48.2	50.1
In constant 1975 £b.	*£b.*	*£b.*	*£b.*
Total tax revenue	*20.3*	*37.4*	*44.0*
National income	*58.7*	*77.6*	*87.8*

Fig. 8.4: Taxes as a proportion of national income, 1960 to 1980.

The type of tax may be of interest, as well as total tax revenue. The *averag* **income tax** rate, for example, represents total income tax divided by tot: income; whereas the *marginal* income tax rate means the percentage tax payabl on any extra ('marginal') income. The distinction may be important, becaus marginal tax rates are likely to affect short-term incentives.

Average UK tax levels are much the same as in many other Europea countries; though Holland and the Scandinavian countries have higher ta levels, and Spain and Switzerland lower. But until recently the UK's *margin* rates of tax on income were much higher than most other countries. Th result was (probably) to damage incentives without raising tax revenue.

In times of rapid inflation taxes expressed as money amounts, like car licen: fees, need to be regularly 'increased' in money terms in order to stay th same in 'real' terms. The same applies to lump-sum personal allowances : the base of the income tax system. Most taxes are now expressed as percentage however, like Value Added Tax or National Insurance contributions, and aut< matically keep pace with inflation.

Taxes on income are sometimes called **direct** taxes, and taxes on expend ture **indirect**. Thus income tax and employees' national insurance wou! count as 'direct', and most other taxes as 'indirect'. The 1979 Budget reduce income tax and increased Value Added Tax, partly because indirect tax: were thought to be less of a disincentive. This is dubious (it depends on th interaction of the 'income effect' and the 'price effect' – see **7.1**); and th resulting sharp increase in the Retail Price Index delayed expectations of low: inflation.

Figure 8.5 sets out the main UK taxes in 1981, and their revenue yie as a proportion of total tax revenue. Of the income tax yield of 29 per ce: of total taxes, less than 1 per cent comes from the graduated part: the bas: rate of 30 per cent raises nearly all the money.

Direct **70%**	29% Income Tax	*Personal incomes*
	21% National Insurance	*Wages*
	4% Corporation Tax	*Company profits*
	4% Petroleum Revenue Tax	*North Sea oil*
	11% Local rates	*Property*
	1% Capital taxes	*Capital transfers and capital gai*
Indirect **30%**	14% Value Added Tax	*Most consumer spending except food*
	11% Excise taxes	*Drink, tobacco, petrol*
	5% Other spending taxes	*Miscellaneous*

Fig. 8.5: Main sources of tax revenue, 1981.

8.2.2 **Redistributing Income**

When taxes on spending, as well as on income, are allowed for, the tax system as a whole hardly redistributes income at all. The average level of total tax per person is about the same percentage of income across a very wide range of income levels. It is mainly government spending which redistributes income, through the welfare services and social security benefits.

A **progressive** tax takes a larger percentage of higher than of lower incomes; a **proportional** tax takes the same percentage of all incomes, whatever their size; and a **regressive** tax takes a larger percentage of lower than of higher incomes. The tax system as a whole is almost 'proportional', except at very low or very high income levels.

Income tax is 'progressive': it takes a smaller percentage of lower incomes, because the lump-sum personal allowance, which is not taxed, is more important to those with lower incomes. Income tax is also **graduated**. The basic rate of 30 per cent applies to taxable incomes up to about £15,000 a year. But a higher rate of tax is payable on incomes above that level, rising to a top rate of 60 per cent on taxable earned incomes above £36,000.

While the poor don't gain much from the tax system, the rich may lose. Top income earners may bear income tax rates rising to 60 per cent of earnings and 75 per cent of investment income. (Until recently these rates were 83 per cent and 98 per cent respectively!) Yet the total tax revenue yielded by graduated (higher) rates of income tax, and from the surcharge on investment income is very small, less than $\frac{1}{2}$ per cent of national income.

The flat amount of tax on each packet of cigarettes is 'regressive'. A low-income smoker spends more of his income on cigarettes than a high-income smoker, so the tax on cigarettes represents a larger proportion of a low-income smoker's total income. It is to avoid Value Added Tax being regressive that most food is exempted from VAT in the UK.

In trying to help 'the poor', we need to distinguish between absolute poverty and relative poverty. In relative terms the 'poor' are always with us, in the sense that some people will always constitute the lowest 10 per cent of income-earners. In exactly the same way, there will always be some people whose incomes are 'above average'. (But, of course, the members of these groups need not always be the *same* people: there is movement between categories from time to time.)

In absolute terms 'the poor' stand to benefit more from a small share of a *growing* cake than from a slightly larger share of a static (or even declining) cake. Imposing very heavy tax rates on those who earn most may be a serious disincentive to the creation of wealth. Yet the poor would probably gain more from this than they do from redistribution of 'existing' incomes.

Official complaints about tax avoidance (which is legal) and tax evasion (which is illegal) date back more than 100 years. But nobody knows how much there is. A recent Inland Revenue estimate was that tax evaded on earnings might be about 5 per cent of total tax revenue. Not all tax avoidance is officially disapproved: a protective tariff may deliberately be set so high that nothing is imported. The revenue yield is nil, but the tax achieves its purpose precisely because everyone chooses to avoid it.

Both motive and opportunity are required for avoidance or evasion of tax. In general, reducing tax *rates* will reduce the motive, and having simpler tax *rules* will probably reduce the opportunity. The British tax system is notoriously complicated; and many of its complexities result from attempts to be 'fair'. These might not be needed so much if the top rates of tax were lower. The 1955 Royal Commission said: 'The statute book becomes encumbered with elaborate provisions against avoidance, some of which rank among the least intelligible portions of English prose.'

8.3 Local Authorities

8.3.1 Receipts

Figure 8.6 shows **local authority** receipts as a percentage of national income from 1960 to 1980. The proportion of local authority receipts coming from local rates (property taxes) has been falling, and that from central government grants rising.

Per cent of national income	1960 (%)		1970 (%)		1980 (%)	
Local rates	3.7	*39%*	4.6	*33%*	5.0	*31%*
Rents etc.	2.0	*20%*	2.7	*20%*	3.0	*18%*
Central government grants	3.9	*41%*	6.6	*47%*	8.2	*51%*
Total receipts	9.6		13.9		16.2	

Fig. 8.6: Local authority receipts, 1960 to 1980, as a percentage of national income.

Local authorities own about one third of the country's dwellings (see Ch. 10) so rents are another major source of income, in addition to local rates. The third source, now more than half the total, is grants from central government.

Local authority spending exceeds their total receipts; but the resulting deficits could be eliminated by further increasing the amount of grants from central government. This would not affect the total size of the Public Sector Borrowing Requirement. Due to the importance of central government grants local authorities may not be as independent as many of them might like. Central government also lays many statutory duties on them.

8.3.2 **Spending**

Figure 8.7 shows the pattern of local authority spending since 1960. It doubled in real terms between 1960 and 1970, and rose from 24 per cent to 31 per cent of total government spending. The real increase between 1970 and 1980 was one sixth. Since total government spending rose by one third in that decade (see Fig. 8.1 on page 154), the local authorities' share of the total fell back to 27 per cent.

Local authorities are responsible for the bulk of all government spending on education, which is easily the largest single kind of spending. They are also the major spenders on other welfare services in kind, on the environment and roads, and on the police. Local authorities also run certain 'trading services' in aerodromes, car parks, passenger transport, ports, etc. It is not easy to judge how much loss these services 'ought' to make, if any; but there may be scope for local authority business to be more commercial.

Per cent of national income	*1960* (%)	*1970* (%)	*1980* (%)
Education	3.9	5.3	6.1
Other welfare services	0.5	1.0	1.5
Housing	1.5	2.1	1.4
Environment	1.2	1.7	1.4
Roads	0.9	1.3	0.9
Debt interest	0.8	1.8	1.6
Police	0.6	1.0	1.3
Miscellaneous	1.4	2.0	2.5
Total spending	10.8	16.2	16.7
In 1975 £ b.:			
National income	*58.7*	*77.6*	*87.8*
Local authority spending	*6.3*	*12.6*	*14.7*
As a percentage of total government spending:	24%	31%	27%

Fig. 8.7: Local authority spending, 1960 to 1980, as a percentage of national income.

In practice it has proved difficult for central government to control local government spending in total. (The precise details are left to local decisions.) A major problem is that the taxpayers (rate-payers) are largely local business firms who do not get a vote. Thus the voters tend to welcome high spending, for which, on the whole, they do not have to pay. This is a modern example of 'taxation without representation'.

8.4 Nationalised Industries

8.4.1 Extent

Nationalised industries in Britain account for about 10 per cent of the employed work force, and about 20 per cent of productive capital investment. They consist mainly of utilities, like gas, electricity, and telecommunications, and transport concerns like the railways. Most nationalisation occurred between 1945 and 1950. But the post office was a government department for hundreds of years, and electricity generating was taken over as long ago as 1926. Recent transfers from the private to the 'public' (government) sector include steel (1967) and shipbuilding (1977). There have also been more recent transfers in the other direction (see **8.4.4**).

Figure 8.8 sets out some key statistics for 11 of the largest concerns, grouped into Energy, Communication, Transport and Manufacturing.

	Profit or (Loss) (£ m.)	Sales (£ b.)	Assets (£ b.)	Employees (thousands)
Energy				
National Coal Board	(460)	5	6	280
Electricity Council	480	8	33	160
British Gas	310	5	11	110
British National Oil	440	6	1	—
Communication				
Posts	130	$2\frac{1}{2}$	1	180
British Telecom	1,030	6	16	250
Transport				
British Airways	(570)	2	$1\frac{1}{2}$	50
British Rail	(940)	2	3	230
Manufacturing				
British Leyland	(500)	3	$1\frac{1}{2}$	120
British Shipbuilders	(80)	1	$\frac{1}{2}$	70
British Steel	(530)	$3\frac{1}{2}$	$2\frac{1}{2}$	100

Fig. 8.8: Main nationalised industries results, 1981–82.

'Profit' above is defined as current cost earnings before interest and tax, and 'assets' as current cost net assets after deducting current liabilities. The figures include so-called 'extraordinary' losses, which were especially heavy for British Airways and British Steel in 1981–82.

There are profits in energy (except for coal) and communication; but in general where there is competition the nationalised industries make losses. Electricity, gas, and telecom are capital intensive, with assets per employee (in £ thousands) of 200, 100, and 70 respectively. All the rest average less than £20,000 assets per employee.

8.4.2 Reasons

There have been several different reasons for taking firms or industries into public ownership. Although there is clearly a mixture, on the whole political reasons, rather then economic ones, seem to have been paramount. A recent official study listed six purposes of nationalisation, which it said 'have not altered significantly over the last 50 years'.

a. To promote greater efficiency. This was probably a major reason for nationalising coal (1947) and steel (1967), though in each case several years elapsed before the work force declined much. Between 1956 and 1970, employment in the coal industry fell from 700,000 to 300,000, while output fell from 210 m. tons to 140 m. In steel, between 1972 and 1983, employment fell from 230,000 to 80,000, and output from 25 m. tons to 12 m.

b. Lack of private risk capital. The emphasis should be on the riskiness, not on the *amount*, of the investment needed. We have seen that some of the industries are capital intensive; but even the government cannot create resources out of nothing. It borrows, it taxes, or state industries may charge monopoly prices. But in each case lenders, taxpayers, and consumers, who actually provide the funds, could equally do so for private enterprise. Governments may, however, be willing and able to take some risks, such as nuclear power stations, which a commercial business would refuse.

c. To regulate certain natural monopolies. We noted this reason earlier (1.3.2), together with the alternative of regulating privately-owned monopolies, as in several foreign countries.

d. To assist national economic planning. This might apply to energy and transport; though workers may not obey orders merely because an industry is government-owned.

e. To obtain employees' legitimate rights. It is not obvious what this means. Perhaps it may be a secondary reason in some cases. But the leader of the largest trade union said not long ago: 'The nationalisation of our basic industries ... has been a disappointment to many who hoped that public ownership would transform the role of the workers in the industries concerned.'

f. To achieve the most equitable distribution of income. It is not clear whether the 'equity' refers to different income levels or to different regions of the country. Nor is it clear how it could be achieved. This seems a minor aspect of nationalised industries, unlike in the welfare services, where it is central.

We may add three further reasons to the six above:

g. For defence or security reasons. Many private firms perform highly secret work for the Ministry of Defence; but the UK Atomic Energy Authority might fall under this heading.

h. To provide a social service. The most obvious example is the £800 m. subsidy to British Rail in respect of 'uneconomic' passenger services. This is nearly as much as revenue from fares.

i. To rescue 'lame ducks'. Two recent examples are Rolls-Royce and British Leyland. Although both were privately-owned at the time, the government was not willing to let either go bankrupt. Parts of British Shipbuilders, British Steel and the National Coal Board probably now fall in the same category.

8.4.3 Results

The nationalised industries were supposed to 'break even taking one year with another'. In 1961 this was taken to mean over a five-year period, after charging interest on loan capital. But the target has not been met. Over the 30 years from 1950 to 1980, the nationalised industries in total made zero profit *before* charging any interest. With average capital employed (in 1982 pounds) of more than £60 b. throughout the period, in real economic terms there have been huge losses.

But it is not possible to judge performance solely in accounting terms. For instance, the government may have told some industries to hold down their prices, which could lead to losses. Or because of their monopoly position, others may be able to charge unduly high prices, as with British Gas. Indeed, the lack of any clear-cut way to judge performance is a serious problem.

A recent survey suggested that 'where nationalised undertakings face direct competition ... a decline in their share of the market will constitute prima facie evidence of inefficiency'. On this basis, British Steel has not been doing very well; public sector transport has been losing market share, both in passengers and freight; and the National Coal Board seems to need protection against cheaper imports.

On the face of it, any concern that cannot go bankrupt, because it has access to 'unlimited' taxpayers' funds, has little incentive not to waste money. It may also permit unfairly low pricing where there is a competitive threat from private enterprise. Another result has been that trade union 'industrial' action against the employer has been transformed into *political* action against the government. Thus taxpayers not consumers become the ultimate arbiters.

In practice nationalisation may have impeded, rather than helped, sensible business planning. The official study quoted earlier reported that: 'Boards of most nationalised industries feel strongly that governments intervene excessively ... the trend towards more frequent and *ad hoc* interventions has delayed decisions, disrupted previously agreed plans, invalidated criteria for planning and assessing performance, resulted in financial deficits, and damaged corporate morale ...'

Finally, how satisfied are the customers of state monopolies? The Post Office, British Telecom, and British Gas have all been subject to fierce public complaints. On the other hand, thousands of satisfied customers are not news. Nor are privately-owned monopolies by any means exempt from similar criticism.

8.4.4 Privatisation

The nationalised industries are in the public sector for many different reasons; and their results, while hard to judge, mostly seem less than adequate. So a government favouring competition might want to transfer some of them to private enterprise. This would make the industries more responsive to consumers' wishes, relieve taxpayers from bearing any future losses, change the climate for wage-bargaining, and reduce political interference. (An example of the latter was telling British Steel in 1983 not to close one of its five main plants, even at an annual cost of at least £50 m., for at least three years.)

When Mrs Thatcher became Prime Minister in May 1979 there were more than 50 'public corporations'. Within four years, four had been transferred to the private sector, in whole or in part, together with some other government-owned enterprises, as set out in Fig. 8.9. British Airways and British Telecom may soon be transferred, and privatisation of many of the rest could occur in several different ways.

		Per cent		*£ m.*
1981	British Aerospace	51	Offer for sale	150
	Cable and Wireless	49	Offer for sale	224
1982	National Freight Corporation	100	Management	54
	Amersham International	100	Offer for sale	71
	Britoil	51	Tender	548
	Associated British Ports	49	Offer for sale	22
1983	British Rail Hotels	100	Separate Tenders	30
	International Aeradio	100	S.T.C.	60
	Victraulic (British Steel)	70	Management	15

Fig. 8.9: Privatisation since 1979.

Merely relaxing a statutory monopoly might suffice (as happened earlier with the BBC and on some British Airways routes); or the government might sell only part of the equity share capital (as with British Aerospace and Britoil), or only parts of the business (for example, British Gas showrooms or British Rail hotels), or separate subsidiaries (for example, International Aeradio and Amersham International). The equity might be sold to the public, or to the enterprise's own management (as with National Freight Corporation and Victraulic).

Such sales of publicly-owned assets would require financial investment from the private sector, and the proceeds would, directly or indirectly, go towards reducing the National Debt. To transfer *control*, the government need sell only 51 per cent of the equity (or even less if the government's shares became non-voting). Thus an industry with £1,000 m. net assets might be recapitalised with loan capital of, say, £400 m., and equity of £600 m.; in which case selling only £301 m. of the equity shares would be enough.

The financial institutions invest about £10,000 m. a year in government stocks and company securities. So the capital market has the capacity over, say, a 10-year period, to absorb extensive transfers of state industry assets. But some of the industries concerned have serious problems. Just as national-isation itself could make little difference in the short-term, so perhaps with the reverse. The benefits, if any, would partly be long-term.

8.5 Miscellaneous Intervention

With government spending and tax revenue exceeding 50 per cent of the national income, it is clear that in the modern UK economy the government is in a very powerful position. But in addition to these easily measurable instru-ments of government intervention, there are many many other kinds which are hard to measure and to classify. Figure 8.10 sets out some of the main kinds of government economic intervention, and the economic objectives to which they are related. The rest of this section goes on to discuss four types of controls in more detail: foreign exchange controls, price controls, capital market controls, and consumer protection laws.

Growth	Tax incentives for investment
	Infant industry support
Balance of payments	Foreign exchange controls
	Import tariffs
Inflation	Price controls
	Monetary policy
Labour	Prices and incomes policies
	Trade union immunities
Miscellaneous	Regional policies
	Capital market controls
	Consumer protection laws

Fig. 8.10: Some types of government intervention.

8.5.1 **Foreign Exchange Controls**

Foreign exchange controls were introduced as a 'temporary' measure restricting freedom on the outbreak of the Second World War. They were abandoned 40 years later, in 1979, though the Exchange Control Act 1947 itself remains. That Act in effect forbids any British resident from doing anything at all connected with foreign currencies without government permission. Abandoning exchange controls in 1979 merely means that, for the time being, government permission is automatically granted.

The government estimated in 1968 that exchange controls 'saved' only £25 m. a year, less than ¼ of 1 per cent of all imports. Yet it was extremely complicated to administer. A detailed 422-page Exchange Control Manual outlined the regulations, the first page for some reason saying it 'should not be made available to the general public'. Over the years 81 separate Notices were issued, on such subjects as cash gifts, coin collecting, education, gold, Hong Kong, insurance, shipping and aviation. There were also 11 Commodity Notices dealing with metals, sugar, vegetable oil, fishmeal, cocoa, coffee, grain, copra, rubber, cotton and wool.

For many years there was a 'travel allowance'. That is a typical official euphemism meaning a travel *restriction*! As recently as 1970 the British travel restriction was reputed to be the lowest of any country in Europe except Albania. It was relaxed in that year to allow British fans – and voters – to visit Mexico for the World Cup.

Some of the detailed restrictions may seem incredible. British citizens were searched at airports to see that they did not take more than £25 in currency abroad. The Post Office used to open thousands of letters sent abroad each year, to make sure they contained no currency. On emigration, British families could take only £5,000 with them to last for *four years*; after which time they might be permitted to take the balance of their UK assets. Lord Cromer, a former Governor of the Bank of England, called the post-war British exchange control system 'as stringent, inhibiting and corrupting as any seen in a leading country in peacetime this century'. One should be aware that this kind of bureaucratic control is always likely to be part of the 'cost' of government intervention.

8.5.2 **Price Controls**

Of all government economic controls, **price controls** are probably the most far-reaching. They prevent a firm from changing the selling price of any of its products without government permission. As a result, prices no longer represent market signals relating consumers' wishes to the scarcity of resources. Instead they merely quantify government orders. But in a changing world, yesterday's money price may not be 'right' for today.

When the price system is suppressed, some other way must be found to ration economic (i.e. 'scarce') resources. This may be by queues (as in the National Health Service), by rationing (e.g. petrol coupons), or by other means (e.g. Cup Final tickets). Some people then object strongly if pricing creeps back in, as when 'ticket touts' sell Cup Final tickets. (I remember the amazement on one such person's face when I congratulated him on doing such a good job in satisfying consumers!) And where governments allocate resources directly, there may be openings for bribery, which in effect represents a less-than-ideal attempt to reintroduce the price mechanism.

In general, fixing prices above the level they would be in a competitive market will tend to lead to surpluses (for example, butter mountains, unfilled airline seats). Similarly, fixing prices below the competitive market level will tend to lead to shortages (for example, rented accommodation, hospital beds). Figure 8.11 illustrates these effects.

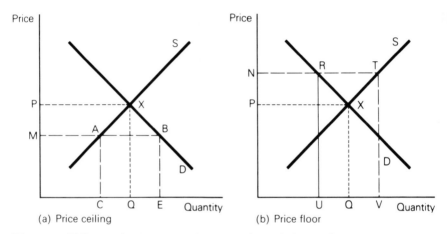

Fig. 8.11: Effects of price control on supply and demand.

Figure 8.11 (a) shows the effect of a price ceiling M at a level *below* the competitive market price P. Supply falls from Q to C, while demand rises from Q to E. Thus there develops a *shortage* of CE (equal to AB). Figure 8.11 (b) shows the effect of a price floor N at a level *above* the competitive market price P. Demand falls from Q to U while supply rises from Q to V. Thus there develops a *surplus* of UV (equal to RT).

There can be detailed problems with price controls in practice. For instance, there is a time-lag between the event supposed to 'justify' a price change (under the rules) and permission being granted. And if they cannot increase the price, suppliers may reduce product *quality*, which is often hard to check.

Price controls may form part of a wider prices and incomes policy (see 7.4.2), intended to reduce inflation or suppress its effects. For several years in the 1960s and 1970s there was a Price Commission to administer price controls. From time to time it used to boast about how much it had 'saved' consumers by rejecting firms' requests for price increases. But it could not tell how much extra *supply* its decisions might have deterred. It is absurd to suppose that lower prices are necessarily 'better' than higher prices. If that were really so, a Price Commission should simply order all prices to be reduced at once to zero.

8.5.3 Capital Market Controls

a. New issue controls. For about 15 years after the Second World War, no British company was legally permitted to raise more then £10,000 by borrowing or by an issue of ordinary shares without first obtaining government permission. What may now strike a modern reader is not merely how restrictive such a regulation appears, but how long after the war the restriction persisted. Whereas it seems possible (though difficult) to reintroduce exchange controls, there is surely little chance of such controls on new issues being reimposed. The main continuing 'restriction' is simply that the Bank of England can control the *timing* of issues over £3 m., to ensure that large issues do not coincide.

b. Dividend controls. For 10 of the 13 years between 1966 and 1979, **dividend controls** limited (usually to less than the rate of inflation) any increase in cash dividends paid by companies to their shareholders. As a result, over the period total 'real' dividends fell by about one third. The controls were normally presented in the context of some kind of general 'prices and incomes policy' (see 7.4.2), though there are important economic differences between dividends and wages. (For instance, it is not usual for employees to do without any wages – not merely any *increase* in wages! – when a company has a particularly bad year. Yet this does happen with shareholders.)

Dividend controls were scrapped in 1979, but they seem quite likely to be reintroduced if a future government imposed another prices and incomes policy. In various ways the UK tax laws still tend to discourage the free flow of capital between companies and shareholders, thus obstructing the movement of economic resources to their potentially most profitable use.

c. Monopolies and mergers. Mergers may lead to economies of scale and allow the transfer of economic resources from less competent to more competent managements. On the other hand mergers may create monopolies and restrict competition. Hence the net economic results are not always clear; and UK government policy has not been 'against' mergers *per se*, but has tended to look at each case as it arises, to see whether on balance it is likely to operate against the public interest.

The Monopolies and Mergers Commission (MMC) can prevent mergers or require monopolies to change their behaviour. Proposed mergers may be referred to the MMC (by the government) where assets over £5 m. are involved or where the merger would create a 'monopoly share' (25 per cent or more) of the 'relevant market'. In practice only two or three mergers a year since 1965 have actually been prevented. An important precedent was set in 1982 when the government over-ruled the MMC's rejection of a proposed merger. Until then the MMC's adjudications had always been accepted by the government. The immediate result is likely to be to increase uncertainty about government policy.

8.5.4 Consumer Protection

Once the rule used to be *caveat emptor* – let the buyer beware. Of course there were legal rules about implied conditions of sale, and to prevent fraud. But the general view was that competing suppliers would prosper in the long run only if they fostered their reputation for quality. The risks to consumers of financial or physical damage were tempered by awareness of the costs of regulation.

Nowadays there is a mass of legislation protecting consumers. There are also consumer organisations, such as the separate Consumer Councils for most nationalised industries. And the privately-run Consumers Association publishes (in *Which?*) regular comparisons of quality and price for most consumer appliances, foodstuffs, etc. Apart from protection for children, adult consumers may be thought to need protection for two main reasons: risk of financial loss, or risk to health and safety.

Consumers may be vulnerable with large purchases, say of houses, cars, or expensive equipment. They cannot always judge technical qualities for themselves, and a mistake might involve significant loss. For some products there are minimum technical standards. Rental markets, e.g. for television sets, also reduce the risk of loss to consumers: if their set breaks down they simply get a free replacement from the lessor. Customers can now change their minds within a few days, if 'over-persuaded' by door-to-door salesmen. And there are provisions about truth in advertising.

There are many regulations to do with pricing: how price 'cuts' may be advertised; how petrol prices must be displayed; disclosure of the real annual interest rate in credit deals; standard measures for drinks, to allow price comparisons; other requirements on weights and measures, both the practice and disclosure.

Health and safety laws prevent the sale of certain 'dangerous' drugs and other substances, or require definite labels disclosing the contents of food products. There are limits on permitted shelf lives. A health warning must be printed on cigarette packets; which may imply that any product not so labelled must be 'safe'. But who is to decide what is 'too dangerous'? Drugs that could never possibly harm anyone may not be much use. And to what extent should adult consumers be protected against themselves, as with seatbelts in cars?

Work Section

A. Revision Questions

A1 What percentage of national income was government spending in 1980?

A2 Name three reasons for the recent increase in welfare state spending.

A3 Name three kinds of 'costs' of government spending.

A4 What three ways were suggested to reduce government spending?

A5 Name three possible difficulties in trying to eliminate 'wasteful' government spending.

A6 What are the two main purposes of taxation?

A7 How much did total tax revenue increase between 1960 and 1980, as a percentage of national income?

A8 What is the difference between 'average' and 'marginal' tax rates?

A9 Why does it matter whether tax rates are expressed as money amounts or as percentages?

A10 What is the difference between 'direct' and 'indirect' taxation?

A11 If taxes as a whole do not significantly redistribute income, how does most redistribution occur?

A12 What is the difference between 'progressive' and 'regressive' taxes?

A13 If income tax is progressive, how can the tax system as a whole be proportional?

A14 Give two reasons why income tax is progressive.

A15 What is the difference between 'absolute' and 'relative' poverty?

A16 What proportion of local authority incomes comes from (a) local rates? (b) central government grants?

A17 What proportion of the country's dwellings are owned by local authorities?

A18 What proportion of total government spending is incurred by local authorities?

A19 What proportion of local authority spending goes on education?

A20 Why may it be argued that local rates are an example of 'taxation without representation'?

A21 What percentage of the total work force is employed in nationalised industries?

A22 Which three nationalised industries are most capital intensive?

A23 Name three reasons given for nationalisation.

A24 Name three sources of finance for capital investment by nationalised industries.

A25 Why may a profit not represent a 'good' performance for a nationalised industry?

A26 Why may a loss not represent a 'bad' performance by a nationalised industry?

A27 Name three nationalised industries which have lost market share.

A28 How does nationalisation affect trade union wage-bargaining?

A29 Name three arguments for denationalisation.

A30 Name three possible ways to denationalise a public corporation.

A31 How long did 'temporary' exchange controls last?

A32 What is the likely result of fixing prices (a) above and (b) below the level they would be in a competitive market?

A33 Why is it hard to judge whether price controls have, on balance, been of benefit to the economy?

A34 Name one economic advantage and one economic disadvantage of mergers.

A35 What two reasons were suggested why adult consumers may need protection?

B. Exercise and Case Studies

B1 If the *marginal* rate of tax on income above a certain minimum level is 40 per cent, what is the *average* rate of income tax on annual income of:
    i. £4,000   ii. £7,000   iii. £10,000
    if the minimum level (below which no tax is payable) is:
    a. £1,500 per year   b. £2,500 per year?

B2 Refer to **8.4.2** (a) on page 163.
    Calculate the apparent change in output per employee:
    a. for the National Coal Board between 1956 and 1970;
    b. for British Steel between 1972 and 1983.

B3 Refer to Fig. 8.1 on page 154.
    a. Which items fell (as a percentage of national income)
        i. between 1960 and 1970?
        ii. between 1970 and 1980?
        Comment on possible reasons.
    b. Which headings would you expect to contain most of
        i. transfer payments?
        ii. capital goods?
        Explain your reasons.
    c. Express each of the three 'economic categories' as a percentage of total government spending for

      i. 1960   ii. 1970   iii. 1980.

      Try to explain the reasons for any major changes.

B4   Refer to Fig. 8.8 on page 162.

     a. Rank the profitable nationalised industries in order of:

       i. return on net assets;

       ii. profit margin

     b. Rank the loss-making nationalised industries in order of loss per employee.

B5   Refer to Fig. 8.8 on page 162.

     From reference material determine the latest figures for as many national-ised industries as you can. Comment on significant changes from the 1981–82 figures shown.

B6   **Growthland and Egalitaria**

     Two hypothetical countries start with identical levels and dispersions of income. In each country, incomes of the top quartile amount to 50 per cent of the national income, of the next quartile to 25 per cent, of the next to 15 per cent, and of the bottom quartile to 10 per cent of national income.

     In Egalitaria the top quartile is to lose each year 1 per cent (of national income) of its excess over 25 per cent, which is to be split pro rata between the bottom two quartiles (i.e. two-fifths to the bottom quartile, three-fifths to the second quartile). In 25 years, therefore, all four quartiles will receive exactly 25 per cent of an (assumed) unchanged national income.

     In Growthland, by contrast, the shares of each quartile will remain in the existing proportions; but national income is assumed to grow each year in real terms.

     If Growthland's rate of growth is 2 per cent a year:

     a. How will total national incomes in Growthland and Egalitaria com-pare after:

       i. 10 years   ii. 25 years   iii. 50 years?

     b. What will each quartile's income in Growthland amount to after:

       i. 10 years   ii. 25 years   iii. 50 years?

     c. How will the bottom quartile's income in Growthland compare with the *top* quartile's income in Egalitaria after:

       i. 50 years   ii. 75 years   iii. 100 years?

     d. Recalculate answers to (a), (b), and (c) above on the basis that Growth-land's rate of economic growth is:

       i. 1 per cent a year   ii. 3 per cent a year.

B7   A number of organisations are partly government-owned. Which of the following would you classify as a 'nationalised industry'? What are your criteria?

     a. British Leyland 99½ per cent owned (through the National Enterprise Board)

     b. Cable and Wireless 51 per cent owned

    c. British Aerospace 49 per cent owned

    d. British Petroleum 32 per cent owned

    e. Investors In Industry 15 per cent owned (through the Bank of England).

B8   Would it make sense to 'consolidate' (i.e. add together) the results of all the nationalised industries and present accounts as if they were a single enterprise? What would the results mean? If your answer is 'No' how would you justify consolidating the accounts of Imperial Chemical Industries?

B9   Select an economic good or service of your choice. What consumer protection is necessary? What is currently provided? To what extent is *government* intervention required?

B10 Try to assess the effects on the UK economy of the abolition of foreign exchange controls in October 1979.

B11 Refer to Fig. 8.1 on page 154.

    a. From reference material, determine the money amounts of government spending under the appropriate headings for the most recent year for which figures are available.

    b. Express these amounts as percentages of national income.

    c. Compare the results with those shown for 1980; and comment on any significant differences.

B12 Refer to Fig. 8.4 on page 157.

    a. From reference material, determine the money amounts of tax revenue under the appropriate headings for the most recent year for which figures are available.

    b. Express these amounts as percentages of national income.

    c. Compare the results with those shown for 1980; and comment on any significant differences.

B13 Refer to Fig. 1.13 on page 22.

    a. What would happen if the government fixed the maximum price of brief-cases at £40?

    b. What would happen if the government fixed the minimum price of brief-cases at £70?

C. Essay Questions

C1 'If swimming pools are being provided free, put me down for six!' (Lord Harris of High Cross, on the welfare state.) Discuss.

C2 'Health and education are important. So are food and clothing; but that is no reason for the government to finance them out of tax revenue in order to provide them "free" to consumers.' Discuss.

C3 'It would be better for most people to pay directly for welfare services like education and health, instead of paying indirectly, by means of taxes, for a government bureaucracy to administer a state monopoly providing these services free of charge to consumers.' Discuss.

C4 Explain why you agree or disagree with the view that, for any given total amount or percentage, it makes little economic difference how national insurance contributions (= social security taxes) are split between employer and employee.

C5 To what extent is tax avoidance undesirable?

C6 'Privatising profitable nationalised industries is unfair to tax-payers, while privatising unprofitable ones is impossible.' Discuss.

C7 Is privatisation desirable? Why or why not?

C8 'The "commanding heights" of the economy seem to have turned into "bottomless pits".' Discuss.

C9 What should be done about 'lame ducks'?

C10 Which if any of the nationalised industries should be privatised? On what criteria would you decide?

C11 Do price controls raise more problems for business firms than they solve for governments?

C12 Should foreign exchange controls be reimposed?

C13 'The ultimate result of shielding men from the effects of folly is to fill the world with fools.' Herbert Spencer. Discuss, with reference to consumer protection legislation.

C14 Is private industry any better equipped than the government to make decisions about capital investment?

C15 As resources become scarcer, further government intervention in the economy becomes both inevitable and desirable. Do you agree?

Chapter 9

Fiscal and Monetary Policy

Objective: *To outline three different approaches to fiscal policy; to discuss the two main components of monetary policy; to describe the overall economic and political objectives of government policy and the inter-relationship of fiscal and monetary policy; and to identify two opposite schools of thought in political economy.*

Synopsis: *British governments traditionally aimed to balance the budget in every peacetime year. Since the war, a proposed alternative has been to balance the budget only over the whole period of the trade cycle. In fact, however, UK governments have run 'permanent deficits'. Borrowing to finance these deficits has been eroded in real terms by substantial inflation.*
  Recent emphasis in monetary policy has shifted to controlling the rate of growth in the money supply, away from trying to control the level of interest rates. But both definition and control of the money supply has proved difficult.

Government overall policies try to influence growth, the balance of payments, inflation, and unemployment. Fiscal and monetary policy are inter-related, the effects of deficits (the Public Sector Borrowing Requirement) depending partly on how they are financed. Recent policy to reduce the PSBR has been affected by the unexpected depth of the world recession in the early 1980s. The impact of government policy on business firms is hard to predict, and not the same for different firms.

Two main schools of thought in political economy may be classified broadly as 'market-optimists' and 'market-pessimists'. Putting it the other way round, the two groups may be regarded respectively as pessimistic and optimistic about the results of government intervention.

9.1 Fiscal Policy

9.1.1 The Trade Cycle

Figure 9.1 outlines the simple pattern of the trade cycle. It has four main stages: the slump, the upswing, the boom, the downturn.

The slump (A) is marked by heavy unemployment (of labour and production capacity), and low consumer demand. Prices, if not actually falling, may be rising less rapidly than usual. Confidence in the future will be low, as will the amount of new capital formation.

When the slump turns into the upswing (B), after a time the pace of the recovery begins to quicken. Expectations improve, and production in many areas can quickly increase by using existing spare capacity. Upward pressure on prices starts to get stronger.

Towards the top of the upswing (C) bottlenecks become more common as existing capacity is fully used, and labour shortages begin to occur. It now becomes less easy to increase output merely by putting unused resources to

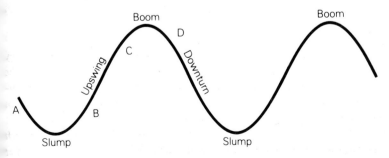

Fig. 9.1: The pattern of the trade cycle.

work. Prices for scarce factors of production are rapidly bid up, and money profits tend to be high. Much new capital investment will now seem worthwhile if boom conditions continue.

When the boom ends, consumption starts to slow down (D). Investments that promised to pay off if the boom continued now appear unprofitable, and may have to be liquidated. High interest payments, which were tolerable when sales and profits were expected to be high, now become a heavy burden. Business failure become more common. Production and employment decline.

The above general description says nothing about how long the trade cycle takes, nor about the extent of its peaks and troughs. It also tends to assume that all industries move together, which need not be so. Figure 9.2 lists seven different kinds of trade cycle theory. The question is not so much why output fluctuates (see **4.3.3**), but why there often appears to be some *regularity* (or 'cycle') of fluctuation over a long period of years.

Monetary:	expansion and contraction of bank money and credit.
Over-investment:	not too little, but too much *misdirected* investment causes recessions.
Political:	periodic political clamping down on creeping inflation.
Psychological:	people infect each other with pessimistic or with optimistic expectations.
Under-consumption:	too much income goes to wealthy or thrifty people compared with what can be invested.
Innovation:	clustering of important inventions.
Sunspot:	external events.

Fig. 9.2: Seven kinds of trade cycle theory.

Businessmen are naturally very keen to tell when 'turns' in the trade cycle are going to occur, since these can have important implications about the level of future demand in many industries. Experience suggests that certain economic statistics (known as **leading indicators**) may signal future peaks and troughs in the trade cycle. 'Longer' leading indicators (about 12 months in advance) include: interest rates, dwellings started, stock market price indices, CBI surveys of 'optimism' among businessmen. 'Shorter' leading indicators (about six months in advance) include: credit extended, new car registrations, CBI surveys of changes in new orders and of expected changes in stocks of materials.

9.1.2 Balanced Budgets

Government **budgets** reflect the relationship between government revenue (mainly taxation) and government spending. They come under the heading of fiscal policy – so-called because of the Latin word *fiscus*, meaning 'state treasury'. Business budgets normally refer to some kind of estimate for the future, but a government 'budget' can mean both the plan and the outcome. Thus one might say: 'The government budget deficit in 1980 turned out to be larger than forecast.'

In the eighteenth and nineteenth centuries, governments expected taxation and other receipts to cover total government spending, except in war-time. A more recent approach required the government to balance its budget only over the period of the trade cycle, taken as a whole. The idea, as Fig. 9.3 shows, was that in times of recession the government would run a deficit in order to counteract the economic slow-down. In times of boom the government would run a budget surplus in order to damp down the expansion. Over the whole trade cycle, the surpluses and deficits should more or less cancel out.

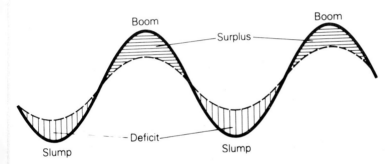

Fig. 9.3: 'Smoothing out' the trade cycle.

The solid line represents the sharp fluctuations of the trade cycle with a balanced government budget each year. The broken line shows the much gentler variations if the government runs deficits in slumps and surpluses in booms to 'smooth out' the cycle. Such government action is called 'demand management'.

Experience has revealed serious problems with the 'cycle-smoothing' approach to budgets. It can be hard to interpret the *current state* of the economy; nor is it always easy to predict even in which *direction* any government action will operate, let alone its *extent*. Moreover, the *time-lags* inherent in political actions tend to vary unpredictably. And many kinds of government spending cannot be changed at short notice.

These difficulties have tended to mean either that short-term policy measures, such as cutting capital spending, turn out to be harmful in the longer run; or that the same capital goods industries (motor cars, domestic appliances) are continually the subject of **stop-go** measures if the government tries to 'fine-tune' the economy. It has also meant that tax changes, rather than government spending changes, have been used as short term 'regulators'. Indeed, some observers believe that government efforts at demand manage-ment in the past may actually have *accentuated* the trade cycle rather than damping it down.

9.1.3 Permanent Deficits

The idea of balancing the budget over the period of the trade cycle has remained only an idea. Post-war fiscal policy in the UK has *not* aimed to balance the government budget, either every year or over the trade cycle. Instead the actual policy has been to run a deficit *every* year – though it might be smaller in boom years than in recessions.

Orthodox theory would predict that the policy of 'permanent **deficits**' would lead to permanent inflation, since most of the government deficit would probably be financed, in effect, by increasing the money supply. And so it has turned out. Since 1967 the pound has lost more than 80 per cent of its purchasing power (see **6.2.2**), and the average rate of inflation over the next 15 years exceeded 10 per cent a year.

Figure 9.4 shows since 1966 the annual government budget deficit (the Public Sector Borrowing Requirement) as a percentage of gross domestic product at market prices. Since 1947 there has been only a single year of surplus (1969) and one of break-even (1970). In all 10 years since 1973 the budget deficit has exceeded 4 per cent of GDP. So much has the intellectual

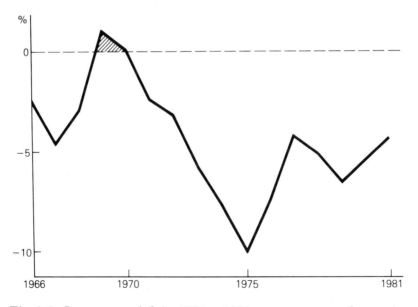

Fig. 9.4: Government deficits 1966 to 1981 as a percentage of gross domestic product.

climate changed, compared with the previous 250 years, indeed, that a projected 1981 budget deficit exceeding 4 per cent of GDP was widely labelled as 'deflationary'.

9.1.4 The National Debt

Modern UK government policy, as we have seen, is to run permanent budget deficits, which are financed mainly by domestic borrowing. In 1970 the **National Debt** stood at £33 b., which equalled 65 per cent of gross domestic product. Extra net borrowings in the next 10 years totalled £62 b., bringing the National Debt in 1980 to £95 b. But by 1980 this represented only 42 per cent of GDP.

If the government needs to borrow more each year to finance its deficits, how are these domestic borrowings ever 'repaid'? Largely by means of inflation. The national debt consists of pounds which continually shrink in real purchasing power. Thus the extra net borrowing to finance each year's deficit is mostly, in effect, merely 'topping up' the national debt in real terms.

In terms of 1982 purchasing power, the national debt in 1970 was equivalent to £152 b.; and the net borrowings over the next 10 years totalled £124 b. Yet at the end of the period, in 1980, the actual national debt outstanding was only £124 b. The 'missing' £152 b. – the entire opening national debt in 1970! – is the amount eroded by currency debasement in the decade.

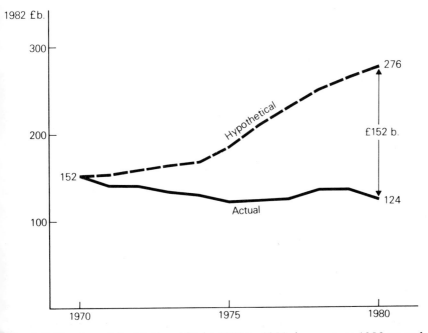

Fig. 9.5: Erosion of the National Debt 1970 to 1980, in constant 1982 pounds.

Figure 9.5 shows, in terms of 1982 pounds, both the actual national debt between 1970 and 1980 and the 'hypothetical' amount if there had been no inflation. Since the interest rates payable presumably, in the long run, come to reflect the anticipated inflation (see **3.3.1**), not all of this huge amount is really a 'gain' to the government from debasing the currency. (It must be offset against the 'high' nominal interest payable on the national debt.) Only *unanticipated* inflation would provide such a gain: an example is shown in Figure 9.6.

Figure 9.6 shows an example of a specific government security which formed part of the national debt. 6½ per cent Exchequer Stock 1976 was issued at £95½ per £100 stock in March 1971, and repaid at par in March 1976. The apparent **redemption yield** was 7.7 per cent (= 6.8% Flat Yield plus 0.9% gain on redemption); but the *real* annual rate of return (before tax) amounted to *minus* 4.8 per cent! In this case the 'gain' from currency debasement was £223 m. (in March 1976 pounds) – 20 per cent of the amount borrowed.

	Current £. m.	Constant March 1976 £. m.
Received		
March 1971: Issued £600 m. at 95½	573	1,111
Paid		
Total half-yearly gross interest	195	288
March 1976: Repaid £600 m. at 100	600	600
= 'Gain' from currency debasement		223

Fig. 9.6: Government view of 6½ per cent Exchequer Stock 1976.

9.2 Monetary Policy

9.2.1 Controlling the Money Supply

We noted earlier the two main definitions of the 'money supply' (see **6.1.2**) M1 consisting of notes and coins plus bank current accounts, and M3 consisting of M1 plus bank deposit accounts. In each case, credit accounts with commercial banks represent an important part of the supply of 'money'. Hence with **fractional reserve banking** (see **6.1.1**), control over the money supply depends mainly on control over the banks' reserve base.

There are two main ways in which the central bank may exercise such control:

1. Open market operations. These refer to sale purchase of government securities (**gilts**). When the central bank *sells* gilts to commercial banks or their customers, this reduces their balances with the **Bank of England**, and so *reduces* the money supply. (The *purchase* of gilts by the central bank *increases* the money supply.)

2. Special deposits. From time to time the Bank of England may call in 'special deposits' from the banks (which may or may not bear interest). In effect these reduce the banks' balances, and hence reduce the money supply. Calling in special deposits can check bank lending, if they are at maximum capacity; but *releasing* special deposits may not necessarily *increase* bank lending. (It has been compared to pushing on a piece of string.) In general, business borrowing in recent years has been limited far more by lack of profitable investment opportunities than by lack of finance.

The monetary authorities may aim to control either the stock of money or the level of interest rates; but, if there is a definite relationship between interest rates and the demand for money, they cannot control both volume and price at the same time. Thus the authorities may try to control the money supply, as they have been doing in recent years, and let market forces determine interest rates. Or they may try to set a particular level of interest rates (see **9.2.2**), in which case they will have to supply whatever quantity of money is needed.

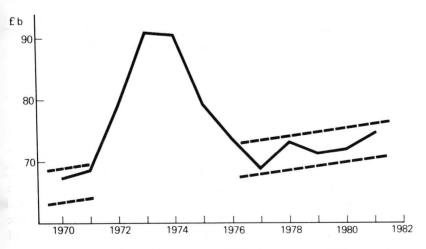

Fig. 9.7: Money supply M3, 1970 to 1981, in constant 1981 pounds.

Apart from the problem of defining the 'money supply', experience has shown that financial institutions may, to some extent, be able to circumvent monetary controls. Another problem, as we saw in **6.1.4**, is that the velocity of circulation may not be stable, especially in the short run. Figure 9.7 shows M3 money supply figures from 1970 to 1981 expressed in terms of constant 1981 pounds (that is, after allowing for inflation). The substantial real increase in 1973 and 1974 is clearly revealed, as is the subsequent decline to the 'normal' trend.

9.2.2 Controlling Interest Rates

The monetary authorities may desire a particular level of interest rates for several reasons:

a. To limit the cost of servicing the national debt. This cost £14 b. in 1982, more than 5 per cent of the GDP.
b. To maintain a particular sterling exchange rate. If international interest rates are out of line, 'hot money' (see **5.2.3**) can move rapidly and affect exchange rates.
c. To avoid high or variable interest rates for business finance. The long-term corporate finance market almost completely dried up in the late 1970s because of the prevailing high interest rates.
d. To avoid high mortgage interest rates. These are counted directly as part of the Retail Price Index, and hence affect the reported rate of inflation.

Will increasing the money supply reduce the rate of interest? In the long run, no; but in the short run it may do so, depending on people's *expectations*. (Recall the very large real **negative interest rate** in 1974–5 in Fig. 6.8 on page 125.) The difference between anticipated and unanticipated inflation is crucial.

The long-run answer is plain. Increasing the supply of money, by more than any increase in output, is likely to cause (or at least to accompany) inflation. Hence the **inflation premium** included in the overall market rate of interest will rise as the market comes to expect higher inflation. That is why interest rates are higher in countries where inflation is (expected to be) high than in countries where the rate of inflation is low.

In the short run, however, an increase in the supply of money may lead to a *temporary* reduction in the 'real' rate of interest (i.e. the overall nominal money rate of interest minus the rate of inflation). This may happen if too small an inflation premium is added to begin with, as inflation accelerates. The same thing can happen in reverse, as the rate of inflation declines. Indeed, one of the problems in reducing the rate of inflation is that until the market is convinced that it will happen (and reduces the inflation premium accordingly), real interest rates may rise to high levels.

9.2.3 Indexation

Indexation means applying an index of the rate of inflation to certain items expressed in terms of money. It can be used to adjust parts of the tax system (personal allowances or tax thresholds), social benefits (pensions), or even wage-rates (as in 'threshold agreements' in the early 1970s). The link with Constant Purchasing Power accounting (see **6.4.1**) is apparent.

Indexation by itself cannot *stop* inflation: the proper monetary and fiscal policies would also be required. There are opposing views about indexation:

a. it can help reduce inflation, by soothing people's fears of being 'left behind';
b. it doesn't reduce inflation, but it can help people to 'live with' continuing rising prices, by mitigating some of their adverse effects;
c. it actually makes inflation worse, by putting a floor under the rate and perpetuating cost-push.

Indexation is complicated to manage if applied universally, but might be regarded as unfair if applied selectively. Perhaps it is more a political than an economic question. The fierce resistance to any proposals to modify index-linked pensions suggests that phasing out indexation might prove difficult.

9.3 Overall Government Economic Policy

9.3.1 Objectives and Constraints

Among the government's economic policy objectives may be:

a. the rate of economic growth (see Ch. 4);
b. the balance of payments position (see **5.3**);
c. the rate of inflation (see Ch. 6);
d. the level of unemployment (see Ch. 7);
e. smoothing out the trade cycle (see **9.1**).

There may also be more political aims, concerned with:

f. income distribution (see **8.2.2**);
g. 'merit goods' (see **1.3.4**);
h. winning the next election.

Thus the government's budget problem is extremely complex. In trying to achieve their *objectives*, policy-makers need to take into account the various policy *instruments* available to them, as well as the various economic and political constraints. They must consider the total amounts of taxation and government spending, and their detailed economic and social effects. They must also try to judge the likely effects of any *changes* – their direction, extent, and timing. **Politicians** will also be concerned with the effects on particular *groups* of people.

Clearly fiscal and monetary policies are inter-related. The size of the Public Sector Borrowing Requirement, and how it is financed, will affect the money supply or interest rates or both, as Fig. 9.8 shows. Since 1970 the non-bank private sector has financed about 85 per cent, and the banking sector the remaining 15 per cent. Either method can lead to undesirable results. But the alternatives are either increasing taxation or else reducing government

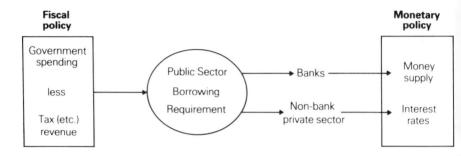

Fig. 9.8: The inter-relationship of fiscal and monetary policy.

spending (in order to reduce the PSBR). Both may seem politically unattractive in the short term.

Increasing direct taxation may tend to reduce incentives, either for individuals to earn more income (or for the unemployed to seek work) or for business firms to invest. Putting up indirect taxes will tend to increase the Retail Price Index, and may thus affect inflationary expectations. Raising taxes will also tend to reduce demand for goods (which may affect imports as well as domestic production).

Cutting government spending will reduce aggregate demand. Cutting government spending on goods and services will probably reduce some people's perceived benefits, and hence may be politically difficult. It may also be hard to reduce current spending plans at short notice. Cutting social security transfer payments may be unpopular, since those affected are vulnerable without trade unions to bargain for them. With over 9 m. retirement pensioners, the political implications are serious. Cutting subsidies will tend to put prices up, and thus increase inflationary 'cost-push' pressures. So one can see why it may be politically tempting in the short run to cut back on government capital formation (see **3.4.1**). In the short run it will not hurt many voters. It may also have a smaller effect on unemployment than cutting back current government consumption.

A recession is likely to exacerbate these problems, especially if the rate of inflation is still high. There will then be political pressure to reduce interest rates without cutting government spending or increasing taxes, and pressure to reduce unemployment without increasing inflation. But reducing interest rates could also reduce the sterling exchange rate, which might adversely affect the balance of payments. There is also the difficult problem of trying to balance short-term and long-term considerations.

In contrast, if the government wishes to inject more purchasing power into the economy, the options may seem more attractive. It can reduce taxes or increase spending. Tax changes can be made fairly quickly (say within three months), while transfer payments can be increased within about six months. Major changes in spending on goods and services may take rather longer to work through the system.

It must be remembered that in nearly all the aggregate statistics to which the government has access there is likely to be a substantial margin of error. When there is doubt about an appeal in cricket, the batsman gets the benefit. Given the political pressures, it is perhaps not surprising that when there is doubt about the economy, the tendency is usually to increase rather than reduce the government deficit.

9.3.2 Demand Management

In terms of aggregate demand management, fiscal policy and monetary policy often complement each other. There is thus a link between monetary explanations of economic changes and those based on 'circular flow' models (see Ch. 2).

The effect of a government budget deficit $(G > T)$, for example, depends partly on how it is financed. To finance the PSBR by borrowing from the non-bank private sector, government securities will have to offer high enough **yields** to attract investors. This will tend to drive up interest rates, so that government borrowing may **crowd out** private borrowing. (This helps to explain why long-term corporate borrowing has been at such a low level in recent years.) At the extreme it may be argued that extra government spending effectively reduces private spending by an equivalent amount.

But if the government finances the PSBR by borrowing from the banks, this will increase the money supply, and hence may tend to lead to inflation. Banks' loans to the public sector increase their assets, thus enabling them to increase their lending to the private sector by a multiple of that amount.

Similarly, a balance of payments surplus $(X > M)$ also increases the domestic money supply. In increasing its foreign currency reserves, the Bank of England buys the foreign currency by the creation of bank balances.

A major reason for a low real rate of economic growth was once thought to be lack of aggregate monetary demand. The classic expression of disillusionment with that view was a statement in 1976 by the Labour Prime Minister James Callaghan:

> We used to think that you could just spend your way out of a recession and increase employment by cutting taxes and boosting government spending. I tell you in all candour that that option no longer exists, and that insofar as it ever did exist, it worked by injecting inflation into the economy. And each time that happened the average level of unemployment has risen. Higher inflation, followed by higher unemployment. That is the history of the last twenty years.

Now it is fashionable to put far more emphasis on the 'supply' side; for example, by concern about structural rigidities in the economy. Figure 9.9

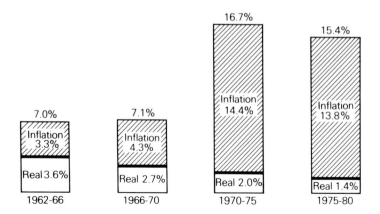

Fig. 9.9: Total annual rates of increase in money GDP 1962 to 1980 split between inflation and real growth.

analyses the increase in money GDP since 1962 between a real increase in GDP and an increase in the level of money prices (inflation). The lower rate of real increase in GDP in recent years certainly does not seem to be due to a failure to supply enough money.

9.3.3 Medium Term Financial Strategy

The Thatcher government's objectives for the medium-term were stated in 1980 to be to bring down the rate of inflation and to create conditions for a sustainable growth of output and employment. To achieve the reduction in inflation, the government would 'progressively reduce the growth of the money stock'. While the relationship between the PSBR and the growth of money supply is important, 'it is not a simple one'. Nevertheless there was no doubt that 'public sector borrowing has made a major contribution to the excessive growth of the money supply in recent years'. If interest rates were to be brought down to acceptable levels 'the PSBR must be substantially reduced as a proportion of GDP over the next few years'.

Although the government was generally viewed as '**monetarist**' – in contrast to the supposedly **Keynesian** outlook of previous post-war governments of both political parties – it clearly recognised the interrelationship of fiscal and monetary policy. Indeed, as the problems of defining and controlling the money supply became more evident in 1981 and 1982, the emphasis

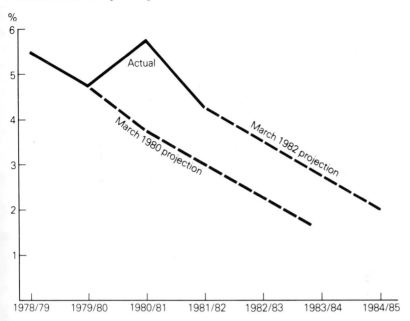

Fig. 9.10: Medium term financial strategy. PSBR as percentage of GDP, projections.

may have shifted. But the attempt to pursue the **medium-term financial strategy** was persisted with. Figure 9.10 sets out the projections (stated not to be 'targets') for PSBR as a percentage of GDP, as published in the Budgets of 1980 and 1982. It will be seen that the actual PSBR for 1980–81 was about 2 per cent of GDP larger than had been projected. This was mainly because the recession turned out to be deeper than had been expected.

9.3.4 Effects on Business Firms

Fiscal policy can have a major impact on business firms.
1. It affects the *general* level of spending in the economy.
2. It tries to balance the main *components* of total demand, like consumption and investment.
3. It may encourage or discourage *particular types* of economic activity.

Fiscal policy may aim at stimulating or reducing personal consumption by changes either in income tax or in welfare payments like unemployment benefits or pensions. The impact on business firms will depend on which income groups are affected by the changes. Changes affecting low-income groups which spend most of their incomes on basic necessities will have a different impact from changes which affect higher income-earners.

The *extent* to which consumers increase their purchases as their incomes change varies considerably from one product to another. The demand for consumer durables, for instance, like cars or washing machines, is likely to be very responsive to income changes (**income-elastic**). Thus a 10 per cent rise in real incomes might lead to a 20 per cent increase in the number bought. But for necessities like bread or milk, a change in income may not make much difference to the amount bought.

Monetary policy can also be significant for business firms. It can have important implications for interest rates and for the rate of inflation. Clearly, therefore, business firms need to study the government's fiscal and monetary policies very carefully. In practice they also need to try to assess how likely these policies are to succeed; or whether changes will be required. (Monetary policy can be changed more quickly than can fiscal policy.)

Businesses must try to allow for the likely effects of government economic policy on their own sales forecasts, financial needs, and so on. Moreover not all business firms are likely to be affected in the same way or to the same extent. For example, a change in the sterling exchange rate might be far more important to a travel agent than to a bakery. That is why it is so difficult for any organisation such as the Confederation of British Industry (CBI) to claim to speak for 'business' as a whole. In this book we have tended to discuss aggregates; but it is crucial not to forget that actors in the market economy are individuals and firms, with their own particular problems and opportunities.

9.4 Two Schools of Thought

Economists hold widely different views about the desirability of various kinds of government action. Their views can differ for two kinds of reasons: they may not agree about the technical results of certain actions, or they may not agree about the desirability of certain objectives.

An example of disagreement about technical results would be the debate over the likely outcome of reducing the rate of increase in the money supply whether it will bring down the rate of inflation with little long-term effect on the rate of unemployment, or whether it will make little difference to inflation, but will exacerbate and prolong unemployment.

An example of disagreement about the desirability of objectives would be the debate about growth versus equality: to what extent a faster rate of economic growth is the best way to benefit the poor, rather than relying on redistributive measures of taxation and government spending. The debate may hinge on whether one is referring to 'absolute' or to 'relative' poverty.

A widely-advertised split in recent years has been between so-called 'Monetarists' and so-called 'Keynesians'. There has been some tendency for the two groups to shift ground towards each other, as the more extreme views have sometimes been disproved by events. In any event, there is a natural tendency for attention to focus on the areas of *disagreement*, rather than on topics where virtually all economists would be agreed. Thus the extent of the split may tend to be exaggerated.

Perhaps the most useful way to categorise two main schools of thought is between '**market-optimists**' and '**market-pessimists**'. In general the classical economists and the 'monetarists' would be counted as market-optimists and Keynes and his followers as market-pessimists. If one regards the question in terms of *laissez-faire* versus government intervention, then the former group would incline to leave the market alone, to be optimistic about the market and at the same time *pessimistic* about the likely results of government intervention. The Keynesians, in contrast, would be much more concerned about likely 'market failure', and far more inclined to advocate some kind of government action to 'correct' it. Categorising the two schools

	Market-optimists	*Market-pessimists*
Members		
a. Historical	Classical economists	Mercantilists
b. Modern	Monetarists	Keynesians
General views		
c. View of market	'Optimistic'	'Pessimistic'
d. Time horizon	Long run	Short run
e. Output determinant	'Real' factors	Total money demand
f. Major concern	Supply side	Aggregate demand
g. Adjustment mechanism	Price changes	Volume changes
h. View of government	'Pessimistic'	'Optimistic'
Specific views		
i. Economic growth	Harmed by 'stop-go'	Fiscal policy can help
j. Stabilisation	Harmful or futile	Desirable and feasible
k. Balance of payments	Float exchange rate	Import controls can help
l. Money supply rise	Leads to inflation, but leaves 'natural' rate of unemployment unchanged	Increases output, and reduces the level of unemployment
m. To cut inflation	Reduce money supply (demand-pull)	Prices and incomes policy (cost-push)

Fig. 9.11: Two schools of thought in political economy.

of thought in this way combines their economic and political views. Although most economists in the last 200 years can broadly be placed in one group or the other, political opinions, as well as economic views, have changed a good deal in that time. Thus even 'market-optimists' today may be prepared to tolerate a good deal more government intervention than many 'market-pessimists' might have wanted in the middle of the nineteenth century.

The contrast between the two groups can be useful if it is understood to refer to tendencies only, and is not taken to predict specific policy recommendations on any particular issue. Thus Fig. 9.11 outlines the general and some of the specific differences between market-optimists and market-pessimists.

It must be emphasised that the contrast is not absolute, but it exists. Most people would be concerned both with the short run and the long run: but it was Keynes (market-pessimist) who said: 'In the long run we're all dead.' Most people would recognise that government actions could be harmful as well as helpful; but it was Adam Smith (market-optimist) who said: 'Though the profusion of government must undoubtedly have retarded the natural progress of England toward wealth and improvement, it has not been able to stop it ... If governments' own extravagance does not ruin the state, that of their subjects never will.'

Work Section

A. Revision Questions

A1 What are the four main stages of the trade cycle?

A2 Name four different theories explaining the trade cycle.

A3 How was it suggested that the government might try to 'smooth out' the trade cycle? What is the implication for balancing the budget?

A4 Identify three problems in using fiscal policy to 'smooth out' the trade cycle.

A5 Why cannot the whole of that part of the National Debt 'eroded' by inflation be regarded as a real 'gain' to the government?

A6 In what two ways can governments try to control the money supply?

A7 Name two problems in trying to reduce inflation by controlling the growth of the money supply.

A8 Name two reasons why the government might desire a particular level of interest rates.

A9 Why won't increasing the money supply reduce the rate of interest in the long run? Why might it in the short run?

A10 What is indexation?

A11 Name three likely areas for government economic policy to focus on.

A12 What are the two main alternative ways to reduce the PSBR?

A13 Why may increasing taxation be thought undesirable?

A14 Why may reducing government spending be thought undesirable?

A15 In what two main ways can government finance the PSBR?

A16 What is meant by 'crowding out'?

A17 Between 1970 and 1980 roughly what proportion of the increase in money GDP went into real growth and what proportion into inflation?

A18 What is meant by the Medium Term Financial Strategy?

A19 How may fiscal policy affect business firms?

A20 Define 'income-elastic'.

A21 For what two different kinds of reasons may economists differ about the desirability of particular government actions?

A22 Why may the extent of the contrast between 'market-optimists' and 'market-pessimists' tend to be exaggerated?

A23 Of the two groups, which would tend to be concerned more with the short run, and less with the long run?

A24 Of the two groups, which would tend to be concerned more with 'supply' factors and less with 'demand' factors?

A25 Which of the two groups tends to emphasise the price mechanism as a key adjustment factor?

B. Exercises and Case Studies

B1 Refer to Fig. 9.4 on page 180. Update the chart by calculating government deficits (or surpluses) since 1981 as a percentage of Gross Domestic Product at market prices.

B2 Refer to Fig. 9.6 on page 182.
   a. Prepare a similar table to show the 'government view' of £600 m. of 14 per cent Treasury Stock 1982, issued in November 1976 at 98 and redeemed at par in March 1982. Assume that only four months' interest was paid in March 1977.
   b. Compare the outcome of the two government securities over their lives. How do you account for the difference?

B3 Refer to Fig. 9.9 on page 188. Use reference material to determine the approximate split between a 'real' change in GDP and the amount of inflation stemming from the increase in *money* GDP between 1980 and the most recent year for which figures are available.

B4 **The June 1979 Budget**
   The longer-term context
   Since the war, four main objectives of government economic policy have been to:
   1. Keep unemployment low;
   2. Promote economic growth;
   3. Keep inflation low;
   4. Stabilise the economy.
   a. Unemployment. By historical standards unemployment had been low until the mid-1970s. The proportion of the workforce unemployed was $1\frac{1}{2}$ per cent in the early 1960s, $2\frac{1}{2}$ per cent in the late 1960s, and $3\frac{1}{2}$ per cent in the early 1970s. But in the last few years, partly as a result of depressed conditions in all the industrialised countries, UK unemployment had risen to more than 5 per cent (about $1\frac{1}{4}$ m.). With evident overmanning in many UK manufacturing industries, and with an extra 1 m. young workers coming into the work force over the next five years (= 4 per cent of the work force), the medium-term prospects for employment seemed bleak. Apart from the personal unhappiness and the loss of output involved, the cost in social security benefits would be a heavy burden on the government budget.
   b. Economic growth. Post-war economic growth in real national income

per head, at about 2 per cent a year, had been at least as rapid as during any other 30-year period in UK peacetime history. But other countries had done better; and Germany in particular had enjoyed a post-war real growth rate of about 5 per cent a year. More recently the UK growth rate had been slowing down. In fact, latest estimates suggested virtually no growth at all between 1973 and 1980. Since the electorate had come to take growth for granted, and since many government spending plans had been based on the assumption of continued growth, any failure of the economy to recover quickly to its 'normal' growth trend could cause severe political problems.

c. Inflation. The average rate of UK inflation in the 20 years to 1967 was just under 4 per cent a year. Historically it was unusual not so much because of the annual *rate* of inflation experienced, but because prices had risen in every single year. There was no 'fluctuation' in the price level, but inexorable increase. Since the 1967 devaluation of the pound, however, the rate of inflation had accelerated to around 7 per cent a year over the next six years. That was bad enough; but since 1973 the rate of inflation had risen even more sharply to reach unprecedented year-after-year average peacetime rates of around 15 per cent a year. This was causing the most serious social and financial strains.

d. Stabilisation. Although the UK economy was thought to have suffered from 'stop-go' policies ever since the late 1950s, government policy continued to emphasise stabilisation as a major aim. Unfortunately since 1972 the economy appeared to be getting less stable. Real GDP growth of 8 per cent in 1973 was followed by two years of *decline* in GDP. Interest rates, which before 1957 used to change at most once a year, started twitching in the 1960s, and by the mid-1970s were fluctuating sharply within short periods. Since 1976 the Bank of England's Minimum Lending Rate had moved from 9 per cent to 15 per cent, then back down to 5 per cent, then back up to 14 percent – all within the space of less than three years. This instability was having many undesirable consequences. In particular, businesses were reluctant to invest in long-term projects, both because of the political and economic uncertainties and because high long-term interest rates made long-term borrowing appear extremely expensive.

One of the few bright spots recently had been the discovery of large quantities of oil and natural gas in the North Sea. But the pessimists were afraid that this 'windfall' might be squandered by financing expensive social programmes for a few years more than would otherwise have been possible. When the oil ran out (about the end of the century?) the underlying economic structure might be less competitive than ever. At all events, judged by four fundamental economic policy objectives, the new Chancellor of the Exchequer was confronted with a British economy which in the last five years or so had been failing sensationally on all four at once!

The shorter-term context

In May 1979 the Conservatives won the General Election on a Manifesto which promised income tax cuts and a reduction in government interference in the economy. The 'free market' philosophy fiercely advocated by the new Prime Minister appeared to mark a break with the practice of all previous post-war governments (of both parties). The previous Conservative government of 1970–74, under Mr Edward Heath, had reversed its similarly 'non-interventionist' Manifesto policies less than two years after taking office; and many experienced commentators seemed to be expecting a similar 'U-turn' from Mrs Thatcher – probably even more quickly.

There were a number of specific short-term difficulties facing the Chancellor of the Exchequer as he set about preparing his first Budget early in June 1979, some five weeks after taking office:

a. Government spending. Cuts in government spending are difficult to produce in a budget part of the way through the fiscal year (running to 31 March), since significant changes in policy commitments need time to take effect. Moreover the previous government had already tried to make some of the easier cuts in government spending, as well as leaving several 'post-dated cheques' for the incoming government.

b. Taxes. The Conservatives had promised significant cuts in taxes on income at all levels. If introduced in this first budget, any such cuts would apply (and reduce government revenue) for the *whole* current fiscal year (starting in April 1979). But any increases in *indirect* taxes could take effect for only *part* of the year to 31 March 1980. In particular, any increases in Value Added Tax would apply for only just over six months in the current fiscal year 1979–80, since there was a three-month time-lag in collecting the revenue.

c. Budget deficit. The Public Sector Borrowing Requirement (PSBR) for 1978–79 had amounted to £9½ m. (about £1 b. more than forecast), which amounted to some 5 per cent of gross domestic product. On unchanged policies the PSBR was estimated at £11¼ b. in 1979–80, roughly 6 per cent of GDP. Yet the Conservatives were committed to a PSBR of less than £8½ b. in the current year 1979–80.

d. Money supply. The money supply (defined as Sterling M3) was rising at a rate of about 13 per cent a year, above the top of the previous Chancellor's target range of 8 to 12 per cent. Inflation, as measured by the Retail Price Index, was running at 10 per cent a year and rising.

Question. What should the new Chancellor of the Exchequer do in his June 1979 budget?

B5 Refer to Fig. 9.1 on page 177. Try to fit the years since 1971 into the pattern shown. Which years seem to be hard to fit, if any? Why do you think this is?

B6 What should the Chancellor of the Exchequer do in *next* year's Budget? Why? What do you see as his main problems?

C. Essay Questions

C1 How does the trade cycle affect any specific business of your choice?

C2 What causes the trade cycle? Does it matter?

C3 Should the government aim to balance its budget? Why or why not?

C4 What are the advantages and disadvantages of using fiscal policy in demand management?

C5 'The "money supply" cannot be defined adequately; and even if it could, the monetary authorities cannot sufficiently control it.' Discuss.

C6 'Instead of being called "monetarists", those who subscribe to monetarist propositions might be called "realists". Real things in the long run are determined by real factors.' (Professor R. J. Ball.) Discuss.

C7 Are we 'all monetarists now'?

C8 Argue for or against Indexation as part of a government's approach to reducing the rate of inflation.

C9 Argue for or against a prices and incomes policy as part of a government's approach to reducing the rate of inflation.

C10 'The more the state plans, the more difficult planning becomes for individual firms.' (Professor F. A. Hayek.) Discuss.

C11 What are the broad objectives of governments' economic policy, and how may they be achieved?

C12 How might a decision by the government to deflate the economy affect the operation of a business?

C13 What are the main internal and external constraints hindering the process of government decision-making in economic matters?

C14 Would political economy be more successful if politicians weren't in charge of it?

C15 How would a market-optimist and a market-pessimist be likely to differ in their views of (a) economic growth, (b) the sterling exchange rate, and (c) unemployment?

Part IV Industry Study

Chapter 10

The Housing Market

10.1 The Construction Industry

10.2 Demand for Private Housing
10.2.1 The Existing Stock of Houses
10.2.2 Population and Social Trends
10.2.3 The Level of Disposable Incomes
10.2.4 House Prices
10.2.5 Cost of Mortgage Finance
10.2.6 Public Sector Housebuilding and Rents
10.2.7 Existing Owners Moving

10.3 Supply of Housing
10.3.1 Costs
10.3.2 The Housebuilding Cycle
10.3.3 Variations Between Small and Large House-building Firms

10.4 Housing Stock
10.4.1 Existing Stock of Houses
10.4.2 Changes in Housing Stock

Objective: *To note how the construction industry is split; to discuss the main influences on demand for private housing; to describe some important aspects of supply; and to analyse annual changes to the existing stock of houses by tenure.*

Synopsis: *Government policy affects house-building more than most industries. New house-building represents only about one fifth of the construction industry's total output. The industry contains many small firms, mostly specialist sub-contractors.*
   Houses last a long time, so the number of new houses built each year is only a small proportion of the existing stock. About 80 per cent of the average cost is covered by mortgage finance. The rate of mortgage interest – which is tax-deductible – varies in line with the general level of interest rates. In recent years council house rents have risen sharply and tenants have been encouraged to buy their homes.

The four main elements in house-building costs are: land, materials, labour, and credit. Since 1968 the number of new houses built has fallen, especially in the public sector. Gross investment in housing showed a four-year cycle until a sharp decline in the years after 1978.

More than half of all houses are owner-occupied, about one third rented from local authorities. In the private sector since the war there has been a continuing move from renting to owning, partly due to rent controls.

10.1 The Construction Industry

The construction industry, of which house-building is part, is mainly domestic. It is of interest in the context of macro-economics because government policy probably affects it more than most industries.

New house-building is only about one fifth of total construction industry output. Figure 10.1 analyses the industry's output between its three main divisions:
1. New work and repair and maintenance work.
2. Housing and other (industrial and commercial).
3. Private sector and public sector (mainly local authorities).

Percentages	New works				Repair and maintenance			
	Housing	Other	=	Total	Housing	Other	=	Total
45% Public	6	18*	=	24	7	14	=	21
55% Private	12	24†	=	36	12	7	=	19
Total	18	42	=	60	19	21	=	40

* = Nationalised industries, schools, hospitals, roads
† = Factories, offices, shops

Fig. 10.1: Construction industry: analysis of output, 1981.

Much building work is still craft-based and labour-intensive, with little scope for economies of scale. Moreover scheduling all the various activities would be difficult for a single large firm. Thus the construction industry contains many small firms. About 95 per cent of firms employ fewer than 25 people and account for 30 per cent of output. But the 1 per cent of firms employing more than 115 people account for 50 per cent of output. This wide variation in size makes it impossible to speak of a 'typical' firm in the industry.

The small firms tend to be specialist sub-contractors, such as carpenters, electricians, painters and plumbers. The main building contractors use them to minimise their 'fixed' costs in a fluctuating market for new houses; while the sub-contractors aim to survive the ups and downs in demand for new buildings by concentrating on the more stable repair and maintenance work.

10.2 Demand for Private Housing

Many factors affect the demand for private housing, which we discuss in this section in turn: the existing stock of houses; population and social trends; the level of disposable incomes; house prices; cost of mortgage finance; public sector house-building and rents; and existing owners moving.

10.2.1 The Existing Stock of Houses

The number of new houses built each year is very small relative to the stock of existing houses. This is because most houses last a very long time. Thus 1982's 180,000 new houses represented less than 1 per cent of the stock of 22 m. houses. Of all houses in Great Britain, about 30 per cent were built before 1919, 20 per cent between 1919 and 1944, and 50 per cent since 1945. (For Greater London the split is more nearly equal between the three periods.) About 10 per cent of houses in use are over 100 years old. In the end their age affects the rate at which existing houses are demolished; though in the short term demolitions and repairs can be postponed.

10.2.2 Population and Social Trends

The 'bulge' of births in the 1960s (see Fig. 1.12 on page 21) affected schools in the 1970s. The same 'bulge' will cause more households than usual to be formed throughout the 1980s. The gradual fall in the average number of people per household (from 4.2 in 1931 to 3.1 in 1961 and to 2.6 in 1981) has also increased demand for housing units.

10.2.3 The Level of Disposable Incomes

Expenditure on housing is probably related to 'permanent income' (see 3.2.3 on page 55) rather than to current income levels. Thus expectations about future real income levels may be important in making long-term decisions about housing requirements. Total consumer expenditure on 'housing' (including local rates and water charges, but excluding depreciation of dwellings) has risen from about 10 per cent of total consumer expenditure in 1960 to $12\frac{1}{2}$ per cent in 1970 and 15 per cent in 1980.

10.2.4 House Prices

Figure 10.2 shows quite sharp variations since 1970 between average house prices and retail prices in general. There have been peaks in 1973–74 and in 1979–80, and troughs in 1977 and 1982.

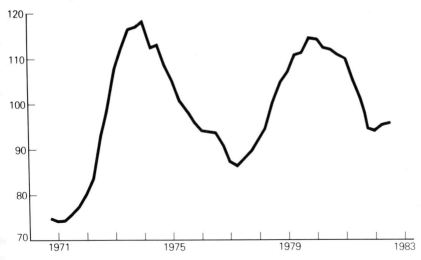

Fig. 10.2: House prices relative to retail prices, 1971 to 1982.

10.2.5 Cost of Mortgage Finance

The availability and cost of mortgage finance affects demand for private houses. About 80 per cent of the average purchase price of building society-financed houses is covered by the mortgage. The banks have recently increased their share of net mortgage advances, from under 10 per cent during the 1970s to more than 25 per cent in 1981–82. Figure 10.3 shows the varying cost of mortgage finance since 1971, which is related to changes in the general level of interest rates. Tax relief on mortgage interest was limited from 1974 to 1983 to loans of not more than £25,000. So inflation since 1974 (see Fig. 6.4 on page 118) reduced the 'real' mortgage ceiling for tax relief by more than two thirds.

10.2.6 Public Sector House-building and Rents

Public sector house-building has fallen sharply in recent years, from 170,000 completions in 1977 to about 50,000 in 1982 (see Fig. 10.6 on page 204). Figure 10.4 shows that average council house rents rose by about 40 per cent in real terms between 1980 and 1982; and government policy encouraged tenants to buy council houses on favourable terms. This led to about half a million homes being transferred from the public to the private sector between 1980 and 1983. But in any year local authorities may either overspend or underspend the amount made available by central government for public housebuilding. The dispersion of decision-making in the public sector makes it impossible to regard 'government' as monolithic with respect to housing policy.

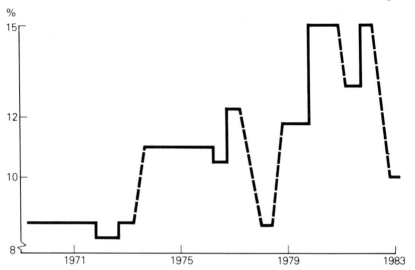

Fig. 10.3: Building society mortgage interest rates, 1971 to 1983.

10.2.7 Existing Owners Moving

In addition to the demand for houses by 'first-time purchasers', another major factor in the housing market is demand from existing owners who are moving. But since purchases and sales between existing owners offset each other, in looking at aggregate statistics it is normal to consider only the *net* new

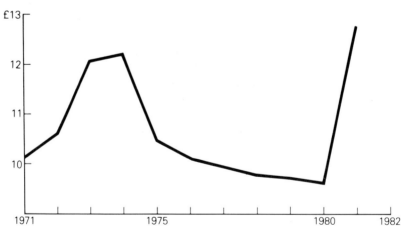

Fig. 10.4: Average council house rents, 1971 to 1982 (in constant 1982 pounds per week).

demand. Certainly the 'second-hand' market is extremely important in the housing market: indeed, some of the older houses must have had dozens of owners. The main reasons for moving would probably be related to a change in income and wealth, a change in household status (for example, when children are grown-up) or a change of jobs.

10.3 Supply of Housing

10.3.1. Costs

Average house prices rose 4.7-fold between 1971 and 1981, compared with a 3.7-fold increase in the Retail Price Index. There are four major elements in building houses: land, materials, labour, and credit. Fig. 10.5 sets out changes in each of these since 1971.

1975 = 100	Site values	Housing materials	Construction earnings	Treasury Bill rates (%)	House prices
1971	56	53	47	7– 4	48
1972	94	57	53	4– 9	63
1973	146	68	69	7–13	86
1974	145	85	80	13–11	91
1975	100	100	100	9–12	100
1976	100	123	112	8–15	108
1977	106	146	125	12– 4	119
1978	129	158	140	6–12	143
1979	183	182	161	11–16	183
1980	241	218	191	17–13	220
1981	250	237	216	11–16	225
1982		256		14– 8	

Fig. 10.5: Changes in building costs, 1971 to 1982.

Housing materials rose faster than average earnings in construction between 1975 and 1977, but otherwise the two have risen roughly in line with each other. In contrast, site values rose very rapidly between 1971 and 1974, then fell back sharply in 1975 and stayed flat until 1977. Thereafter site prices rose faster than other items.

10.3.2 **The Housebuilding Cycle**

Figure 10.6 shows (in thousands) the number of houses completed between 1968 and 1982. Clearly there has been a substantial decline, from 425,000 in 1968 to 180,000 in 1982. The number of private houses completed fell by around 40 per cent over the period (from 220,000 to 130,000), while public house completions fell by no less than 75 per cent (from 200,000 to 50,000).

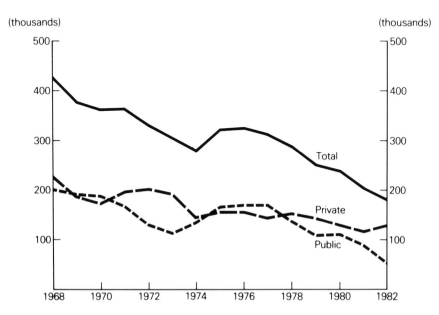

Fig. 10.6: Number of houses completed, 1968 to 1982.

The number of demolitions also fell sharply, from 120,000 in 1968 to 50,000 in 1982. The reduction of 70,000 demolitions is significant: it represents about 40 per cent of 1982 completions.

Figure 10.7 shows the expenditure (in real terms) on gross domestic fixed capital formation in dwellings between 1968 and 1982. The picture here is not quite the same as completions, partly because houses take time to build, and partly because the average cost of a house increased in real terms during the period. Figure 10.7 shows the four-year building cycle between 1968 and 1977; and the severe drop since 1978.

10.3.3 **Variations Between Small and Large House-building Firms**

Differences between small building firms and larger ones make it hard to define any 'typical' firm. In phases of rapid expansion, such as 1972–73 and 1975–76, many small firms can keep their profit margins high by means of well-balanced operating plans. They maintain a high volume of work by

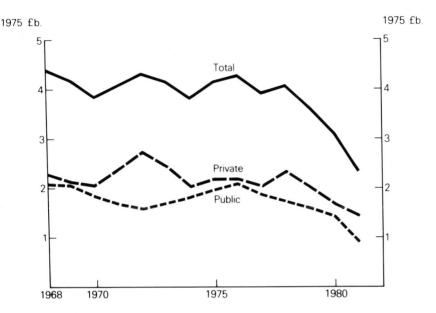

Fig. 10.7: Gross fixed capital formation in dwellings 1968 to 1982 (in constant 1975 pounds).

acquiring medium-sized sites only when needed and turning each one over quickly. They keep costs low by incurring few overheads and where possible financing each stage of development from building society advances. The net result is to provide a fast high rate of return on low capital employed.

Large and medium-sized firms try to meet the heavy pressure of demand for houses in all price ranges. But their scale and structure are different from smaller firms. They may keep the volume of work high, but can seldom turn sites over quickly because of their size. In addition to high operating costs, they may incur large head office overheads, with substantial sums tied up in **work in progress**. Increasing the size of 'land banks', often with rapidly inflating prices, is expensive; ensuring the flow of work requires large stocks of materials; and labour costs may rise unduly if shortages force firms to use marginal sub-contractors.

Under such conditions returns may be neither quick nor high. Firms tend to borrow heavily at high short-term cost in order to solve their immediate cash flow problems. Possible sudden changes in supply and demand factors can then leave larger firms highly vulnerable.

10.4 Housing Stock

10.4.1 Existing Stock of Houses

More than half of all houses are owner-occupied, about one third are rented from local authorities ('council houses'), and the remainder from private landlords. The main exception to this pattern is in Scotland, where more than half of all houses are council houses.

Figure 10.8 sets out the distribution of houses by tenure in 1971 and 1981. The main changes have been an increase of 2.2 m. houses (11½ per cent), and a noticeable switch from private renting to owner-occupation. The latter has been partly due to rent controls.

Millions	*TOTAL* (%)	*PUBLIC* (%)	*PRIVATE* (%)	*Owner-occupied* (%)	*Rental* (%)
End of 1971	19.0 *100*	5.9 *30*	13.1 *70*	9.6 *50*	3.5 *20*
End of 1981	21.2 *100*	6.6 *31*	14.6 *69*	12.0 *57*	2.6 *12*
Change (10 years)	2.2	0.7	1.5	2.4	(0.9)

Fig. 10.8: Distribution of houses by tenure, 1971 and 1981.

10.4.2 Changes in Housing Stock

Figure 10.9 analyses reasons for the change in housing stock between 1971 and 1981, splitting the decade into two five-year periods. The average annual rate of increase in total houses has remained fairly steady at about 220,000 per year; but whereas this was split evenly between the public and private sectors between 1971 and 1976, the net addition to private sector houses has been much larger between 1976 and 1981.

Thousands	Public Sector			Private Sector		
	1971–76	1976–81	*Total*	1971–76	1976–81	*Total*
New Construction	+ 135	+ 120	+ 130	+ 165	+ 130	+ 150
Demolitions, etc.	– 0	– 20	– 20	– 75	– 20	– 40
Council houses sold	– 25	– 60	– 40	+ 25	+ 60	+ 40
Total	+ 110	+ 40	+ 70	+ 115	+ 170	+ 150

Fig. 10.9: Annual average changes in tenure of housing stock 1971 to 1981.

Work Section

A. Revision Questions

In the construction industry:

A1 What are the three main divisions?

A2 Roughly what proportion is new housebuilding of total output?

A3 What proportion of output is produced by firms with less than 25 people?

A4 How do main building contractors try to cope with new housing fluctuations?

A5 How do smaller sub-contractors try to cope with new housing fluctuations?

A6 Why is annual production of new houses such a small proportion of the existing stock?

A7 Roughly what proportion of all houses in use was built:
a. before 1880?   b. before 1918?   c. since 1945?

A8 How will the 'bulge' of births in the 1960s affect demand for houses in the 1980s?

A9 How does inflation affect the cost of mortgage finance?

A10 How did council house rents change between 1980 and 1981?

A11 What are the four major cost elements in building houses?

A12 Which two cost elements have fluctuated most in real terms, and which two least?

A13 How has the annual rate of new houses built changed in the dozen years since 1970? In what respect have private and public sectors differed?

A14 How has the annual rate of demolitions changed since 1968?

A15 Name two reasons why real expenditure on building new houses shows a rather different year-to-year pattern from new housing completions.

A16 What proportion of the housing stock in Great Britain is council housing?

A17 Roughly what proportion of new houses built is offset by demolitions?

A18 Why did the stock of public housing grow so little between 1976 and 1981?

A19 How many council houses were purchased annually by tenants in 1976–1981? What proportion of council houses does this represent each year?

A20 Roughly what proportion of the existing stock of houses is represented by net annual additions?

B. Exercises and Case Studies

B1   Refer to Fig. 10.1.
     What is the split of total construction industry output in 1981 between:
     a. New work and repair and maintenance work?
     b. Housing and other?
     c. Private sector and public sector?

B2   Firms employing between 25 and 115 people account for what proportion
     of:
     a. The total number of firms?
     b. Industry output?

B3   From reference material update:
     a. Fig. 10.2.
     b. Fig. 10.3.
     c. Fig. 10.4.
     d. Fig. 10.5.
     e. Fig. 10.6.
     f. Fig. 10.7.
     g. Fig. 10.8.

B4   Refer to Figs. 10.8 and 10.9.
     Account for the change in housing stock between the end of 1981 and
     the latest year for which figures are available.

C. Essay Questions

C1   How would you expect rent controls to affect the housing market?
C2   How should an optimal level of slum clearance be reached? What role
     if any, should the government play?
C3   Why is the availability of mortgage funds important in influencing the
     amount of private housebuilding?
C4   Is tax relief in respect of mortgage interest desirable?
C5   If other businessmen use housing starts as 'leading indicators' of change:
     in economic conditions, what should builders use?
C6   How can governments affect the demand for private housing?
C7   How can governments affect the supply of private housing?
C8   Should council houses be subsidised out of general tax revenue?
C9   Should local authority housing be privatised?
C10 Should private ownership of housing be (a) forbidden? (b) tolerated?, o
     (c) encouraged?

Abbreviations

CAP = Common Agricultural Policy (of EEC)
CBI = Confederation of British Industry
CCA = Current Cost Accounting
CPP = Constant Purchasing Power (accounting)
CSO = Central Statistical Office
EEC = European Economic Community
EMS = European Monetary System
GATT = General Agreement on Tariffs and Trade
GDP = Gross Domestic Product
GNP = Gross National Product
IMF = International Monetary Fund
LDC = Less Developed Country
MMC = Monopolies and Mergers Commission
MNC = Multinational Company
MPC = Marginal Propensity to Consume
MTFS = Medium Term Financial Strategy
NIC = Newly Industrialising Countries
NNP = Net National Product
OECD = Organisation for Economic Co-operation and Development
OPEC = Organisation of Petroleum Exporting Countries
plc = public limited company
PSBR = Public Sector Borrowing Requirement
RPI = Retail Price Index
VAT = Value Added Tax

Circular Flow Model

C = Consumption
G = Government spending (on goods and services)
I = Investment (real, private sector)
M = Imports
S = Savings
T = Taxes
X = Exports
Y = National Income

Quantity Theory of Money

M = Money supply
P = General level of Prices
T = Volume of Trade
V = Velocity of circulation

Glossary

refers to another Glossary entry.

Accelerator Theory: Hypothesis that a change in demand for consumer goods causes even larger changes in demand for capital goods* used to make them.

Aggregate: Total, which risks ignoring heterogeneity* of components.

Agoraphobia: 'fear of markets'.

Annuity: Regular annual amount paid or received for a given number of years (in personal affairs, until death).

Average Cost: Total cost divided between number of units produced.

Bads: Opposite of economic goods*. Objects of which people prefer less.

Balance of Payments: Balance of (nation's) payments and receipts of foreign currencies. May refer to current* or overall* balance.

Balancing Item: Residual unexplained item in balance of payments account

Bank of England: UK central bank* whose main responsibility is integrity of currency. Also manages the National Debt*.

Bankruptcy: Legal process of sharing out one's assets between creditors who are owed in total a larger amount.

Barter: Exchanging goods against other goods rather than money.

Bilateral: 'Two-sided', usually referring to international trade deals; in contrast to normal 'multi-lateral' ('many-sided') deals using (international money.

Black Economy: Unrecorded economic transactions, which need not be illegal. Also called: informal, hidden, parallel, underground, etc economy.

Bretton Woods System: International monetary system from 1945 to 1971 with national currencies 'fixed' against US dollar (itself 'fixed' against gold at $35 per ounce), subject to occasional changes on fundamental disequilibrium.* Abandoned due to US inflation.*

Budget: Plan for a period normally expressed in money. A business budget may cover cash, profit, production, sales, etc. A government budget relates revenue from taxation* and other sources to government spending,* the difference being the budget surplus or deficit.

Capital Consumption: Estimated decline in economic value of capital goods,* caused by physical wear and tear, technical obsolescence, etc. In national income statistics calculated at current replacement cost.*

Capital Formation: Usually regarded as new expenditure on capital goods;* but, in principle, value of capital goods could be increased by using existing ones better.

Capital-Output Ratio: The relation between the value of capital assets employed and the annual value of the goods and services they produce.

Central Bank: Banker to government and to clearing banks,* often with a monopoly over issue of paper banknotes. In UK, the Bank of England.*

Centrally Planned Economy: Economy in which use of factors of production* is directed by a central government planning agency using compulsion, rather than by individual voluntary market participants.

Chain of Production: Network of producers, from primary,* through secondary* and tertiary* producers, to final consumer.

Circular Flow Model: Model* of national economy, showing flows of income between groups.

Classical Economists: In England (and Scotland) school of political economists from about 1776 to 1870, including Adam Smith, David Ricardo, and John Stuart Mill. Advocated *laissez-faire** and free trade;* and opposed mercantilist policies.*

Commerce: Exchange of services or wholesale merchandise.

Comparative Advantage: Theory that value of output will be maximised if each of two or more parties specialises in those productive activities in which he has a greater advantage (or smaller disadvantage). Held, with qualifications, to justify a policy of free trade.*

Competition: 'A discovery procedure' – F. A. Hayek. Process of rivalry between entrepreneurs* which tends to reduce costs of production to lowest possible levels. Actual 'imperfect' competition* is not to be confused with hypothetical 'perfect' competition.*

Constant Purchasing Power (CPP) Accounting: Method of inflation accounting which treats money amounts of different dates as 'foreign currencies', using the Retail Price Index* as the 'exchange rate'.

Consumer Durable: Consumer good which lasts for some time, e.g. car, washing machine. Does not usually refer to dwellings (treated as capital goods* in national income statistics), nor some consumer goods of less value which last for years (e.g. curtains, books).

Consumer Surplus: The e.cess of a good's subjective value (V) to a consumer above its market price (P). If a consumer would be willing to pay up to V for something, then (V − P) may be thought of as the consumer's 'profit'.

Consumption (C): Process of deriving utility from a commodity or service, which need not imply 'using it up', e.g. looking at a picture.

Cost/Benefit Analysis: Process of comparing activities in money terms which tries to allow for 'social' costs (and benefits) ('externalities') as well as financial and opportunity costs and benefits. For example, where to site London's third airport.

Cost-Push Inflation: Type of inflation held to be caused by firms 'passing on' increases in costs (whether from wages, imports, or taxes), but requiring 'accommodating' increase in money supply.*

Counter-Cyclical Action: Government attempt to reduce amplitude of trade cycle,* e.g. by running a surplus in time of boom.

Crowding out: Process by which government spending reduces private spending, in the extreme by an equivalent amount.

Currency Debasement: Process of reducing purchasing power of currency (money), originally by fraudulently adding base metal to precious metal, now by more sophisticated methods.

Current Account: (Also called 'Demand deposit' or 'Sight deposit'.) Account with bank which (usually) bears no interest and is withdrawable 'on demand', i.e. with no period of notice. Contrasted with Deposit account* (also called 'Time deposit').

Current Balance: Balance of payments* on 'current' account of international trade in goods and services.

Current Cost Accounting (CCA): Form of current value accounting (not strictly 'inflation' accounting) which uses current (usually replacement*) costs in place of original historical costs.

Customs Union: Free trade area* between countries with common external tariff.*

Deficit Financing: Policy of running (permanent) deficit on government budget,* financed immediately by borrowing, often ultimately by inflation.*

Deflation: Fall in general level of prices, *not* simply a reduction in the rate of increase.

Demand Management: Government manipulation of the aggregate demand for goods and services, by fiscal,* monetary,* or other means.

Demand-Pull Inflation: Inflation caused by excessive aggregate money demand in relation to output.

Deposit Account: (Also called 'Time deposit'.) Account with a bank, withdrawable by giving a definite period of notice (often seven days) and bearing interest. Contrasted with Current account.*

Depreciation (asset): Amount written off cost of fixed asset and charged as expense in business accounts; spreads the total net cost over the fixed asset's economic life, usually in equal instalments.

Depreciation (currency): Reduction in value of domestic currency against foreign currencies in a floating exchange rate* system.

Devaluation: Reduction in value of domestic currency against foreign currencies in a fixed exchange rate* system.

Direct Investment: Investment abroad including control of a business enterprise. Contrasted with Portfolio investment*.

Direct Tax: Tax levied directly on the taxpayer, such as income tax or corporation tax. Contrasted with indirect tax.*

Dirty Float: System of floating exchange rates* subject to government intervention, ostensibly only to 'smooth out' trends.

Discount Rate: Interest rate used in making present value calculations.

Disposable Income: Personal income less direct income taxes.

Dividend: Cash payment to shareholder out of profits, declared by a company's directors.

Dividend Controls: Compulsory restrictions on amount of dividends payable by companies, in force in UK for 10 years between 1966 and 1979.

Division of Labour: Specialisation.

Dumping: Selling goods abroad at less than 'cost', or at less than selling price in home market.

Durable Consumption Goods: See Consumer durable.*

Economic Good: Scarce valuable resource. 'Goods' are tangible, 'services' intangible, but the term 'goods' may include both.

Economic Growth: Increase in real national income* per head.

Economic Rent: The excess of a factor of production's market price over the minimum amount ('transfer earnings'*) needed to attract it from an alternative use.

Economies of Scale: Reductions in unit costs arising from increase in scale of operation, e.g. due to greater technical efficiency of larger plant sizes, spreading of fixed costs over more units, etc. There may also be *diseconomies* of scale, often due to organisational factors, e.g. increased difficulty of communication or cost of administration.

Elasticity of Demand: Responsiveness of demand to a change in a variable, usually price or income. If volume of demand changes proportionally more than the other variable, it is said to be 'elastic' with respect to that other variable; if not, 'inelastic'.

Entrepreneur: Individual with initiative to seek profit* by organising factors of production* with a view to sale.

Equilibrium: State of 'balance', with no inducement to change. In the circular flow model,* the level of national income* at which aggregate withdrawals* equal aggregate injections.*

Equity: Residual financial interest in a firm's assets.

European Monetary System (EMS): Arrangement for monetary cooperation within EEC, involving (a) 'snake'* – which the UK has not yet joined – within which exchange rates of members' currencies move, (b) fund into which members deposit 20 per cent of their gold and currency reserves, and (c) lending and borrowing facilities.

Exchange Controls: Government restrictions on free movement of foreign (and domestic) currencies across national boundaries. Abolished by UK in 1979.

Expenditure Taxes: Taxes on consumer spending, e.g. Value Added Tax.

Exports (X): Domestically-produced goods or services sold to foreigners.

Externality: Social cost or benefit not taken into account by private decision-makers.

Factor Cost: As opposed to market price: in national income statistics, GDP* at factor cost equals gross domestic production at market prices less expenditure taxes, plus subsidies.*

Factor of Production: Scarce resource which contributes to valuable output.

Financial Institutions: Major organisations in the capital and money markets, such as commercial banks, insurance companies, pension funds.

Financial Investment: See Investment, Financial.*

Finished Goods: Stocks of completed goods, held for sale.

Fiscal Policy: Government policy with regard to spending and taxation, contrasted with (or complementing) monetary policy.*

Fixed Cost: Cost which is fixed (in the short run) regardless of the volume of output (in contrast to a variable cost*).

Fixed Exchange Rate: International monetary system under which rate of exchange of two currencies is 'fixed' within a narrow band, and alterable only infrequently (by means of devaluation* or revaluation*).

Floating Exchange Rate: International monetary system under which rate of exchange of two currencies is not fixed but free to 'float' according to market conditions of supply and demand, possibly modified by government intervention ('dirty floats'*).

Forecasting: Guessing the uncertain future, often in quantified form. 'A pretence of knowing what would have happened if what did happen hadn't —Ralph Harris.

Fractional Reserve Banking: System under which banks can lend many times as much money as has been deposited with them; hence their reserves are only a 'fraction' of the total amount lent out to customers.

Free Good: Desired, but not scarce, resource, which has no market value.

Free Trade: System of inter-regional trade without government restrictions (such as tariffs,* quotas,* exchange controls,* etc.).

Free Trade Area: Group of nations with free trade between them, but with different external tariffs* (in contrast with Customs union*).

Frictional Unemployment: Unemployment of labour due to continual shifting of employees between jobs, stemming from lack of knowledge about jobs, wage-rates, etc. in labour market.

Full Employment: Maximum practicable level of employment of labour, but less than 100 per cent due to frictional unemployment.*

Fundamental Disequilibrium: Long-term disequilibrium in exchange rate of one currency against another, held to justify devaluation* or revaluation under Bretton Woods fixed exchange rate system.*

Gilt-Edged Security: UK government loan stock.

Gold Reserves: Official government holdings of gold.

Gold Standard: International monetary system under which all currencies have a fixed exchange rate* against gold, with paper banknotes convertible on demand into gold at that rate.

Government Spending (G): Comprises (a) current spending on goods and services, (b) capital formation, and (for some purposes) (c) transfer payments.*

Graduated Tax: Tax whose rates increase as income (or expenditure or capital) increases. Contrasted with a flat-rate (proportional) tax.

Gross Domestic Product (GDP): Measure of gross output of economy before allowing for capital consumption,* estimated in three ways: (a) people's income, (b) people's expenditure, and (c) firms' output (value added*).

Gross Fixed Capital Formation: Capital investment in fixed assets, such as land improvements; buildings; plant, machinery and equipment.

Gross National Product (GNP): GDP* plus net property income from abroad.

Heterogeneous: 'Of different kinds', not homogeneous.* Aggregates* or averages* may need interpreting with caution if dissimilar kinds of items have been added to calculate them, e.g. 'the labour force', 'UK industrial companies'.

Homogeneous: 'Of the same kind', hence legitimately additive.

Hot Money: In international monetary system, short-term capital which is free to move from one financial centre to another depending on relative interest rates, confidence, etc.

Human Capital: Abilities of individuals, either inherited or acquired by 'investment' (in education, training, etc.). In a non-slave economy, not a marketable asset as such, but individuals can increase their own future earning power by diligent study!

Hyper-Inflation: *very* rapid rate of inflation,* of at least 50 per cent per month.

Imperfect Competition: The best kind of competition we have (usually), since perfect competition* is rare. The 'imperfections' stem from ignorance, transactions costs, entry barriers, etc.

Imports (M): Foreign-produced goods or services purchased domestically.

Import Quotas: Compulsory limit, by volume or value, on the amount of specific foreign goods or services allowed to be imported in a period.

Import-Substitute: Domestically-produced good which competes with imports.

Import Tariff: Tax which raises the price of imports to domestic consumer.

Income-Effect: The extent to which people may prefer leisure to working as their income increases.

Income-Elastic: The extent to which demand for a good varies with income.

Incomes Policy: See Prices and incomes policy.*

Income Tax: Tax payable on personal incomes, such as wages, dividends, or profits of unincorporated firms. Basic rate is 30 per cent, in addition to which there are graduated* rates on taxable incomes above about £15,000, plus a surcharge on investment incomes above £7,500.

Indexation: Process of linking money amounts to the rate of inflation as measured by the Retail Price Index*, e.g. government securities, pensions, tax thresholds.

Indirect Tax: Tax, usually on expenditure, which is not directly assessed on the individuals bearing it. Thus business firms *pay* Value Added Tax, although customers *bear* it.

Industrial Revolution: Transformation of the British economy between 1750 and 1850 through adoption of machine methods of production resulting in division of labour★ and significant economies of scale.★

Industry: Business activity, often manufacturing.

Infant Industry: New firm or industry, argued to 'require' protection★ until it is able to compete with established rivals, either at home or (more probably) abroad.

Inflation: Rise in the general level of money prices, usually measured by the (annual) rate of increase in the Retail Price Index.★

Inflation Accounting: See Constant Purchasing Power (CPP) accounting.★

Inflation Premium: Part of the rate of interest, depending on the anticipated future rate of inflation.

Injection: In the circular flow model,★ an addition to the income of domestic households or firms that does not arise from the spending of domestic firms or households respectively. Examples: Investment (I), Government spending on goods and services (G), Exports (X).

Institutions: See Financial institutions.★

Interest-Elastic: The extent to which an economic aggregate, like saving or investment, varies with a change in the rate of interest.

Interest Rate: Annual rate of compensation for borrowing or lending money for a period of time, comprising: (a) pure time-preference, (b) risk premium, and (c) inflation premium.

Intermediaries: Business entities which act 'between' producers and consumers, e.g. distributors, or financial organisations which split borrowing from lending and may alter the time-maturity of loans.

Intermediate Goods: Goods used to produce other goods, not themselves for direct consumption.

International Monetary Fund (IMF): World agency formed in 1945 to act as a sort of 'central bank' to trading nations.

Investment, Financial: Acquisition of ownership of a financial security, often from an existing holder. Hence need not imply 'real' investment, i.e. new capital formation.

Investment, Real: Capital formation, investment in fixed assets, to be used in production of other goods or in stocks (inventories).

Invisible Trade: International trade in services, such as banking, insurance, shipping, tourism.

J-Curve Effect: Phenomenon under which currency devaluation★ may worsen the balance of payments in the short run, due to price-inelasticity of imports.★

Keynesians: Followers of J. M. Keynes, a Cambridge economist who was influential from 1919 to his death in 1946 and beyond. 'Keynesian' doctrine may now differ considerably from anything JMK himself said.

Laissez-Faire: 'Leave alone'. Doctrine of political economy urging no government intervention in economic affairs as a rule (though there are several exceptions). Advocated by most classical economists from Adam Smith (1776) to John Stuart Mill (1871).

Lame Ducks: Failing firms calling for financial help from taxpayers via government.

Leading Indicators: Economic statistics thought to signal future 'turn' in the trade cycle.★

Leisure: Time freely available, in which person is voluntarily not occupied in work.

Less Developed Country (LDC): Country with relatively low level of national income per head, e.g. Afghanistan, Tanzania. This characteristic encompasses countries which may otherwise be heterogeneous.★

Limited Company: Form of business organisation with a separate legal identity, whose owners (shareholders) are not personally liable for the entity's debts (unlike members of a partnership firm). Larger companies are now called 'public limited company' (plc).

Local Authorities: Government organisations elected regionally, and responsible for public spending on education, environment, etc. Half their funds come from central government grants, the rest from local rates (property taxes), rents, etc.

Loss: Negative profit. Though not the aim, often the result of business enterprise.

Marginal Cost: The additional cost incurred by producing one more unit of output.

Marginal Propensity to Consume (MPC): Proportion of any change in income which 'tends' to be spent on consumption.★

Market: May mean the 'capital market' for loans and equity (financial securities★). More generally refers to the system of voluntary exchange of goods and services based on competition★ and private ownership of factors of production,★ in which consumer preferences are signalled to producers via market prices which also reflect the relative scarcity of resources.

Market Imperfections: Respects in which a market fails to meet criteria for 'perfect' competition,★ e.g. ability of sellers to influence demand (by product differentiation, advertising, etc.); barriers to entry; imperfect knowledge about prices and profits.

Market-Optimist: Someone who thinks in the long run the market system, aided by the price mechanism, will usually produce the goods better without government intervention.

Market-Pessimist: Someone who thinks in the short run the market system, hampered by price inflexibility ('stickiness'), can usefully be 'corrected' by government intervention.

Market Segmentation: The process of analysing conditions in a market to enable an enterprise to focus on a specific part of the total market. The basis may be demographic (age, region, income, sex), technical, etc.

Medium of Exchange: The primary function of money, to act as a means by which goods and services can be exchanged indirectly, as opposed to direct exchange by barter.★

Medium Term Financial Strategy (MTFS): Setting targets several years ahead for key aggregates,★ such as the money supply★ and the Public Sector Borrowing Requirement.★

Mercantilist Policies: Policies of government intervention in seventeenth and eighteenth centuries opposed by Adam Smith and the classical economists. The three 'pillars' of the mercantile system were said to be: the Corn Laws, the Navigation Acts, and the Protection of Industry.

Merger: A combination of two (or more) formerly independent business units into a single enterprise.

'Merit Goods': Goods or services about which governments think individuals should not be allowed to choose, either because of lack of knowledge about their effects, good or bad, or because individuals might knowingly make the 'wrong' choice.

Mixed Economy: An economy in which some of the means of production are privately-owned and some are owned by the government. Nearly all economies are 'mixed' in this sense, but the proportions vary widely between 'free market' economies and centrally-planned 'command' economies.★

Model: Simplified representation of a state of affairs aiming to explain how key variables are related.

Monetarists: Economists emphasising importance of monetary★ as against fiscal★ policy. Often contrasted with Keynesians.★

Monetary Policy: Control of the banking and monetary system, usually by a government.

Money Supply: The quantity of 'money', which may be defined in several ways, e.g. M1 = Notes and coins plus current accounts★ with banks; M3 = M1 plus deposit accounts★ with banks.

Monopoly: 'Single' or dominating seller in a market. In the UK legally reckoned to be a seller with over 25 per cent of the 'market' (precise definition of which is crucial). The emphasis is on the *market*, not on 'concentration of production' which may overlook competitive imports.

Multinational Company (MNC): Company which operates in many countries, usually with production facilities as well as marketing operations.

Multiplier: In the circular flow model,★ the final change in national income★ divided by a causal change in government spending★ or other injection.★

National Debt: Aggregate debt of government, accumulated by borrowing, eroded in real terms by inflation.★

National Income (Y): Value of output of economy, plus net property income from abroad (= Gross National Product★), less allowance for capital consumption.★ Sometimes also called Net National Product.

Nationalised Industry: 'Public corporation'. Firm or industry owned by government. Precise definition somewhat vague, e.g. British Leyland, London Transport, UK Atomic Energy Authority, are *not* public corporations.

Negative Interest Rate: 'Real' interest rate net of inflation,* which may be negative because the actual inflation rate may exceed the inflation premium* (representing the anticipated inflation rate). May also be affected by asymmetrical tax treatment.

Net National Product (NNP): American name for national income.*

Newly-Industrialising Country (NIC): Country with medium level of national income per head, which is increasing fast, e.g. Brazil, South Korea.

Non-Tariff Barriers: Obstructions to imports* other than tariffs,* usually government-imposed, e.g. needless licensing requirements, customs regulations, etc.

Official Exchange Rate: Value of domestic against foreign currency, set by or used by government officials. Not applicable when rates are free to float.

Opportunity Cost: The hypothetical revenue or other benefit that might have been obtained by the 'next best' alternative course of action, which has been forgone in favour of the course actually taken.

Overall Balance: The sum of the current balance (of payments on international trade) and the capital account balance. It must be met by 'official financing', i.e. changes in borrowing and in reserves of gold and foreign currencies.

Overmanning: Employing more people than necessary for efficient operation.

Paradox of Thrift: In the circular flow model,* with its special assumptions, the 'paradox' that an increase in savings (a 'withdrawal'* from the circular flow) leads to a fall in national income.*

Partnership: Form of enterprise with two or more owners ('partners'), each of whom has unlimited personal liability for the firm's debts.

Paternalism: Practice of treating people as if they were children. In economics, usually applied to government ('the gentleman in Whitehall knows best'); but maybe to employers' treatment of workers.

Perfect Competition: Analytical model of the form a market would take if: there were (a) many small sellers of identical products; (b) complete knowledge of prices and opportunities; (c) no significant economies of scale,* (d) no barriers to the movement of factors of production* or of entrepreneurs.*

Permanent Income: Expected long-run level of income; used in relation to level of consumption in contrast to 'current income', which may be affected by temporary factors.

Phillips Curve: Alleged relationship between rate of inflation and level of unemployment, thought to exist in UK in 1960s.

Politician: 'That insidious and crafty animal ... whose councils are directed by the momentary fluctuations of affairs.' Adam Smith.

Portfolio Investment: Financial investment* not involving direct control of an enterprise.

Potential National Income: = Full-Employment National Income. The level that national income *would* reach if there were no unemployment of labour above a necessary minimum due to frictional reasons.

Present Value: Discounted amount of future cash flows, equivalent to the (present) 'value' of an asset.

Price: The exchange value of a commodity, usually determined by the interplay of supply and demand on the market. Not synonymous with 'subjective value'; hence Wilde's definition of a cynic as one who 'knows the price of everything and the value of nothing'.

Price Controls: Government restrictions on free movement of market prices.

Price-Effect: The extent to which people may work more hours as the (after-tax) wage-rate increases (or vice versa).

Price-Elastic: The extent to which demand for a good varies with price. Strictly a good is said to be 'price-elastic' if the percentage change in the volume of goods purchased exceeds (in the opposite direction) the percentage change in price.

Price-Inelastic: Relatively unresponsive to price changes (of demand). Does *not* mean that a change in price induces no change at all in the volume of goods purchased; but that the percentage change in the volume of goods purchased is less (in the opposite direction) than the percentage change in price.

Prices and Incomes Policy: System of government controls over prices, including wage-rates and (sometimes) dividends. May be compulsory or 'voluntary'.

Primary Sector: The extractive industries, including agriculture, forestry, fishing, mining, quarrying, and the extraction of oil and gas.

Private Sector: The privately-owned part of the economy, independent of government control, comprising the personal sector and companies.

Privatisation: 'Denationalisation'. Transfer of a public corporation, or another part of the public sector,* to the private sector.*

Production Possibility Curve: A graphical representation of the various combinations of output possible from an economy at full employment, often applied to a hypothetical two-commodity world.

Profession: Vocation; job involving advanced learning.

Profit: Sales revenue less expenses for a period.

Progressive Tax: A tax whose rates increase as income (or expenditure or capital) to which it applies increases.

Proportional Tax: Flat-rate tax.

Protection: Government measures, such as import quotas* or tariffs,* designed to 'protect' domestic producers against the competition of foreign producers. More widely, may refer to measures to 'protect' consumers, employees, investors, etc. against various evils.

Public Corporation: See Nationalised industry.*

Public Goods: Commodities or services which (a) can be consumed by an increasing number of people without diminishing the amount available to others; (b) are available to everyone within a catchment area and cannot be withheld from non-payers, e.g. national defence.

Public Sector: Government-controlled part of economy, comprising activities of (a) central government, (b) local authorities, and (c) the nationalised industries.

Public Sector Borrowing Requirement (PSBR): Government deficit, the excess, if any, of government spending★ over tax★ and other revenue.

Purchasing Power: Value of money. What money will buy in 'real' terms, often measured by the 'basket of goods and services' comprising the constituent items in the Retail Price Index.★

Quantity Theory of Money: $MV = PT$; where M is the money supply,★ V is the velocity of circulation,★ P is the general level of prices, and T is the volume of trade (output). The Quantity Theory (oversimplified) holds that for a given level of output, the value of money will in the long run be related to the amount of money issued.

Raw Material: Input to manufacturing process, often held for a time as stock.

Real Terms: After excluding the effects of inflation.★

Redemption: Repayment of a loan. See also: Yield to Redemption.

Regressive Tax: A tax whose rates effectively increase as income falls, normally applying more to expenditure taxes★ than to income tax.★

Reliability Gradings: Estimates by the Central Statistical Office of the margins of error attaching to various economic aggregates.★

Replacement Cost: Estimate of what it would cost to replace an asset, either 'gross' (new) or 'net' (in the asset's existing partly-used condition). In accounting, replacement cost (= current cost★) contrasts with historical (original) cost.

Residual Error: The balancing item in national income statistics to reconcile estimates based on income or on output with those based on expenditure. This treatment is purely for convenience: it does *not* imply that the expenditure estimates are less inaccurate.

Retail Price Index (RPI): Monthly statistic measuring (against base date January 1974 = 100.0) money prices of representative 'basket of goods'. The year-on-year rate of increase in the RPI is commonly regarded as 'the' rate of inflation.★

Revaluation: In a fixed exchange rate system,★ the up-valuation of a domestic currency against a foreign currency.

Saving (S): Income (of individuals or companies) not spent on current consumption★ of goods and services.

Secondary Sector: Manufacturing and processing industries, including construction.

Second-Hand Market: Market on which used goods are exchanged for cash, either directly between ultimate consumers, or via middlemen.

Security (share): Any stocks or shares, which may be 'quoted' on a stock market, issued either by governments or by companies.

Snake: In the European Monetary System, band within which members' currencies fluctuate.

Social Costs: 'Externalities'. Costs arising from an action, not taken into account by private decision-maker. Example: pollution for which he will not be liable to pay damages.

Sole Trader: Form of enterprise where an individual owner bears unlimited personal liability for what the business owes.

Stagflation: Combination of stagnation and inflation.

Stock (inventory): Holding of goods as (a) raw materials,* (b) work-in-progress,* or (c) finished goods,* with a view to re-sale (perhaps after further processing) in the ordinary course of business. May also refer to consumers' holdings of finished goods awaiting consumption.

Stock Appreciation: Increase in value of stock due solely to price increases, not to 'real' (volume) increase.

Stop-Go: Oscillations in UK government demand management* (in the 1960s) between restrictions and relaxations of aggregate demand. Probably counter-productive attempts to 'stabilise' economy.

Store of Wealth: Traditional function of money,* impaired by inflation.*

Structural Unemployment: Form of unemployment of labour caused by structural imbalances in the economy, due to technical changes or to institutional obstructions to mobility.

Subsidies: Government grants of money to industries or firms to reduce the price or encourage the production or particular goods, or to consumers to encourage consumption.

Taxation (T): Compulsory levy payable to government by individual or firms.

Terms of Trade: A measure of the purchasing power of exports in terms of imports.

Tertiary Sector: Service industries, including utilities, distribution, transport, communication, and personal and commercial services.

Time Preference: Ratio between valuation of a good now and valuation of an otherwise identical good at some future date. Usually expressed as an annual 'rate', e.g. value now 100, value in 2 years 121, gives a 'rate' of 10 per cent a year.

Trade: Business, especially employment in industry or commerce, as opposed to a profession.*

Trade Creation: Process by which customs union* may increase international trade by causing individuals in member countries to buy from outside the customs union what would previously have been bought within it.

Trade Cycle: Fluctuation in level of activity and output in economy, often thought to exhibit some regularity.

Trade Diversion: Process by which customs union* may reduce international trade by causing individuals in member countries to buy from inside the customs union what would previously have been bought from outside it. May be caused by height of common external tariff.

Transfer Earnings: What a factor of production could earn in an alternative use (= 'opportunity cost'*).

Transfer Payment: Payment, usually by government, other than in exchange for goods or services, e.g. retirement pensions, unemployment benefit.

Unemployment: Unused resources, usually referring to labour, and usually assumed to be involuntary (e.g. 'leisure'* would be excluded).

Unit of Account: Numeraire in accounting. Traditionally the monetary unit; but in times of inflation an alternative 'constant purchasing power' unit has been suggested.

Value Added: Difference between sales revenue and cost of bought-in materials and services. Roughly equals profit plus wages.

Velocity of Circulation (V): Gross National Product* per year divided by the money supply*. Various definitions of the latter will, of course, give different values for V. Monetarists* tend to assume V is stable.

Vested Interest: Interest of some one or group in a particular state of affairs; e.g. UK coal miners have a vested interest in coal imports being forbidden by government.

Visible Balance: Balance (of payments) arising on 'visible' international trade (in goods), as opposed to 'invisible' trade* (in services).

Visible Trade: International trade in goods, as opposed to 'invisible' trade* (in services).

Voucher System: Proposal for allowing producer competition* and consumer choice in welfare services, especially health and education, while maintaining government (i.e. taxpayer) financing.

Wealth: Well-offness, expressed in terms of money, usually related to (ultimately) marketable assets.

Withdrawal: In circular flow model*, any income which is not passed on, e.g. Saving (S), Taxes (T), or Imports (M).

Work in Progress: Partly-completed stocks in manufacturing process.

Yield: Rate of return on investment or security. Interest or dividend divided by the current market price.

Yield to Redemption: Yield on loan stock including element of capital gain (or loss) anticipated when principal (nominal amount) is repaid 'at par' on maturity, in addition to the 'flat' yield of annual interest.

Index